THE PEER AND THE GANGSTER

THE PEER AND THE GANGSTER

A Very British Cover-up

DANIEL SMITH

The
History
Press

For Rosie, Charlotte and Ben

First published 2020

The History Press
97 St George's Place, Cheltenham,
Gloucestershire, GL50 3QB
www.thehistorypress.co.uk

British Library Cataloguing in Publication Data.
A catalogue record for this book is available from the British Library.

ISBN 978 0 7509 9329 6

Typesetting and origination by The History Press
Printed and bound in Great Britain by TJ International Ltd.

MIX
Paper from
responsible sources
FSC® C013056
FSC
www.fsc.org

Contents

Acknowledgements

A book like this relies on the efforts of a large cast of individuals and organisations who generously offer up their time and expertise. I certainly could never have written it without access to a host of wonderful archives and libraries. I extend my thanks to the staff of the National Archives, the British Library, the Special Collections at the National Library of Scotland, the Parliamentary Archives at Westminster, the BBC Written Archives Centre, Christ Church Archive in Oxford, the Labour History Archive and Study Centre, and the Bodleian Library. Gratitude too to the Soho Society, the Metropolitan Police History Group, the National Association of Retired Police Officers, the Association of ex-CID Officers of the London Metropolitan Police, the Association of *Mirror* Pensioners, the BBC Pensioners' Association, the Labour History Group, *East End Life*, the *East London* Advertiser, the *Jersey Evening Post*, the *Aberdeen Press and Journal*, Gay's the Word bookshop and Boxing News Online.

Then there are the many individuals who either shared their memories with me or else pointed me in the direction of others who might. At the top of this list must go John Pearson, who was the first to alert the world that the saga of the 'Peer and the Gangster' was not all that it had at first seemed. I will be forever grateful to him for giving me his blessing to write this book. Special thanks to Val Wilson for her help with research in Scotland, and to Ray Rose, who generously shared a few of the fruits of his exhaustive research with me late on in the writing process. Thanks also to: Matt Barber, Michael Brotherton, Ian Brown, Paul Callan, Duncan Campbell, Caro Cluskey, Jess Conrad, Monty Court, Roger Crowhurst, Judith Curthoys, Anthony Daly, Simon Danczuk, Tony Delano, Beverley Edwards, Bob Fenton, Georgia Glover, Roy Greenslade, Jeffrey Hackney, Bill Hagerty, Joe Haines, Dr Henry Hardy, John Jackson, Lord Lexden, David Little, Linda Mallard, Leah McGrath Goodman, Paddy O'Gara, Jeremy Reed, Greg Rosen, Mike Smith, Angela Swinn and Walter Harris, John and Nelly Symonds, Lord Taverne, Michael Thornton, Richard Tracey, Phyllis Trachy, Barry Turner, Jon Vickers-Jones, Philip Webster and Bradley Wakenell. I also owe a debt of gratitude to all those who have gone on the public record with their personal experiences of the Krays over the years, many of whom are no longer with us.

Also, to my agent, Andrew Lownie, who 'got' this book from the outset and who was ready with good advice throughout. And to Mark Beynon, Jezz Palmer, Caitlin Kirkman, Simon Wright, Alex Waite and the team at The History Press who have given it such a good home.

And, as ever, to my family. In particular, to Mum and Dad for their constant support and encouragement (which I call upon more often than I ought), to Matt for his interest in general and especially for his advice in navigating Freedom of Information requests, and to Celia who should surely have had a career in PR! Finally, of course, to Rosie, who has been with me every step of the way, and Charlotte and Ben (who I suspect were, during the writing of this book, the only under-6s in the country who could pick out Bob Boothby in a photograph). I couldn't have done it without you.

Daniel Smith
March 2020

Prologue

Homosexuality is equally prevalent among what used to be called 'the higher and lower orders'; and sometimes these are attracted to each other. This is known in homosexual circles as 'plain sewing'.

Bob Boothby, Recollections of a Rebel (1978)

Saturday, 11 July 1964

The Mirror Building, Holborn Circus, London

It was the sort of front-page splash that editors dream of. 'PEER AND A GANGSTER: YARD PROBE'[1] screamed the headline in the *Sunday Mirror*, suggesting much even as it revealed so little. By the following morning, breakfast tables up and down the country were aflutter with the news. There was a collective spluttering of tea, a choking upon cornflakes, the whiff of kippers surrendering to the stench of scandal.

The libel legislation of the day ruled out the paper naming the subjects of its headline. But that was almost beside the point for the time being. Here was a story hinting at revelations that may yet surpass those of even the Profumo affair, which had fatally undermined Harold Macmillan's government the previous year.

As the front page revealed, a 'prominent peer' – a 'household name' no less – and 'a leading thug in the London underworld' were under Scotland Yard investigation. Their alleged crime – for it was still a criminal matter at the time – was their involvement in a homosexual relationship. Moreover, there was the suggestion that the story had broader dimensions. There were allusions to 'private weekend activities of the peer and a number of prominent public men during visits to Brighton' and 'relationships between the East End gangsters and a number of clergymen'.[2]

The story broke just a fortnight before the release of the latest *Carry On* film and promised to match every bit of the high campery and innuendo of those movies. If, as Philip Larkin held that it did, sexual intercourse had begun sometime between the *Lady Chatterley* obscenity trial of 1960 and the Beatles' first LP in 1963, it was still all rather vanilla. The Beatles professed only to want to hold your hand and even the Profumo narrative – that of the older man having his head turned by a beautiful, younger woman – was distinctly orthodox. But now the *Sunday Mirror* was hinting at something less vanilla and more tutti-frutti.

The underworld thug in question was a man who was as yet little known to the public but who would in due course take his place alongside the likes of Jack the Ripper and Dr Crippen in the pantheon of British criminality. He was Ronnie Kray and, along with his twin Reggie, he had spent several years establishing one of London's most feared criminal enterprises.

The politician, meanwhile, was one of the grand old men of the British political scene – Lord Boothby, better known as Bob to his friends. Eton- and Oxford-educated, he was a scion of the upper class. A Conservative parliamentarian from the age of 24, he had stood shoulder to shoulder with Churchill in the 1930s as they railed against those who called for appeasement. He was there in Churchill's wartime administration too, until a financial misstep forced him out and put paid to his ambitions of high office. Now in his sixties, he was a regular on television and radio – an acerbic and amusing guest and commentator, always ready with some delicious anecdote or another and instantly recognisable from his long flop of grey hair and his deep, melodious voice. National treasure status had seemed to beckon.

For Norman Lucas, the *Sunday Mirror's* dogged crime reporter, the front page represented another journalistic notch on the belt. Able to sniff out a potential front page at a thousand paces, these days the juiciest stories more often than not found their way to him, such was the extent of his network of informants who operated on both the right and the wrong side of the law. He had been tipped off about this story by a source within C11, Scotland Yard's secretive intelligence-gathering arm. The Krays had been under surveillance since the start of the year, prompting scrutiny of their web of social contacts that spanned many tiers of British society. None, according to Lucas's informant, was more prominent than Boothby.

The story had come to Lucas at just the right moment. Reg Payne, the *Sunday Mirror's* rough-and-tumble editor, had got the Krays in his sights but was unsure how best to shine a light on their nefarious activities. Now here was the perfect opportunity not only to take on the twins but to attack the government, too. The proudly left-leaning *Sunday Mirror* was no friend of the Conservative Party and with the Tories still reeling from Profumo, here was a story that might see them put out of office altogether.

Come Sunday morning, a photographer from Clapton called Bernard Black read the story with particular interest. He knew exactly to whom the story referred. In fact, a few months earlier – and at Ronnie Kray's request – he had photographed the gangster with Boothby on a sofa at the politician's flat. On the Monday, he made his way to the Mirror Building and deposited a package of photos with the *Sunday Mirror*'s young picture editor (and a future editor of the *Daily Mirror*), Derek Jameson. Jameson was delighted by the pictorial evidence to back up the Scotland Yard insider's tip-off. When Boothby was unmasked as the peer and Kray as the gangster, as they doubtless soon would be, surely they could not now deny that the story had substance? A libel action? 'Bring it on!' thought Jameson to himself.[3] The next Sunday, the paper ran a follow-up front page in which, although the image could not be printed, details about it were described against a wry headline: 'THE PICTURE WE MUST NOT PRINT'.[4] The net was closing in.

But then, as suddenly as it had arrived, the story went away. The saga of the peer and the gangster became the century's greatest British scandal that never was. This, then, is the tale of how that story was killed.

1

The Nation's Favourite

It was 13 October 1963 and Lord Boothby was in a lift heading down to the lobby of the BBC Television Centre in London's White City. He was accompanied by a producer and old friend, John Irwin. There was nothing in the air to suggest anything out of the ordinary. But as the lift doors opened and he stepped out, an imposing figure emerged from the shadows. For a moment Boothby was disorientated, then he recognised his assailant. It was Eamonn Andrews. 'Lord Boothby, we're on the air – sound and vision. In fact and at last, tonight's the night – This is Your Life!'[1]

That episode of *This Is Your Life* – the long-running and always celebratory biography-themed show – ought, perhaps, to have marked Boothby's transition into something like quiet retirement. Born in 1900, he had been a fixture of British public life throughout a tumultuous century. His friends had died in the trenches of the First World War. His maiden speech in the Commons was witnessed by his political hero, David Lloyd George, then still in his pomp. He was Churchill's ally in the 1930s and his foe for much of the rest of the time. And in the 1950s he had earned a reputation as one of the hardest-hitting and most effective backbench voices in the House of Commons, warning against British aggression during the Suez Crisis, championing the European project and fighting for gay rights. Moreover, he was perhaps the first British politician to really 'get' the power of radio and television. There had been plenty of talented parliamentary communicators among his generation, but no one who quite understood as he did how you might go about becoming a political personality via the airwaves. He was, after all, the man Winston Churchill used to refer to, not altogether warmly, as 'The Hon. Member the Star of Television'.[2]

By his own admission, Boothby got away with much in his life thanks to his ability to charm. A significant component in this was his voice – a feature that never failed to impress those who met him. He possessed a velvety rich baritone and in his youth there was talk that he might become a singer. As a student at Oxford, he encountered Freddie Grisewood, who taught him the secrets of voice production. It was a skill he put to good use wherever he went, captivating individuals in personal conversation, commanding the attention of his parliamentary colleagues and winning giant audiences on the radio and television. It was as a regular panellist on the political discussion show *Any Questions?* – helmed, as chance would have it, by Grisewood, who had forged a successful career as a BBC broadcaster – that Boothby first became a regular interloper into parlours and drawing rooms throughout the nation.

The transition from politician to personality came naturally enough. To go with the voice, Boothby had long ago developed a distinctive fashion style. The sumptuous hair – which retained its lushness even as it greyed – was typically set off by a well-cut suit complete with carnation in the buttonhole. His mind, meanwhile, overflowed with anecdotes, often caustic and always fascinating, about the famous and notorious – tales he needed little encouragement to share. Cutting a dash and with a reputation for having been either eyewitness to or key player in many of the landmark events of the century – in 1959, he was asked to host a series of films giving a retrospective on the century to date[3] – little wonder he was a natural favourite with radio and television audiences and producers.

On *This Is Your Life*, Eamonn Andrews was typically effusive, summing up Boothby as 'Peer of the Realm, Titan on Television, Man of Independent Spirit'. One of the guests recalled him on the campaign trail ahead of the 1924 general election, when he'd fought for the seat of East Aberdeenshire. A picture was painted of the youthful Old Etonian dressed in knickerbockers, telling the assembled group of hardy farmers and fishermen exactly what needed to be done and how he would go about doing it. 'Who's this raw boy who thinks he knows it all?' the guest had wondered at the time, only to have been won over during the subsequent thirty-plus years of Boothby's service as local MP.[4]

Sir Compton McKenzie – writer, social commentator and co-founder of the Scottish National Party – came on to confirm what a grand chap Boothby indeed was, while his former neighbour, Noel Coward, commended him for his tireless condemnation of Hitler in the period when the government had instead pursued appeasement. Someone else recalled Boothby receiving the *Legion d'honneur* and celebrating the next day at Versailles by devouring a huge ice cream cornet. Andrews, meanwhile, knowingly pointed out Boothby's reputation as someone rather fond of the company of women, before introducing the MP Jennie Lee, who suggested she had been asked to appear as she was the only woman the BBC could find who had never been in love with him. Here was Boothby laid out for the nation – the Establishment figure with a devilish streak of rebellion, a man of integrity and culture who nonetheless couldn't always resist the finer things in life. Boothby for his part maintained an air of surprised delight, mixed with the usual bonhomie. It was all tremendously good fun.

Boothby was now 63 years old. He had the public adoration, the plaudits, the titles. He had done his bit in public life. His most productive days were surely behind him. So why not head into the sunset? It was a case of both nature and necessity. On the one hand, Boothby was a show-off. Rarely could he resist making himself the centre of attention, whether at a family gathering or on a panel show. He continued to speak with regularity in the House of Lords after his ennoblement in 1958 and found it hard to turn down an invitation for a television or radio appearance. Moreover, he could not afford to. Despite having fingers in numerous entrepreneurial pies, he was no good with money. His lifestyle did not come cheap and he had appearances to keep up. There was a staff to pay, fine wine to buy, entertaining to be done. And his expensive tastes extended to a passion for gambling that ensured he was rarely out of debt to someone or other.

He needed the BBC's patronage to keep his head above water. His problems were compounded by the fact that the Beeb had recently become rather less willing to employ him as extensively as they once did. Several on-air comments – delivered with Boothby's characteristic off-the-cuff good humour – had caused problems for the broadcaster, most notably a costly run-in with the newspaper baron Lord Beaverbrook. He had taken umbrage at Boothby's assertion on a 1962 episode of *Any Questions?* that given the chance, he would pass 'an Immigration Bill to keep out the Canadians [of whom Beaverbrook was one]' since they 'have done nothing but damage to this country'.[5] Boothby claimed with some justification that he had been speaking with tongue firmly in cheek – he was, in fact, on reasonable terms generally with Beaverbrook – and argued that he would probably never had said anything of the sort if he had not been wined and dined rather too well by the BBC beforehand on the occasion of the programme's 500th episode.[6] Nonetheless, the saga rumbled on at great expense and no little embarrassment to the BBC. It was clear that the Corporation would now have to accept legal responsibility for anything said in its live broadcasts, which immediately made Boothby a less appealing guest than he had previously been.

Eamonn Andrews even hinted at the trouble Boothby represented in his introduction to the *This Is Your Life* episode. Boothby was, he said, 'not only larger than life, and to the ladies, twice as handsome, he's a compound of all the qualities that make us here in *This Is Your Life* quake in our shoes. Unpunctual, unpredictable, and with more than a touch of fire and brimstone. Hold on to your hats …'[7]

To the world at large, then, Boothby was the lovable elder statesman of British politics. Funny and charismatic, he could be wise and avuncular, indiscreet and irreverent, not to mention ferociously iconoclastic, and sometimes all at the same time. It was a heck of a trick to pull off. His political career was at once one in which he could point to a remarkably consistent record of having been on the right side of history, while remaining largely unstained by the sort of climb-downs and compromises that tend to attach to those who hold high office. All this had turned him into that rarest of things – a household name from the House of Lords who was not an ex-Prime Minister. But such a level of fame meant that when the *Sunday Mirror* came calling with their story about gangsters and peers in 1964, Boothby did not have much of a hiding place. Admittedly, Viscount Montgomery, hero of El-Alamein, briefly considered suing on the basis that he believed the British public would assume the allegations referred to him.[8] But once Monty was out of the picture, there were few other obvious targets on which the finger of suspicion could alight.

The situation was critical for Boothby. While he might have been able to bat away aspects of the tabloid story that would not stand up to scrutiny, he knew his life could not bear too much close examination. Perhaps if there had been a country pile, a dutiful wife, a couple of grandchildren and a bounding Labrador awaiting him somewhere, he would have exited the scene quietly and without too much fuss. But there was none of that. Instead there was his manservant, Gordon Goodfellow, and his flat – 1 Eaton Square, in the heart of Belgravia – that served as his gateway to the capital's exotica; to the exclusive gentlemen's clubs, the high-rollers' casinos, not to mention the after-hours dives and the nightclubs where, if you searched hard enough, you could find whatever sort of companionship you desired.

Boothby was a man split in two. There was the Boothby who craved attention from a public that generously lavished their affection on him in these, his later years. Then there was the Boothby of the secrets and lies, the man who guarded his private life with a keenness that verged on ferocity. In his 1962 memoirs, *My Yesterday, Your Tomorrow*, he insisted somewhat pre-posterously – and presumably to throw any interested parties off the scent – that 'I have had no private life at all.'[9] In fact, even though London and a few other of the UK's metropoles were really starting to swing by 1964, they still had a way to go to catch up with the type of fast living that the nation's upper classes had been perfecting for centuries. For real dissolution, the Eton-and-Oxford man was always likely to have a head start on the up-and-coming cats of Carnaby Street.

Boothby understood that better than most and so had constructed for him-self a precarious house of cards. For all that he gave to the public, he was clear that their access to his inner life must be restricted. In 1975, Elaine Grand suggested to him in a televised interview that it was an illusion that the public knew him. 'Yes,' Boothby replied. 'I don't think you do know me altogether. Not very well, anyway.'[10] But there had already been a couple of close shaves before the 'Peer and the Gangster' headline – unfortunate dealings with the police seized upon by a Fleet Street pack who enthusiastically reported pro-ceedings with a nudge and a wink. And now the *Sunday Mirror* was taking things several stages further. Unchecked, they would topple his house of cards and he lacked both the time and opportunity to rebuild. The choice was stark: shut down the story or face ruin. And Boothby was nothing if not a survivor.

2

Death of a Story

When the *Sunday Mirror* story broke, Boothby was not in the country. He was holidaying in Vittel, north-eastern France, with an old friend, Colin Coote, the urbane editor of the *Daily Telegraph*. Coote had worked wonders in his fourteen years at the helm of the *Telegraph*, adding not far off 50 per cent to its circulation. But he was a man who knew how to enjoy himself, too. With Boothby, he shared a profound love of good food and fine wine (and, when in England, golf too). Vittel was an ideal destination to unwind, away from the hurly-burly of their London lives.

Nonetheless, the 'Peer and the Gangster' headline did not evade them for long. The air mail editions of the British papers arrived cross-Channel over the next few days, and they settled down to explore the *Sunday Mirror's* chatter about Mayfair parties, dubious visits to Brighton and ties to clergymen. The *Sunday Mirror* also alleged that several people aware of the alleged relationship between the peer and the gangster had been subject to blackmail. Moreover, Scotland Yard was set to unleash an all-out offensive against the criminal parties involved.

The pair had great fun trying to guess who the peer in question might be. It was a conversation that entertained them even on the flight home. Boothby arrived back in London on Friday the 17th and promptly got on the phone to Tom Driberg, a fellow MP who had started out as a journalist and had retained his links to Fleet Street. If anyone would know who was the subject of the story, Driberg would. But imagine Boothby's horror as Driberg told him, 'Sorry. It's you.'[1]

This was roughly the train of events as Boothby told it. It bore little relationship to the truth, however. The moment he saw that headline, Boothby must have known he was in trouble. Even before he read the contents of the article – a good deal of it admittedly some way off-beam – he could have been in no doubt that he was the peer and Ronnie Kray the mobster in question. The Lords might not have been a cradle of virtue, but he was well aware that there were only a limited number of members actively associating with underworld figures. And those who could be described as household names …?

The *Sunday Mirror*'s revelations were, unsurprisingly, quick to cause consternation in Downing Street. In the days that followed, Boothby's name was ever more frequently proffered as the man in question in countless private conversations around Fleet Street and Whitehall. It was clear that here was a story that was not going away. No. 10, moreover, was conscious that the Conservatives were not in a position to easily withstand a scandal such as the one implied.

In power since 1951, the party had in recent times been buffeted by a series of debilitating and embarrassing tales of official wrongdoing. In 1962, it had been John Vassall, a relatively junior civil servant at the Admiralty, who found himself in the eye of the storm. Vassall was just short of his 38th birthday when he was arrested in the September that year, charged with treason after passing secrets to the Kremlin over several years. A rather sad and lonely figure, his story followed a classic Cold War blueprint. In 1952, he had found himself working at the British embassy in Moscow, where he routinely struggled to deal with the complex social interactions of diplomatic life. His sense of isolation was exacerbated by the fact that he was homosexual, too. Moscow was every bit as uninviting to the gay community as post-war England. Nonetheless, Vassall fell in with a Polish colleague who offered to serve as his guide through the Russian capital's gay demimonde. But it was a classic honeytrap. Vassall drank too much at a party and was photographed in a series of compromising positions, and thereafter found himself at the mercy of the Russian authorities. In return for his non-exposure, Vassall's price was to spy for the Kremlin.

It turned out that Vassall was rather good at espionage. Sufficiently low level to keep largely under the radar of suspicion, he nonetheless had access to large volumes of sensitive information that he passed on to his Soviet blackmailers skilfully and discreetly. In the end, he was undone by a combination of evidence from Soviet defectors and his own exuberance – it became obvious to several colleagues that his decadent lifestyle was not sustainable on his income from the civil service alone. He was duly sentenced to eighteen years in prison (going on to serve ten) while the episode served as a source of acute embarrassment to both Harold Macmillan's government and the security services. His arrest coming just a few weeks before the Cuban missile crisis, it looked very much like the British authorities were struggling to keep on top of the peculiar demands of the Cold War age. For a while there was also the suggestion that Vassall had been under the protection of Tam Galbraith, who had served as Civil Lord of the Admiralty from 1957 to 1959. The rumour was that there had been an inappropriate relationship between the two, although Galbraith was subsequently cleared of any wrongdoing. Nonetheless, the episode contributed to the sense that government ministers needed to appear whiter than white.

Yet the Vassall controversy would soon pale in comparison to the scandal that engulfed the Secretary of State for War, John Profumo, less than a year later. Profumo's crime was to embark on an extra-marital affair in 1961 with a strikingly beautiful teenage showgirl called Christine Keeler. While a little illicit bed-hopping was part and parcel of public life and might have gone largely uncommented upon, unfortunately for Profumo, Keeler counted among her other lovers Yevgeny Ivanov, a Russian naval attaché. At the end of 1962, a clash between two more of Keeler's paramours culminated in gun shots being fired – shots that, it turned out, were boldly announcing Profumo's imminent downfall. With the press declaring open season on Keeler's personal life, it was not long before the unfortunate Anglo–Soviet *ménage à trois* was brought into the open.

While it is unlikely that Keeler picked up much in the way of pillow-talk intelligence from Profumo that she could pass on to Ivanov, it was regardless a perilous set of alliances. Then, in March 1963, Profumo made his fatal mistake, telling the House of Commons that there was 'no impropriety whatsoever in my acquaintanceship with Miss Keeler'.[2] His story would fall apart in the weeks and months that followed amid a slew of criminal investigations into Keeler's social circle. Forced to admit that he had indeed lied in his assertions to the Commons, Profumo resigned in early June. It was, said *The Times*, 'a great tragedy for the probity of public life in Britain'.[3]

By October, Macmillan had gone as Prime Minister, too. The Vassall and Profumo debacles had undermined his government and diminished him personally. Both his stature as a public figure and his health went into steep decline. Alec Douglas-Home came in to succeed him and while his aristocratic pedigree and stiff personal style hardly chimed with the age, it was hoped he might at least steady the Tory ship. He was known to be disgusted that Profumo's lapse had caused the public to doubt if Britain was being run by 'men who have the highest sense of integrity and public duty'.[4] The scandals had piled up so that the public was unlikely to indulge many more cases where the private peccadillos of powerful men threatened the well-being of the nation. If nothing else, Douglas-Home could surely navigate a path through to the next elections without crashing into yet another crushing iceberg of scandal.

Boothby insisted that, at first, he was disposed to shrug off the *Sunday Mirror*'s damaging report. That, though, was never a realistic option. For one thing, the party hierarchy were not content to stonewall. The Home Secretary, Henry Brooke, was put in charge of getting to the bottom of the story. On Sunday, 19 July, a week after the initial revelations, the newspaper had returned to its theme. It revealed that it had come into possession of a photograph showing 'a well-known member of the House of Lords seated on a sofa with a gangster who leads the biggest protection racket London has ever known. On a nearby table drinks have been poured out …' Only legal issues concerning copyright of the image precluded publication and, the editorial continued, '*The Sunday Mirror* will continue to build up its dossier on the frightening growth of lawlessness, extortion, blackmail and intimidation in London.'[5] The suggestion was clearer than ever – powerful figures in society were abetting the activities of the most serious criminals.

That evening, Brooke received a handwritten letter from Boothby. 'In view of certain rumours which some of my friends in Fleet Street tell me are now circulating,' Boothby began, 'I think I ought at once to put you in possession of the facts so far as I am concerned.'[6] He proceeded to explain that some six months earlier, Ronald Kray had asked to meet him regarding an opportunity to invest in a house-building project in Enugu, Nigeria in which he thought he might be interested. Kray wanted Boothby to serve as chairman or director of a development company he was expecting to form. The meeting occurred in Boothby's Eaton Square flat and he had been impressed with Kray's plans, details of which 'had been confided to the Tunniff Construction Company, which I knew to be of high repute'. Ernest Shinwell – the son of the former Labour Minister of Defence, Lord Manny Shinwell – was also involved (although he himself would be arrested on suspicion of fraudulent share dealing in August 1964). Nonetheless, Boothby felt he was already stretched by work commitments and so was disinclined to get involved. Kray left a large file of papers for him to study, with the intention of returning the following week for a definite answer one way or the other.

Kray duly came back, accompanied by another man, and Boothby confirmed that he would not be taking up a role in the project. 'He was evidently disappointed,' Boothby wrote, 'but took it in good part, and I offered him a drink.' Before Kray left, he asked if his friend could take a photograph of the two of them, as he was a great fan of Boothby from his appearances on radio and television. Considering it churlish to refuse, Boothby agreed and so came about the photograph that had come into the possession of the *Sunday Mirror*. According to Teddy Smith, an associate of the twins, Ronnie was initially thrilled with the photo as it was 'the next best thing to getting one with Churchill' (Kray was a huge fan of the former prime minister and had a penchant for listening to his speeches on LP).[7]

Boothby was unequivocal in denying there was anything more to his association with Kray. 'This is the sum total of my relationship with Mr Kray,' he assured Brooke. 'I knew then, and know now, nothing of his background. I have never met him anywhere except in this flat – and then for no more than 20 minutes on each occasion. He seems an agreeable chap; but I had no opportunity of judging his character or his financial standing. Nor, in the circumstances, did I wish to do so.' Moreover, he had never attended any Mayfair parties and if he were a homosexual – which he was categorically not – 'I should not choose either gangsters or clergymen'. 'I thought that this information might be useful to you,' he continued, 'because it can be substantiated in every particular.'

Then Boothby went on the attack. If the paper had positively identified him as the subject of its story, he would expect to receive something in the region of £100,000 in a libel action. 'It seems to be a frightening thing that rumours of this kind can be given currency by the gutter press,' he opined, 'although, in this case, every other newspaper has held off it. Perhaps it is a hangover from the Vassall and Profumo cases. Perhaps it cuts deeper. In recent months I have been uneasily aware of a revival in this kind of witch-hunting atmosphere which, emanating from Germany, prevailed in the thirties.'

He cited in evidence a recent speech in the Lords by the much-respected QC, Gerald Gardiner. Speaking in a debate on Crime and Penal Reform four days earlier, Gardiner had despaired of what he perceived to be the spread of criminality since the war. There was, admittedly, a certain snobbishness in his argument. He disparaged those 'places in which "knocking off" things from the railways or "knocking off" things from the docks are so common that if somebody is convicted and fined, when he goes into the pub in the evening nobody refuses to speak to him, because so many of them do it themselves and he has just been unlucky'. By comparison, he spoke of 'another class with which your Lordships are more familiar' in which 'anybody convicted of an offence of dishonesty would have to resign from his club; he would be thrown out of his profession, and few but his oldest friends would ask him out to dinner again'. His underlying concern, though, was hardly extreme – a fear that an underpowered police force was losing ground in the fight against modern criminal enterprises. 'I venture to suggest,' he said, 'that it may begin to look as if the forces of evil are some day going to get the better and be stronger than the forces of law and order.' But Boothby detected 'a note of hysteria' in the speech, all the more worrying given that Gardiner was 'normally so sane and balanced'. 'What good can it do for anyone of his standing to say that the police are being beaten?' agonised Boothby.

Getting into his stride now, he next brought American politics into the debate. Barry Goldwater had just been nominated as the Republican candidate to face Lyndon Johnson in the presidential election scheduled for

November. He had been selected at a Republican Convention notable for its acrimonious atmosphere, fuelled by rivalry between the party's liberal and conservative wings. Goldwater's victory was taken as a sign that old-fashioned conservatism was back on the up. To Boothby, his candidacy was 'a sinister portent'. 'Goldwater-ism,' Boothby wrote to Brooke, 'must be stamped out, at all costs, in this country.'

It was a bravura defence by the peer. Not only had he denied the substance of the story, but he suggested that there were sinister forces behind it. He was not merely innocent, but ought to be protected in the interests of Britain's best liberal traditions. But any hopes that his letter might relieve the pressure upon him were short-lived.

Brooke was keen that Boothby should go on the record with the police. Although he did not see what more he could add to what he had already told the Home Secretary, Boothby agreed and a senior officer was sent to take a statement on the 21st. But worse was to come. The following day, *Stern* – Germany's mass-market weekly – picked up on the story. Unhindered by Britain's libel laws, the magazine not only named Boothby as the subject of rumours but suggested that 'his position in society helps the gangsters towards more lucrative customers who prefer gambling halls and "other queer amusements"'. Lord Boothby, they concluded, was set to become 'the central figure of a scandal that will overshadow the Profumo affair'.[8]

With his name now openly associated with the allegations, the situation had become critical. The option of brazening things out until the furore died down was gone. Boothby did not know where to turn. A heavy drinker at the best of times, he hit the bottle harder than ever. After the publication of *Stern*, copies of which had been relayed to the Conservative hierarchy by a couple of MPs who had been in Germany on other business, Boothby received a middle-of-the-night visit from a party delegation. Although he would not confirm their identities, it likely included the Home Secretary, Henry Brooke, and the Chief Whip, Martin Redmayne. There on orders from the Prime Minister, they wanted to know what Boothby intended to do next. Boothby did not know, beyond sticking to his denials.

Salvation of sorts came in the form of a visit from a friend, Harry Kissin. The German-born son of Russian Jewish parents, Kissin had arrived in

London in 1933 as a 21-year-old. He subsequently made a fortune in the import–export business and since the 1940s had been part of Labour leader Harold Wilson's inner circle. In more recent times, he had also fostered a friendship with Boothby, despite their distant political positions. When Kissin called upon him, he found Boothby in a bad way. He was drunk and talking of ending it all. Kissin did what he could to talk him down and then suggested a practical course of action. Boothby ought to make contact with a solicitor Kissin knew, a fellow called Arnold Goodman.[9]

Boothby knew Goodman by reputation, since the lawyer was a confidante of Harold Wilson. A great bear of a man – he went by the nickname of 'Two Dinners' and famously rearranged his regular evening meetings with Wilson to allow extra time for supper – he was famous for being able to bend others to his will through the use of wit and charm. And when that failed, he would get his way by intimidating opponents into submission. He had come to public prominence back in 1957 when he represented three Labour politicians – Nye Bevan, Richard Crossman and Morgan Phillips – in an action against the *Spectator* magazine, which had published an article accusing the three of having been drunk at an International Socialist Congress in Italy. Under his guidance, the trio denied the story under oath and triumphed in the case. Years later, Crossman's diaries would reveal that they had, in fact, been ferociously drunk at the congress and had compounded the sin by committing perjury.[10] But by then Goodman's reputation as a fixer *extraordinaire* was secure. His loyalties, like those of Kissin, were with the Labour Party, and in 1962 he had worked for Hugh Gaitskell, Wilson's predecessor as Labour leader, during the inquiry that followed the Vassall case. By 1964 he was Wilson's chief legal adviser, although he never held party membership. Nonetheless, he agreed to meet with Boothby in his hour of need.

Fate's pendulum now began to swing back towards Boothby. One of Goodman's first actions was to suggest that Boothby employ the services of a barrister who, once again, was known for his allegiance not to the Conservatives, but to Labour. Boothby, relieved to have a big-hitter like Goodman on side, did not baulk for a moment. The barrister in question was none other than Gerald Gardiner, whose recent performance in the Lords Boothby had bemoaned in his letter to Brooke. But now was not the moment to be fussy. On 31 July, Boothby and Goodman were driven to a meeting with Gardiner. Gardiner posed two direct questions. Was Boothby a homosexual, and had he engaged in any homosexual behaviour in the last ten years. Boothby responded in the same way to both questions: 'Certainly not.'[11]

Gardiner was seemingly convinced, noting that, 'This sort of bad luck can happen to particularly polite people.'[12] Thus assured, Goodman and Gardiner swung into action. A libel writ was the obvious route to take but it was risky, potentially expensive and time consuming. By the time any case was resolved, it was likely the damage to Boothby would already have been done. So, Goodman championed a more aggressive strategy, the type to which he was ideally suited. He would wring a retraction and a pay-out from the *Sunday Mirror* without recourse to the courts.

The first part of the plan was executed the following day. Under Goodman's watchful eye, Boothby composed a letter to *The Times* – the newspaper of record, after all – refuting the *Sunday Mirror* story in the most vigorous terms. Largely echoing what he had already told Henry Brooke, Boothby characterised the allegations against him as 'a tissue of atrocious lies'. He had not and never had been a homosexual, he stated, before concluding:

> I am not by nature thin-skinned, but this sort of thing makes a mockery of any decent kind of life, public or private, in what is still supposed to be a civilized country. It is, in my submission, intolerable that any man should be put into the dilemma of having either to remain silent while such rumours spread, or considerably to increase the circulation of certain newspapers by publicly denying them. If either the *Sunday Mirror* or *Daily Mirror* is in possession of a shred of evidence – documentary or photographic – against me, let them print it and take the consequences.[13]

Goodman knew the power of that letter. By making such a positive statement, Boothby was on the front foot once again. Now it was time to go in for the kill. To his great advantage was the fact that the senior management at the *Sunday Mirror* was starting to wobble over the story. This was in part because the normal chain of command had not been in place when the

story broke. The journalist who initiated it, Norman Lucas, was a redoubt-
able figure but such an incendiary article would usually have gone via his
editor, Reg Payne, to Hugh Cudlipp for sign-off. Cudlipp had enjoyed
an outstanding career, including two stints as editor of the paper itself,
and now served as editorial director of the *Mirror* family of titles. In the
regular scheme of things, he would have been sure to check not only the
credentials of Lucas's story but also any likely political fallout. But he happened to be on holiday when the 'Peer and the Gangster' scoop emerged,
so the job of giving the front page of 12 July the final go-ahead fell to
Cecil Harmsworth King, chairman of the paper's owners, the International
Publishing Corporation.

King was no fool but his eagerness to publish the story – and score
another hit on the ruling Conservatives – perhaps impelled him to act more
precipitously than normal. All might have been well if Joseph Simpson,
Commissioner of the Metropolitan Police, had not then chosen to interpose
himself into events so quickly. On 14 July, Simpson released a statement in
which he denied authorising an investigation into the relationship between
the as-yet unnamed lord and criminal, denied that there were links between
any such figures and members of the clergy, and denied that he was due to
report on said allegations to the Home Secretary. With the boss of the Met
essentially washing his hands of the story, the *Sunday Mirror* found itself in
an uncomfortable place. Even its photographic evidence – the peer and the
gangster seated together on a sofa – did not begin to corroborate the accusations contained in the original article. Sure, there were plenty of whispers
about Boothby that had been doing the rounds for years, but the paper was
meant to be moving away from that sort of hearsay sensationalism. In the
cold light of day, the paper was struggling badly to provide concrete proof
of the story, even if Lucas and the senior editorial staff were convinced that
they had the right people in their sights.

So, when Goodman picked up the phone to King in early August, the
Mirror man found himself with little room for manoeuvre. Goodman went
in characteristically hard. 'I think you should know ...' was his customary way of introducing a legalistic monologue, at the end of which the
other party usually agreed to whatever he was suggesting. And so it was
with King. Having taken over the Cudlipp role to give the original article

the green light, he now feared he had made a terrible mistake. As a result, on 6 August King put his name to a grovelling apology published in the *Daily Mirror:*

> The International Publishing Corporation as owners and publishers both of the *Sunday Mirror* and the *Daily Mirror* wishes to apologise publicly to Lord Boothby ... Neither the *Sunday Mirror* nor the *Daily Mirror*, in that or in subsequent issues, mentioned the name of Lord Boothby, but when Lord Boothby returned to London from France he found to his amazement – as he stated in his letter to *The Times* of August 1 – that Parliament, Fleet Street, and other informed quarters in London, were 'seething with rumours' ... The newspapers concerned communicated with Lord Boothby's solicitors indicating that they were immediately prepared to take all steps to clear Lord Boothby's reputation by the prominent publication of this statement. It is my own view, and the policy of this group, that when a newspaper is wrong, it should state so promptly and without equivocation. I am satisfied that any imputation of an improper nature against Lord Boothby is completely unjustified. In these circumstances I feel it my duty to sign this unqualified apology to Lord Boothby and to add the personal regret of myself and the directors of IPC that the story appeared.[14]

If that were not enough, the IPC also agreed to give Boothby £40,000 in an out-of-court settlement – then a record amount for a British libel pay-off. Goodman, meanwhile, tied up the arrangement so that none of the relevant parties could discuss the matter again in public. Boothby was vindicated. He had been the innocent victim of a ravenous tabloid press. And now he could get on with his life in peace, his good name restored.

There was just one problem. Boothby had been casting a web of lies – and he knew that were plenty of people out there who could prove it. The truth was that while Boothby and Kray were not lovers, a curious relationship had built up over the previous year in which they bonded over their shared love of sex with young men – a passion that Kray helped facilitate for Boothby. The cover-up that had just been executed in his interests would have far-reaching consequences. In the most extreme instances, lives that might have been saved were lost. Nor would Boothby ever find real peace again. How had it come to this? And why, in those few torrid days in the summer of 1964, did a triumvirate of Harold Wilson's most trusted lieutenants combine to save the reputation of a leading member of the opposition party?

It was a drama that had been several decades in the making.

3

The Lost Boys

Thursday, 19 May 1921 was the second day of Eights Week in Oxford. The River Isis bustled with rowing crews, each competing to uphold the honour of their respective colleges. Oarsmen and their acolytes thronged around the boathouses that lined the banks, while the crowds offered enthusiastic support to the racers in between feverish bouts of socialising.

But two particular undergraduates were intent on finding some peace amid all the sporting jollity. The pair, Michael Lewellyn Davies and Rupert Buxton – both students of Christ Church – decided to take advantage of the glorious afternoon sunshine to seek out a more tranquil spot. They set off through the verdant pastures of Christ Church Meadow, down to the river that they followed all the way to Sandford Lasher some miles away. The weir at Sandford created a large pool, some 100 metres across, and it was here that they stopped. The water, unusually low for the time of year, was calm and still, its surface free of weeds. The perfect place for a dip.

A short while later, two engineers from a nearby paper mill heard shouts coming from the pond. They saw the young men struggling in the water. Only their heads were visible above the water line. The engineers rushed for a lifebelt, which they had located, unravelled and thrown into the pond within a minute. Then one of them set off to get help, returning several minutes later with a posse of students from the Radley College boathouse. But by then, there was no sign of either Lewellyn Davies or Buxton.

Their bodies were not recovered until the next morning, when the authorities resumed dragging the river. Buxton was the first to be hauled up, and as he was lifted out of the water it was noted that something heavy dropped off him as he was about 8ft from the surface. This was, it turned out, Llewellyn Davies. According to Thomas Carter, who pulled the pair out, their bodies had been clasped together.[1] They were not the first students to lose their lives at this spot. There was already a memorial on the site commemorating three Oxford alumni who had drowned in the pool between 1843 and 1872. Such was its notoriety that Jerome K. Jerome even referenced Sandford in his 1889 masterpiece, *Three Men in a Boat*. '... the pool under Sandford lasher, just behind the lock, is a very good place to drown yourself in'.[2]

While the circumstances of the deaths of Lewellyn Davies and Buxton were hardly unique then, the impact of the tragedy reverberated for years to come among their friends. Not least among them was Boothby. He had been at Eton with Llewellyn Davies and their friendship had continued at Oxford, despite Boothby being a Magdalen man. Llewellyn Davies possessed a magnetism – albeit one tinged with almost intangible sadness – that was difficult to ignore. It was there even in childhood. He was the fourth of five boys, and in 1897 his older siblings were out with their nanny in Kensington Gardens one morning when they became captivated by a giant St Bernard dog with a penchant for walking on its back legs. The owner of the dog, it turned out, was the author, J.M. Barrie, and their chance encounter sparked an extraordinary series of events.

As the dog captured the imagination of the brothers, so the brothers became an object of fascination for Barrie. In time, Michael – who, like Boothby, was born in 1900 – would become his favourite and served as the principal model for Peter Pan, stories of whom Barrie conjured up for the children's amusement. But having stumbled upon these unexpected creative muses, Barrie was utterly unable to let go of them. He began a process of inserting himself into their family life, and could often be seen out with the boys and their mother, Sylvia, even though both she and he were married to other people. When the boy's father, Arthur, died in 1907, Barrie became still more influential in the family's affairs, including offering financial support. When Sylvia too passed away three years later, Barrie became the boys' guardian.

As Michael grew older, his relationship with the author became more complex if no less intense. Indeed, it was the intensity that was the problem.

There were whispers that Barrie had a sexual interest in Llewellyn Davies, although Boothby never held with the notion. He did, though, acknowledge their attachment as morbid and unhealthy. By the time he arrived at Oxford, Llewellyn Davies – who was strikingly handsome in a boyish sort of a way, and intellectually quite brilliant – was something of an icon to Boothby. Boothby believed that of all his contemporaries, Llewellyn Davies was the one 'touched by genius'[3] although entirely devoid of worldly ambition. Boothby saw a rich future for him, probably as an artist or – like Llewellyn Davies's cousin, Daphne du Maurier – a writer. But that was before Sandford Lasher.

The Coroner's Inquest returned a verdict of accidental death in the case of Llewellyn Davies, with Buxton deemed to have lost his life as he tried to save him. For the university authorities that was certainly a more pleasing verdict than one confirming the suggestion circulating among some that the two men had been lovers engaged in a suicide pact. Exactly what happened in the water that day will never be known for sure but Boothby had been wary of Buxton's influence on his friend for some time. He had warned Llewellyn Davies of a feeling of doom he had about Buxton. His ominous sense of foreboding only accentuated Boothby's pain when Llewellyn Davies died. But, as importantly, it consolidated his sense that life was short and precious, and that he must do all he could to wring as much pleasure from it as possible.

★★★

Boothby was born on 12 February 1900 in Edinburgh, to a family that over its history had won and lost several fortunes. By the time Bob arrived, they were on the up again. Although he would claim that they were never particularly rich, they nonetheless never had fewer than six indoor servants, two gardeners and a chauffeur while he was growing up. In the broadest terms, life was no struggle for the young Boothby.

His father, also called Robert but known as Tom, was a successful banker who would be knighted in 1929. Yet for all his success in the financial world, Tom found work rather a drag. Extremely good looking, he craved leisure time, especially on the golf course, where he could count himself among the very best players in Scotland. Despite his father's easy-going nature, Bob struggled to emerge from his shadow. He too loved golf but never quite reached Tom's standard, and so was the case – at least in Bob's mind – in a great many other strands of life. The son would later suggest that he had entered the world of politics because he suspected it was one area where he might actually stand a chance of surpassing his father.

But it was his mother, Mabel, who was the dominant figure in his life. She was energetic, forceful and boasted a *joie de vivre* that was infectious. She also had a passion for gambling – particularly on the horses – that she would in due course pass on to her son. As an only child, Boothby's early years really were idyllic. By his own admission, he was utterly spoiled by a family that, he would suggest, perhaps 'loved each other too much'.[4]

It was only when he reached the age of 10 that the real world began to seriously encroach upon this idyll. He was sent to a private school in Sussex, a long train ride from home. He could not fathom the decision to relegate him to this outpost, other than that his parents had a sense that it was somehow expected of them and their class. Whatever the reason, Boothby despised his time there and made no secret of the fact. In crushingly sad letters, he begged his mother and father to visit him or, better still, take him back home. Unsurprisingly, his distaste for his school life and all that went with it ensured he made few friends.

At 13 he moved on to Eton, where things were hardly better. In particular, he railed against the strict code of discipline, building for himself a sort of rebel status in the process. Beatings were at this time customarily doled out to rule breakers as long as the senior members of a House were all in agreement that the punishment was warranted. When Boothby eventually found his way onto his House's 'senior command', known as 'The Library', he used his vote to consistently veto beatings regardless of the proposed victim's alleged crimes. It was the first active flexing of his radical, liberal muscles.

Unlike the experience of his previous school, he succeeded in making friends at Eton. Apart from Llewelyn Davies, he was particularly close to Roger Senhouse (who would later head up the publishing house, Secker & Warburg) and the future politician, John Strachey. For all of them, their experience at Eton was defined by the onset of war. Fighting on the Continent was the ever-present backdrop to their teenage years. Each

Sunday a roll call of Old Etonians killed on the battlefield was dolefully read out. Boothby signed up to the Officer Training Corps and, later, the Guards Training Battalion, with a view to entering the fray at the earliest opportunity. His desire to serve was deep rooted and it caused him genuine regret when the Armistice was signed in November 1918. Death held no appeal, but the thought that he would emerge from this extraordinary phase of history as merely a bystander held little appeal, too. The war's end brought not elation but a sense of deflation.

Conflict had moulded his view of life and death in ways that would never entirely change. Among the many names recounted in those Sunday lists of the killed, one affected him more than any other – that of his beloved cousin, Henry Dundas. Henry, three years older than Boothby, had departed Eton to fight in France and was killed at the Battle of the Canal du Nord just a few weeks before the war's end, in circumstances that were not entirely clear. There was the suggestion from eyewitnesses that he had shown signs of depression for some while, before walking towards the German trenches until he was gunned down. For Boothby, Henry's death confirmed the precariousness of existence. 'As we saw all the heroes of our youth being killed, one by one, and not far away,' he would later write, 'our whole attitude to life changed. "Eat and drink and try to be merry, for tomorrow you will surely die" became our motto.'[5]

From Eton, Boothby went up to Oxford alongside many of his contemporaries. He opted to study history at Magdalen College, but he found a university rendered almost unrecognisable by the war. The fighting had virtually cut out a generation of undergraduates. Of those who had not been killed, many simply did not have the appetite to return to their studies. It was left to Boothby's intake to rebuild. Lapsed dining clubs were reinstituted, societies that had floundered were injected with new vigour and the 'eat, drink and be merry' culture prevailed. After the unhappy experience of school, Boothby at last found himself. He kept up those friendships he had cultivated at Eton and added to his circle, forging enduring relationships with the likes of Edward Majoribanks, the stepson of the 1st Viscount Hailsham who would become Lord Chancellor in 1929.

There was much carousing throughout. Boothby rated Magdalen's chef as the best he ever encountered and Boothby's gang joyfully spent evenings draining hock from the Emperor of Austria's cellars at a modest seven shillings and sixpence a bottle. In the holidays, he explored the Continent with friends. One particularly memorable trip saw Boothby staying in a pension at Saint-Servan in Brittany with Senhouse, Clive Burt (another Old Etonian) and Lewellyn Davies. The group would spend their evenings drinking green chantreuse outside the cafés of nearby Saint-Malo, playing boule at the casino and putting the world to rights in the way undergraduates are eternally prone to do. If Boothby's early years in Edinburgh had been an idyll, he seemed to have found a new paradise.

He also cultivated his image as a man of fashion, championing a trend for bright, stripeless shirts partnered with baggy trousers that came to be known as 'Oxford bags'. And still there was time for a little politics. Majoribanks was instrumental in guiding Boothby towards the university's more Conservative organisations, although the party was not an entirely natural fit for Boothby. It was here at Oxford that Boothby also had his first fateful encounter with Winston Churchill.

Then there was the sex. Throughout his life, Boothby never publicly wavered from the line that he had never been a practising homosexual. Suggestions of his prodigious bisexuality nonetheless followed him about for years. Rumours of his delight in intercourse with attractive young men were doing the rounds well before he left university. He himself acknowledged that Oxford in those years immediately after the First World War 'was, basically, a homosexual society'.[6] But he was quick to clarify that this did not mean that all the undergraduates were sleeping with each other. Merely, Oxford was in practical terms an almost exclusively male environment. Aside from a week in the summer when the college put on balls, women had no place there. So it had been at Eton too, where all it took for one young man to achieve almost legendary status as 'the Fornicator' was for it to be known that he had a girlfriend in a nearby town.

While at Oxford, Boothby revealed later in his life, he had gone through what he described as a 'homosexual stage',[7] which he insisted was an emotional rather than physical state. Few of those close to him really believed that particular qualification. Most were quite aware that Boothby had given rather more of himself to this 'stage' than just his emotions. It would certainly explain how he came to be given the epithet of 'the Palladium', said to have been awarded in recognition of his reputation for putting on twice nightly performances. Certainly, one close friend – the career diplomat Archie Clark Kerr – felt compelled to warn Boothby about his conduct.

Clark Kerr was some eighteen years older than Boothby but the pair had bonded when they met at Bushey during Boothby's stint with the Guards Training Battalion. In 1921, Clark Kerr was the Consul-General in Tangier but was soon to finish his time in Morocco, and he invited Boothby to accompany him for a farewell tour of the country. Tangier at the time boasted a large European population, with artists and writers rubbing shoulders with diplomats, spies and shady businessmen. The result was a city that bridged the North African and European cultures, offering intrigue and excitement and, for a young man fresh from Oxford, the opportunity to indulge his tastes and predilections while remaining largely anonymous.

Shortly after Boothby returned to England, Clark Kerr wrote to him concerning his lifestyle. His fear was that private indiscretions might put the brakes on Boothby's ambitions in public life. 'There is only one cure,' Clark Kerr warned, 'and the longer it is put off the harder it will be. I had hoped a little that you would perhaps let the case of old Loulou be a lesson to you …'[8] The 'Loulou' in question was Lewis Harcourt, a Liberal politician who had served as Colonial Secretary from 1910 to 1915. Although ostensibly happily married, Harcourt enjoyed the sexual company of men, women and children. Such was his reputation that boys at his old school, Eton, were warned against going on walks out with him on his frequent returns to the *alma mater*. Eventually, the mother of one of his young victims got wind of what he had been up to with her son, leaving him fearful of imminent exposure. He was found dead in his home at the age of 59 after overdosing on the sedative bromidia. Harcourt lived in Oxfordshire and Clark Kerr's letter implies he and Boothby had enjoyed summer visits to his home. While there is nothing to suggest that Boothby ever felt sexual attraction towards children, that Clark Kerr should have cited Harcourt as an object lesson rather belies the idea that Boothby's experimentation at this time was purely emotional in nature.

As he took the train home from Oxford in 1922 for the last time as a student, Boothby sat alone in his carriage and considered that he should never be happy again. 'I was right,' he would rue many years later.[9] These truly had been – Michael's death apart – the best and most carefree days of his life. He would spend a large part of the proceeding decades striving to recover something like their sense of bliss and possibility. His quest was fundamentally informed – and ultimately blighted – by the loss of, first, Henry Dundas and then Llewelyn Davies. The 'eat drink and try to be merry' mantra was not merely a licence to indulge in Bacchanalian excess but served as a means of striking back against that spectre of death that had stalked Boothby's youth. Shortly after Llewelyn Davies's demise, Boothby wrote to his aunt:

> Michael's death came as a great shock to me: he was the person who, after Henry, I most admired … Now the two people for whom I had the greatest admiration have been taken at 21 and 20 respectively. Who can doubt that they are wanted for finer & more exacting work elsewhere? My faith in an individual future is absolutely firm: it is only strengthened by these things.[10]

In particular, the trauma of Llewelyn Davies's drowning cannot be under-estimated in the strength of its impact on Boothby. He described how Majoribanks wrote a series of hysterical letters in its aftermath, and that Roger Senhouse – who had briefly been Llewelyn Davies's lover at Eton – sobbed uncontrollably at the funeral. Boothby himself – imbued by both parents with a love of the good things in life and, by his mother, an addiction to gambling – now embarked on an arc of reckless hedonism with new abandon. Reflecting on events in 1976, he believed that the drowning had been in some part responsible for the 1932 suicide of Majoribanks, who was by then a high-flying Conservative MP, and for what he regarded as Senhouse's self-destructive relationship with that pillar of the Bloomsbury Group, Lytton Strachey, throughout the 1930s. As for himself: 'I've made a pretty good mess of my life, which would have been very different if Michael had lived. He had a great influence over me, more than anyone else I've ever known. He would have stopped me doing many foolish things, He would have kept me on the rails.'[11]

However, for a while it looked as if Boothby was destined for truly great things before his derailment.

4

Shooting Star

It was a story upon which Boothby dined out often over the years – the first time he came face-to-face with Adolf Hitler. Boothby was invited to Germany in late 1931 to lecture on the economic crisis, packing out lecture theatres in both Hamburg and Berlin with audiences of eight hundred and more. He was a firebrand at home and now his opinions were in demand internationally. Then came a call from a friend, Ernst Hanfstaengl – commonly known as Putzi. German-born and Harvard-educated, Putzi was a debonair socialite who had charmed the upper echelons of American and British society with his ready wit, geniality and precocious skills as a pianist. For the last decade or so, he had also been an ardent admirer of Hitler, rising to become his personal secretary. Now Putzi was inviting Boothby to meet the Nazi leader at his headquarters in Berlin's Esplanade Hotel.

As Boothby would tell it in later years, Putzi said that Hitler had been an interested reader of his recent speeches and was keen to be introduced to him. When the time came, Boothby was led into a long inner room at the Esplanade. The short, spare figure of Hitler was sat at a desk in one corner, dressed in the familiar brown shirt with a swastika on the arm. He did not look up until Boothby was beside him, then he raised what Boothby called his 'limpid blue eyes' before springing to his feet, clicking his heels together, raising his arm and shouting 'Hitler!' His guest, momentarily taken aback, responded by flicking his own heels together, raising his right arm and bellowing back 'Boothby!'[1]

It is likely that this last detail of the story is nothing more than an old raconteur's embellishment, a crowd-pleasing detail from a man who loved the acclaim of an audience. But whether or not he replied to Hitler's salute in exactly this manner, the meeting itself was nonetheless a remarkable one. Boothby was quick to see that Hitler – still a year from beating the odds to become Germany's Chancellor – was not a man to be underestimated. While some in the international community regarded him almost as a figure of fun, Boothby witnessed first-hand how his passion for his political agenda had cut through to a desperate German population. 'The cry "Heil Hitler!" re-echoes through Germany to-day,' Boothby told the readers of the *Evening Standard*. 'We should not underestimate the strength of the movement of which he is the living embodiment. It is impossible to forecast the future.'[2] Around this time, he also confided his thoughts on the situation in Germany in a letter to Winston Churchill. 'At the end of my talk with Hitler I asked him what he was going to do to the Jews, and there was a grand scene, like a Bateman cartoon,' Boothby wrote. 'Eventually he said he would veto "pogroms", which wasn't altogether reassuring.'[3]

The meeting with Hitler marked a pivotal moment in the upward career trajectory of Boothby – a man who had already spent seven years as a Member of Parliament despite being still only 31. His rise up the political greasy poll had begun back in Oxford, where his friendships with some of the university's political heavyweights set him upon a path that might otherwise have taken some significantly different turns. Boothby did not arrive at Magdalen as a party political man. Rather like Winston Churchill – who would become his mentor, ally and eventual nemesis – he could easily have found a home in either the Conservative or Liberal parties. The Liberal leader David Lloyd George was his great political hero for the whole of his life. Indeed, Boothby's entire political being was to a good degree defined by his disinclination to ever be a wholehearted party man.

But it was Edward Majoribanks who persuaded Boothby to make his first political speech at Oxford's Conservative-leaning Canning Club. He spoke on 'The Conduct of Naval Operations during the War of 1914–18', an oration that Boothby considered he had 'got away with'.[4] This was *faux* modesty. His natural skills as a communicator, as he well knew, set him apart. Before long he was the society's secretary and his political die had been cast. In this role he encountered Churchill for the first time. Already one of the great figures of British politics, Churchill had been booked to speak at the Union and Boothby met him at a dinner hosted by the aristocratic young Conservative, Victor Cazalet. Also in attendance was F.E. Smith, Lord Birkenhead, who dazzled the youthful Boothby with his eloquence but whose career rather foreshadowed Boothby's own. A noted *bon viveur*, Birkenhead ended up as a sad drunk whose political life had never come near to meeting its full potential. With that in mind, it is telling that one of Boothby's Oxford contemporaries, Maurice Bowra – who found fame as a critic, academic and insatiable gossip – said of Boothby at Oxford: 'At heart he cherished ambitions of political success but for the moment he was out to enjoy himself, and succeeded on a handsome scale …'[5]

Largely through circumstance rather than ideology, then, Boothby left Oxford in 1922 as a Conservative. He next began a career in the law, harbouring an ambition to be the new Edward Marshall Hall, the 'Great Defender' of the Victorian and Edwardian eras' criminal courts. Marshall Hall's silky oratory saved many a neck from the noose and made him a fixture of public life at the same time. It was not, perhaps, an entirely impossible dream for Boothby to follow in his footsteps and he was welcomed into the chambers of Walter Monckton (later Viscount Monckton of Brenchley) to read for the Bar. But before he had gained any real foothold in the profession, political fate took over.

In 1922, the coalition government of Lloyd George collapsed, with Andrew Bonar Law replacing him as Prime Minister at the head of a Conservative government. When Bonar Law's poor health forced his resignation in May 1923, Stanley Baldwin – who happened to be a friend of Boothby's father – took over and called a general election before the year's end. Boothby had offered his services to the Conservatives in Scotland but was taken aback when it was suggested that, as part of the Tories' strategy of contesting all Scottish seats in a bid to wrest a few from the Liberals, Boothby should stand for Orkney and Shetland.

Walter Monckton granted him three weeks' leave for the project. Few gave Boothby any real prospect of gaining much ground in the staunch Liberal stronghold, but he fought a spirited and much-admired campaign. Where his slick (and largely English-accented) oratory might have been expected to play badly with the voters of Scotland's outlying reaches, in fact his youthful exuberance and impassioned rhetoric won over many, as did his evident political independence. He was not, he told the electorate, 'a Unionist, Conservative, or Tory of the old school. I was brought up in a Liberal family with Liberal traditions …'.[6] As one observer put it, 'when he gets up to speak, he goes off like an alarm clock'.[7]

Boothby never had a chance of winning the seat but his achievement in claiming 45 per cent of the vote got him noticed. Across the nation, however, Baldwin's electoral gamble backfired. He lost his majority and Ramsay MacDonald came in to lead a Liberal-backed Labour minority government. But with the Conservatives set for a period of rebuilding, Boothby now found himself well placed. He opted to leave the Bar and joined Baldwin's opposition secretariat. When MacDonald's administration lost a vote of confidence early the next year, Boothby found himself once more on the campaign trail, for the seat of Aberdeen and Kincardine East. And this time, he won.

Aged 24, Boothby had his parliamentary seat and, when in London, lived out of a rented flat on Pall Mall. He began to nurture many of the political friendships that would, for better or worse, mould his career. Among the new intake of MPs in 1924 was Harold Macmillan, a far less charismatic figure than Boothby but someone with whom he quickly developed a strong rapport, although neither could have had the slightest inkling just how their fates would soon be forever entwined. Meanwhile, Boothby's hero, Lloyd George, was taken with both men. Here were Conservatives that he sensed he could do business with. Boothby in turn was delighted to be taken under the old master's wing. There were plenty more burgeoning alliances too, not least a potentially dangerous association with Oswald Mosley, who had recently ditched the Tories for the Labour Party and who was then fizzing with the latest leftist economic ideas, many of which chimed with Boothby.

Boothby was an early advocate of the economics of John Maynard Keynes, which called for robust public spending in the face of rising unemployment and a depressed economy. It was an outlook that put the young MP out of kilter with Baldwin and the mainstream of his party. He quickly came to be seen as on the radical left of the Conservatives, particularly after he expressed support for Baldwin when he reached out to the unions as industrial relations spiralled downwards in the middle of the decade. In 1926, Boothby raised more eyebrows when he returned from a trip to the Soviet Union to argue that it would be possible to deal commercially and diplomatically with the regime there despite its already well-known dictatorial tendencies. For middle-of-the-road Conservatives still coming to terms with the recent General Strike at home, this truly was Bolshy talk. Churchill admired the courageousness and independent spirit of his young colleague but warned him against sacrificing his political future 'for the sake of herrings' (a reference to the fact that the USSR was a significant importer of the fish, a leading economic commodity for Boothby's Aberdeen constituency).[8]

Boothby was not a man to be cowed, though. In October 1926, he wrote a lengthy note to Churchill, who was then Chancellor of the Exchequer. Boothby listed what he considered to be the various failings of government policy in the aftermath of the General Strike, not least the appearance that the government was siding with mine-owners and industrialists against the interests of the workers. Churchill shook off the criticisms but was impressed by Boothby's incisiveness and self-confidence – enough to invite him to become his Parliamentary Private Secretary. If Churchill hoped this elevated role might knock some of the corners off Boothby, it was soon apparent that any such aspirations were misplaced. Boothby locked horns with his party colleagues on a regular basis, causing him to offer his resignation to Churchill on several occasions. 'I fear I shall always be a bad Party man,' he would note, 'being of a restless and somewhat obstinate disposition.'[9]

Nonetheless, the 1920s were a golden age for Boothby, and not just in political terms. For those with wealth, there was a brief interwar blossoming of hedonistic, bohemian excess, often staged in one or other of the nation's great country houses – a period Adrian Tinniswood has characterised as 'The Long Weekend'[10] – and Boothby for a while was very close to its epicentre, even though his own finances were far from in rude health. In 1928 he joined the stockbrokers Chase, Henderson and Tennant, eventually becoming a partner, but his investment instincts were not the sharpest and money was always a worry. Even as he began to supplement his earn-

ings with paid journalism – having managed to win the appreciation of
Lord Beaverbrook, arguably the greatest press baron of the age – his income
rarely matched his outgoings. For a man of his achievements, it is notable
that he never owned his own home. Nor was his financial situation in any
way improved by his love of the casinos of Venice, Monte Carlo and assorted
other exotic European bolt holes.

But for the time being, he was able to maintain an enviable lifestyle. Aside
from the relationships forged in Westminster, he counted a number of cultural icons among his friends, from W. Somerset Maughan and Noel Coward
to Malcolm Sargent and Arnold Bennett. And through Maud Cunard,
of the famous shipping family, he met one of his musical heroes, Thomas
Beecham. Few were the weekends when there wasn't an invitation to some
get-together or another hosted by one of the nation's great families. There
were, for instance, countless weekends at Cliveden, the Buckinghamshire
estate of the Astor family that provided the backdrop to several pivotal
events in the nation's history throughout the twentieth century.

Some of his happiest times were at the home of Philip Sassoon.
Descendant of the Rothschild banking dynasty and cousin of the war poet
Siegfried, Sassoon was a key figure in Boothby's life at this time – 'For ten
years he shaped my life,' Boothby would say[11] – and the two may indeed
have been lovers. Boothby's reminiscences about life at Sassoon's Trent Park
estate in Hertfordshire gives a taste of the age:

> To-day it all seems like the dream of another world – the white-coated
> footmen, Winston Churchill arguing over the tea-cups with Bernard
> Shaw, Rex Whistler painting alone, an immaculate Sir Samuel Hoare
> playing tennis with the professional, Osbert Sitwell and Malcolm Bullock
> laughing in a corner while Philip himself flitted from group to group, an
> alert, watchful, influential, but unobtrusive stage director.[12]

Boothby could charm with the best of them, erudite and amusing one
moment, coarse and shocking the next. And where he had previously been
exclusively homosexual, he now embarked on a new phase of enthusiastic
bisexualism. He was an enormously skilled flirt who, moreover, professed
an apparently genuine longing to have a family of his own – features that,

he also understood, would do no harm to his political ambitions. He developed a reputation as something of a heartbreaker, leaving behind a string of jilted fiancées, proposed to in haste at moments of high emotion.

Meanwhile, back in the swing of London life, he was considered among the city's most clubable men, in stark contrast to his contemporary, Macmillan. His favourite haunt was White's on St James's Street, regarded by some as the most exclusive of all private gentlemen's clubs since its establishment in 1693. Boothby followed in the finest traditions of several of its clientele, which included the pre-eminent dandy of Regency England, Beau Brummel, and Lord Alvanley, who in the early nineteenth century made a £3,000 bet as to which of two raindrops would reach the bottom of one of the club's window panes first.

In 1930, Boothby narrowly avoided serious injury when his car overturned on a wet and slippery Surrey road (it is difficult to avoid picturing Toad 'road-hogging' his way across the country in Kenneth Grahame's *Wind in the Willows* at this point). But the incident did little to slow him down after an initial few weeks of recovery. He had ceased to be Churchill's secretary the previous year and he often found himself at odds with prevailing opinion within the party, but he was still very much regarded as a 'coming man' – a politician with a distinct political philosophy, a domestic and international profile and an exceptional ability to communicate.

By the time Boothby met Hitler in Berlin, he looked poised to become one of the 'big beasts' of British politics. Perhaps even a future Prime Minister. But the 1930s would prove to be a trying decade for him, as for the entire world. The sweep of global history would put a brake on his personal ambitions. Moreover, behind the scenes things had already begun to go off track. Ask most political observers in 1931 who was a more likely future resident of Downing Street, Boothby or Harold Macmillan, and few would have opted for the socially awkward and introverted Macmillan. But by the end of the 1920s Boothby had embroiled himself in a relationship that would have a cataclysmic effect on the lives of both men.

5

Other Men's Wives

It had all started with the best of intentions. The year was 1929 and Macmillan was in low spirits, having just lost his seat – Stockton-on-Tees – at the general election. Boothby was eager to help lift his friend from his funk. He hit upon the idea of inviting Macmillan and his wife Dorothy for a weekend's shooting at his father's estate, Beechwood, at Corstorphine, a little west of Edinburgh.

Boothby – brash and exuberant – and Macmillan – restrained and serious – had grown close over the five years since they had both entered the House of Commons. They hit it off because they broadly shared a political philosophy, counting themselves among the young progressives who earned themselves the nickname of the YMCA from certain Westminster wags. Boothby and Macmillan in due course worked together on a book – the first either of them was to publish – called *Industry & the State: A Conservative View*. Released in 1927, it was conservative in name only. Here was a radical manifesto for how the state ought to engage with industrial actors – owners, managers and workers – in the new age. The authors, according to the *Daily Mail*, were clearly 'Socialists in Conservative Disguise'.[1]

Macmillan had married Dorothy Cavendish in 1920 at St Margaret's, Westminster, in one of the society weddings of the year. Nonetheless, many regarded it from the outset as a curious mismatch, not least several of the extended Cavendish clan who couldn't fathom what she saw in a man they considered disappointingly dull. The couple had met in 1919 when Macmillan was serving as aide-de-camp to her father, the Duke of Devonshire, who was at the time Governor-General of Canada. The third daughter of the Duke, Dorothy was known as Lady Dorothy from the age of 8 and spent a privileged childhood living on the family's Chatsworth estate in Derbyshire.

To begin with, her relationship with Harold seemed happy enough. While not of aristocratic stock, he hailed from the famous Macmillan publishing dynasty and boasted a sharp intelligence, political ambition and a proud record of service during the First World War. She, meanwhile, offered him a route into one of the nation's great families that would certainly not harm his long-term career aims. That is not to say that their relationship began as merely a matter of convenience. There seems to have been genuine affection early on, and even passion too. By 1926 they were the parents of three children.

But by then, the cracks in their union were already evident. Dorothy was by nature high spirited and fiery. Macmillan was neither. It was becoming clear, too, that his libido did not come close to matching hers. Within a couple of years, Dorothy had started growing bored of her marriage. By the time Macmillan entered the Commons, the long process of drift between them was well under way. Nonetheless, they had made their marital bed and neither had any craving to unmake it – not for the time being at least.

Boothby had met Dorothy several times over the years before the fateful Beechwood get-together of 1929. She found him charming and funny, his excess of energy in distinct contrast to her husband. He certainly cut a dash, speeding his way from one country house to another in his sporty two-seater Bentley. He seems to have considered her engaging enough too, although there was no sign of what was to come. Lady Dorothy was not physically unappealing but nor was she a striking beauty. She was instead handsome and robust, hearty and bright. A well-bred girl with a bit about her, as it were. Not necessarily, though, the sort of woman over whom men swooned.

But then something changed. The shooting party was out on the moors and Boothby stood awaiting his turn, when all of a sudden he felt a hand slip into his and squeeze. It was Dorothy. Here was the slow-burn beginning of what would turn into a blazingly passionate affair after the couple met again during a weekend at Bowood, home of the Marquesses of Lansdowne. It was soon apparent, too, that there was genuine affection underpinning their initial lust. The roots of Boothby's lust for her were far from orthodox anyway. When his cousin, the acclaimed author and journalist Ludovic Kennedy, asked him years later what he saw in her, he replied: 'Dorothy has thighs like hams and hands like a stevedore, but I adore her.'[2] And to Lord Lambton – a man whose own political career expired on the pyre of a tabloid sex scandal in the 1970s – he said she reminded him of a caddy he'd once ravished on a golf course.[3]

For all the unpromising beginnings that these comments hinted at, Dorothy and Boothby soon found themselves in a very serious relationship. They were, it might even be said, in love. In August 1930, their entwinement became even more complicated. Dorothy gave birth to a daughter, Sarah. To the present day, there is mystery surrounding her paternity. The likelihood is that no one really knew for sure. If she was Boothby's, then Dorothy must have fallen pregnant very early in their relationship. Macmillan even turned to Boothby for some closure on the matter in the 1970s, visiting him one day at his Eaton Square flat to ask him for the truth. Boothby insisted that Sarah could not be his because he had been scrupulously careful to take precautions from the outset of the affair. Macmillan's biographer, D.H. Thorpe, many years later learned of a further detail that lends credence to Boothby's denial of paternity. The adult Sarah herself was the target of some sort of amorous advance from Boothby. Even given Boothby's exotic sexual tastes, intentional incest seems an unlikely road for him to have travelled.[4]

Nonetheless, a great many of those in the social circle of Macmillan and Boothby were convinced she was the lover's child and not the husband's. Dorothy even told Macmillan that she was Boothby's, although there was good reason why she might have wanted him to believe that even if it were not true. Dorothy had decided that she no longer wanted to be married to Harold but wanted to spend her life with Boothby instead. She demanded a divorce, and adultery resulting in a bastard child might have offered her a shortcut to that outcome.

Macmillan, though, would not have it. The English upper classes had spent centuries turning a blind eye to private affairs for the avoidance of public scandal and he saw no reason to buck the system now. The actions of Dorothy and Boothby wounded him deeply and he had no wish to heap new humiliation upon himself. He did get as far as discussing the matter with his solicitor, Philip Frere, but Frere convinced him to stick to his guns. If he was serious about ever holding high office, the lawyer suggested, he must rule out divorce once and for all. This he did, writing to Nancy Astor in January 1933: 'Sorry to bother you. But make it clear to her [Dorothy] that I will <u>never</u> divorce her.'[5] He even went as far as threatening to kill himself if she ever absconded with Boothby.

There was a compromise of sorts, with the couple agreeing to what was effectively an open marriage. For five years or so, Dorothy and Boothby virtually lived together, attending public events and doing very little to disguise the nature of their relationship from those in their private circles. Boothby was banned by the Cavendishes from going to Chatsworth but that was about the extent of the sanctions against them. Nor did the public get wind of the scandal; its details never divulged by the press, despite their affair being common knowledge on Fleet Street and to a large swathe of the ruling classes. The Establishment was doing what it customarily does – drawing a veil over that which might excite the lower orders.

When Macmillan regained his seat in the Commons in 1931, he and Boothby found themselves in what might have been expected to be a brutally uncomfortable situation. Yet they hit upon the means not merely to co-exist but to serve as close political allies, even friends. Macmillan simply uncoupled himself from the turmoil of his private life, giving all his energies to his career and compartmentalising his personal relationships. Boothby had made him a cuckold but in Westminster he was his comrade.

Meanwhile, Dorothy and Boothby became an increasingly combustible mix. Each counted Cynthia (Cimmie), the wife of Oswald Mosley, among their greatest confidantes and it was she to whom they repeatedly spilled out their hearts. 'I have not entirely given up hope of getting Harold into a more reasonable frame of mind about divorce,' Dorothy wrote to her in 1932, 'but at present he is hopeless. I am afraid Bob must have led an awful time away. I should think he is sick of everything. He still wants to marry me, but if I don't come to him he probably won't go on waiting and wanting to. The future looks pretty grim.'[6]

She was right that Boothby regularly despaired of the situation. His modus operandi for effecting a break from the *ménage à trois* was to announce an engagement to some third party or other, who more often than not took the form of an American heiress (a type who routinely appealed to the Americanophile in him). Dorothy, though, was highly adept at scuppering such schemes. As Boothby told Macmillan's biographer, Nigel Fisher, in 1977:

What Dorothy wanted and needed was emotion, on the scale of Isolde. This Harold could not give her, and I did. She was, on the whole, the most selfish and most possessive woman I have ever known. Once, when I got engaged to an American heiress, she pursued me from Chatsworth to Paris, and from Paris to Lisbon. But we loved each other. And there is really nothing you can do about this, except die.[7]

Back in 1932, Boothby communicated his sense of the impossibility of it all to Cimmie:

What to do? Go for the high jump, chuck politics, smash up that household, and marry Dorothy? Or cross the Atlantic and marry Iselin [his other romantic interest at that moment]? Or try to stagger on alone? ... I like this girl. And I love Dorothy. As much as I have ever loved her. But can any marriage survive such crushing initial handicaps as a smashed political career (for I could never get back to the House of Commons), and four children in more or less of a mess? ... She said to me tragically yesterday, 'Why did you ever wake me? I never want to see any of my family again. And, without you, life for me is going to be nothing but one big hurt.'[8]

The feeling of entrapment was there too in a letter to his old friend, John Strachey, written the following year: 'The most formidable thing in the world – a possessive single-track woman. She wants me, completely, and she wants my children, and she wants practically nothing else ... I am passionately in love with her. But if I take her, it's goodbye to everything else.'[9]

Then in 1935, he hit upon one of those hare-brained escapades that punctuated his life. He got himself engaged again, and this time to Dorothy's own cousin, Diana Cavendish. He had first met her at a dance in 1929 and the two always got on well, their relationship defined by fun and freedom from the heat and tumult that went with Dorothy. Now, six years later, he was exhausted by the seemingly never-ending saga of his entanglement with Dorothy. He had just enjoyed a convivial dinner with Diana – at which, needless to say, he drank more than was strictly good for him – whereupon he decided to ask her to marry him. They had a marvellous time together, didn't they, and it would put an end once and for all to his Dorothy drama. But when he awoke the next morning, he felt a sudden jolt as the memory of what had transpired a few hours earlier filtered back to him. He immediately sought a way out but, unfortunately for him, Diana had already informed her parents of the good news (although they were, not surprisingly, unconvinced that it was, in fact, good).

The wedding date was set for March 1935, at the Church of St Bartholomew-the-Great in Smithfield. Boothby spent the intervening weeks drinking heavily. Almost as soon as the vows had left their lips, the marriage was doomed. The union went unconsummated on their wedding night, Diana angrily informing him the next morning that he could breathe a sigh of relief as she had her period. 'I've got joyous news for you,' she is supposed to have said. 'It's alright, I've got the curse so you needn't fuck me anymore.'[10] The conversation set the tone for the months and years to come. By the end of 1936 they had agreed to bring the sorry episode to an end and file for divorce. As the law then needed a culpable party in order to permit the separation, Boothby took a woman to a hotel and made sure to be witnessed, making his adultery official. The couple were divorced in 1937.

Socially and professionally, the fallout for Boothby was considerable. The Cavendishes *en masse* were furious with him. Significantly, they included the Tory MP, James Stuart, who was married to Dorothy' sister, Rachel, and who later served as Chief Whip in Churchill's wartime administration and then as Secretary of State for Scotland. He was a powerful enemy to make, as was Lord Balniel, another influential Conservative parliamentarian who had married into the family. Boothby considered that from then on, the Cavendishes were intent on bringing him down. 'Once you get into the clutches of that family,' he ruefully told Susan Barnes in a *Sunday Times* interview in 1973, 'by God, you haven't a hope. They are the most tenacious family in Britain.'[11] He had also succeeded in angering Winston Churchill, a long-time friend of Diana's, and his wife Clementine, who viewed Boothby's behaviour as morally repugnant.

Yet for all these instances of ostracism, Boothby still enjoyed a level of Establishment protection, a security blanket to which he was starting to cling complacently far too often. While behind certain closed doors of high society his name was muck, his misdemeanours were downplayed in the public sphere. It would be impossible to keep news of the divorce out of the papers but he did not suffer the character assassination he might have expected, nor was there any mention of his connection to Harold and Dorothy Macmillan. In part, this was because he used his newspaper connections to ward off the worst. In particular, he appealed to Lord Beaverbrook in a letter of 21 December 1936:

> Dear Max, My marriage crumbled into ruins six months ago, and there is only one thing I can honourably do now. I realise that there must be a good deal of publicity. But don't let your boys hunt me down. Because I am not going to let go of public life; and still believe that one day I may do something. What a hell of an autumn this has been.[12]

Boothby made a hash of his private life in the 1930s, but somehow he got away with it – at least in terms of avoiding public opprobrium. On learning of the affair between Boothby and Lady Dorothy, King George V is said to have warned: 'Keep it quiet.'[13] Elizabeth, wife of George VI, was forgiving too, noting many years later that Boothby was a 'cad' but not a 'bounder' (as measured, presumably, on a scale of dishonour never to be revealed to the average person on the street).[14] While the honest farmers and fishermen of Boothby's Aberdeen constituency were taken aback by the news of his divorce, it was handled delicately enough that they soon forgave him. A man's private life, after all, ought to be his own.

It is Maurice Bowra, though, who most deftly illustrated the capacity of the Establishment to close ranks, keeping scandal 'in-house' and away from the public gaze. Over many decades Bowra relished lampooning the great and the good in verse, which he privately distributed to a select group of friends. In 1942, it was Boothby and Macmillan's turn in 'The Statesman's Tragedy'.[15] Among its many verses can be found the following lines:

A duke's daughter was driven mad,
Was driven mad,
By the soft winning ways I had.
She thought of none but me.
From husband and from marriage-bed
She shrank in horror and in dread.
She sighed to win my lustihead
And manly potency,

...

Her hapless husband, whiskered Hal,
Would gaily greet me in the Mall
As tho' I were his truest pal
And no adulterer.

Even Boothby's bisexuality was considered fair game for poetic rendering:

And little chaps with tender eyes,
With tender eyes,
Would gape on me in mad surprise
And stroke my thick black hair,
Or seated on an eiderdown
Would fumble with my dressing-gown,
And turn on me a puzzled frown
Or little loving stare.

Crucially, these words were never intended for mass consumption. Quite the reverse. They were for the entertainment and titillation of a privileged minority considered able to respond in an appropriate manner.[16] Boothby's conduct had not won the admiration of many in his set, but there was an underlying acceptance that such things went on in these echelons of society. In other words, there were modes of behaviour allowable for the powerful and the influential but unacceptable for the populace at large. The conduct of his private life throughout the decade had seen Boothby earn a few scars, but he emerged largely undamaged in the eyes of the public. Ready to fight another day and to meet the call (and enjoy the benefits) of public duty whenever it might come.

So, it was rather ironic when it was a misstep in his public life that threatened to topple his ambitions once and for all.

6

Czechmate

'This is a very difficult speech for me to make,' Boothby said, as he rose to his feet in the House of Commons. It was 28 January 1941, a few days after combined British and Australian forces had captured Tobruk from the Italians in Libya. There was just the merest sense that the tide of the war might yet turn in the Allies' favour. Boothby ought to have been in his element. Instead, he was stepping down from his post as Under Secretary at the Ministry of Food, a parliamentary select committee having found that his conduct was 'derogatory to the dignity of the House and inconsistent with the standards which Parliament is entitled to expect from its Members'.[1]

For a man tipped not so long before as a future Prime Minister, it was notable that this had been his first ministerial position and a relatively lowly one at that. Now it was all coming to an end, his ministerial career never to be resurrected. His own viewpoint, as he explained to the House, was that he had been undone by bad judgement rather than ill intent. 'Folly I have admitted,' he said. 'Guilt I cannot admit.' His instinct for a rhetorical flourish was as alert as ever. On this occasion, he quoted a few lines of Rabbie Burns to sum up his predicament:

> The poor inhabitant below
> Was quick to learn the wise to know,
> And keenly felt the friendly glow,

And softer flame;
But thoughtless follies laid him low,
And stain'd his name![2]

So, how had Boothby navigated quite such an effective route from coming man to fallen idol in the space of a decade?

Back in 1931, it seemed likely he would get his chance at one of the big posts in government. With the nation facing economic crisis, the Labour Prime Minister, Ramsay MacDonald, agreed to the formation of a National Government that drew upon the talents of Labour, the Conservatives and the Liberal Party. The move, though, was unpopular with many within his own party, including the Foreign Secretary, Arthur Henderson, who led a breakaway group called National Labour into the general election in October that year. The National Government won an overwhelming majority but was now dominated by Conservatives. MacDonald stayed on as Prime Minister but was only titular head of the government. The real power rested with Stanley Baldwin, the Conservative leader and nominally Lord President of the Council.

Before the National Government was formed, it was strongly rumoured that Baldwin would install Boothby as President of the Board of Trade. But when the moment came, there was no such offering. Although he likely did not realise it just then, Boothby's moment had passed. What followed was a spell in the political wilderness as his interests and concerns increasingly diverged from those of his party. Only at the end of the decade was he brought limitedly back into the fold.

For years after Baldwin overlooked him, he cut an increasingly lonely figure. Of his great mentors, Lloyd George was more and more viewed as yesterday's man and Boothby's relations with Churchill were on the decline. Although he would work in concert with Churchill again towards the end of the decade, the roots of their cross-generational friendship had started to wither irretrievably. In the early 1930s, Churchill was tightly focused on India, where he watched with growing concern the activities of Mahatma Gandhi, whom he described as 'a seditious Middle Temple lawyer, now posing as a fakir'.[3] Churchill threw his energies into opposing the granting of Dominion Status, arguing that India was not yet prepared for the demands of Home Rule. Boothby, though, was already more concerned with what was going on in continental Europe.

He was quick to recognise not only the danger posed by Hitler personally – he was, as Boothby put it to Neville Chamberlain in 1938, 'a frantic and ferocious madman, with a destructive genius almost without parallel in history'[4] – but also the deep-rooted nature of the social unrest that underpinned his rise. While others still expected that the Führer could be brought to heel, Boothby had long grasped that it would take more than diplomacy to offset his threat. In his memoirs, he noted:

In order to understand the Germany of the 1930s, you had to go there often, love it, hate it, live it and *feel* it. All this I did. You had to know a great deal about Wagner, homosexuality, racism and anti-Semitism, and the connection between them; and to realise the magnitude of the ferment to which, in combination, they gave rise.[5]

It is noteworthy that Boothby should have considered homosexuality to have been such a significant factor in defining the political and social climate of the decade. Exactly what he meant by the reference is not clear. Possibly, he was suggesting that the rise of Nazism was a response from large sections of German society under severe economic strain to what they perceived as the cultural excesses and sexual liberalism of the Weimar Republic. Looking back on his time in Germany in the 1920s, he recalled:

I got the impression of a demoralised society, desperately trying to find a way out. Among the youth, homosexuality was rampant; and, as I was very good-looking in my twenties, I was chased all over the place, and rather enjoyed it. I used to go to the *Oktoberfest* in Munich every October to listen to operas, drink tankards of foaming *Lowenbrau* beer, sing in the beer cellars with burly Bavarians in *lederhosen* and Tyrolese hats with what looked like shaving brushes, eat one of the thousand chickens roasting in the open in spits, and ride on the big dipper. I loved it all.[6]

That Boothby felt at home in the Weimar's cultural milieu is evident also in his recollections of a New Year's Eve ball at the British Embassy in Berlin

– 'an enjoyable evening, which I have never forgotten'. It was the end of 1931, shortly before his personal audience with Hitler. There was a vast hall, Boothby recalled, with more than a thousand guests 'including some of the prettiest girls I have ever seen'. Returning to his hotel with his host at the end of the night, Boothby gave grateful thanks for the kindness that had been shown him. His host replied: 'It may interest you to know that there was not a single girl there!' Boothby retired to bed, wondering whether this revelation was 'symptomatic of the decadence of a great nation, and decided, rightly, that it was not'.[7]

While Boothby savoured the exoticism that Weimar Germany provided in abundance, not least the chance to explore sexual and gender boundaries, he was also alert to the dark social tensions bubbling up. As the early years of the decade rolled on, he was deeply disturbed by the apparent lack of interest shown by his Westminster colleagues in what was going on around Hitler. Even when Churchill emerged from his Indian fixation, he seemed initially spurred into action more by Germany's rapid rearmament than a recognition that Hitler and his party represented an existential threat in themselves. In 1934, Boothby wrote in the *Daily Mail* of Britain as a 'third-rate military power, and every nation knows it'. He highlighted the growing danger that Germany represented and warned against going down the road of pacifism. 'War will come in two or three years,' he predicted, 'if certain problems are not tackled, if Germany is ready for it, and if the world remains as bankrupt of real statesmanship as it has been since the war ...'[8]

Such attacks inevitably secured him powerful opposition. Boothby's problem was that he increasingly lacked leverage at home. Many on his own benches reckoned his take on domestic and social issues had more in common with the views of the Labour Party, even though his position on international affairs was virtually diametrically opposed. He, meanwhile, believed that the National Government was running out of steam. At the start of 1934, he wrote to Baldwin to tell him as much. 'There is little enthusiasm for the national government,' he wrote, 'and I am firmly convinced we are now moving towards a very considerable electoral debacle.' The problem as he saw it was 'the absence of any political philosophy, or theme, or policy adequate to the needs of the times ...'[9] In the event, Baldwin won the next election in 1935, albeit with a reduced majority, and remained in office until 1937. Boothby, meanwhile, carried on burning bridges with his Conservative colleagues, as when he publicly described the 1935 Hoare–Laval Pact – an initially secret agreement between the British and French governments that would have effectively granted Abyssinia (now Ethiopia) to Mussolini's Italy – as 'one of the most discreditable documents ever issued in the name of the British people'.[10]

At least Boothby and Churchill seemed reasonably back on track by the middle of the decade. Although out of favour among his own ranks, Churchill nonetheless remained a major public figure around whom the anti-appeasers could rally. But there was little appetite in the nation at large for another war and there were powerful figures who for now much preferred to treat Hitler with kid gloves rather than contemplate a confrontation. The likes of Boothby and Churchill were isolated voices both among Baldwin's Conservatives and Clement Attlee's Labour. Away from Westminster, opinion-moulders such as Beaverbrook and *The Times'* editor Geoffrey Dawson (whom Boothby nicknamed 'the Secretary-General of the Establishment') were also vehemently against the idea of another war.

Then came another setback for Boothby with the onset of the abdication crisis in December 1936. With Edward VIII determined to marry the twice-divorced American Wallis Simpson, the constitutional question of whether he could do so while remaining as the monarch and head of the Church of England came to the fore. The government, opposition leaders, other senior members of the royal family and the Church (headed by the Archbishop of Canterbury, Cosmo Lang) held that he could not. Boothby, reluctantly, agreed with them, although he was sympathetic to the predicament of the King – who was being advised by Boothby's former head of chambers, Walter Monckton. Churchill, on the other hand, was determined to do what he could for Edward, urging him to at least delay any decision and exerting pressure on the government to back down. For a while, Boothby, Churchill and the Liberal leader, Archibald Sinclair, thought they had found a workable solution at a meeting in Churchill's Kent home, Chartwell. They drafted a declaration for the King in which he would vow not to marry against the advice of his ministers. In truth, the plan was probably always destined to fail given Edward's determination on the issue. However, before it had any real chance to work, it was effectively torpedoed by Churchill the following day when he addressed the Commons in a state of some inebriation. His demand for government delay on the abdication question was at best clumsy, his interrupting of Baldwin – who was handling the matter with impressive delicacy – prompting the House to turn on him. He was taken aback by the hostility but Boothby was furious. In a hastily written personal letter to Churchill, he accused him of delivering 'a blow to the King, both in the House and the country, far harder than any that Baldwin ever conceived of'. 'What happened this afternoon,' he went on, 'makes me feel that it is almost impossible for those who are most devoted to you personally to follow you blindly (as they wd. like to do) in politics. Because they cannot be sure where the hell they are going to be landed next.'[11]

A few days later, Boothby wrote again, this time to apologise for the first letter written in the heat of disappointment. He sought to explain why the incident in the Commons had so upset him, emphasising Churchill's importance to the country then more than ever and urging him to rely on 'the power of clear disinterested advice, based on your unrivalled intellect and experience' to 'rise to the position of commanding authority which you should always occupy'. That Boothby had an eye to the even greater challenges ahead was evident in his conclusion: 'I believe passionately that you are the only man who can save this country, and the world during the next two critical years. And that must be my excuse for writing this letter.'[12] Or, as he famously put it in a less-guarded, off-the-record moment: 'Churchill was a shit; but we needed a shit to beat Hitler.'[13]

There was a rapprochement of sorts between Boothby and Churchill but the relationship was now thoroughly rooted in mutual need rather than anything more affectionate. A year after the King's troubles, Boothby's own marital strife came to a head with his divorce from Diana Cavendish. The newspapers were kind to him, Beaverbrook's *Express* papers restricting themselves to a brief piece in the Sunday edition of 28 March 1937. There was no condemnation, no editorial comment, not ever a reference to adultery – merely a statement of facts: 'An intimation of a lawsuit against Mr Robert Boothby, MP, by his wife appeared yesterday in the rolls of the Court of Session at Edinburgh.'[14] When the divorce was granted in May – the head receptionist and a chambermaid from the Mayfair Hotel in London having given evidence that Boothby had visited the establishment with a woman in December 1936 – the coverage was even scanter, with barely a mention in the national media.

Boothby now set about opposing the appeasement policy of the government, by then headed by Neville Chamberlain, with greater energy than ever. As he would tell his old Conservative friend, Duff Cooper, the issue at stake was 'between reason and force, civilisation and barbarism'.[15] When Chamberlain returned from his talks with Hitler in Munich in late 1938 declaring 'peace for our time', Boothby considered that it 'could only mean capitulation'.[16] Boothby kept up his criticism of the government, not least in a regular column he wrote for the *Sunday Chronicle*. Matters came to a head in the parliamentary Norway Debate of 7 May 1940. Called in response to Britain's disastrously underpowered intervention in defence of Norway, the debate marked the end of Chamberlain's tenure, Leo Amery famously admonishing him: 'You have sat too long here for any good you have been doing. Depart, I say, and let us be done with you. In the name of God, go!'[17] When Chamberlain entered the Lobby to seek support from his allies, Boothby called out 'Not I.'[18] A vote of confidence was held two days later, which the government won, but Boothby was among the Tory rebels who voted against their leader and the next day Chamberlain was gone. Incidentally, at this most crucial point in the war's progress, it was Boothby who had tea in the Commons with Dorothy Macmillan, rather than her husband.[19]

The Foreign Secretary, Lord Halifax, having stood aside, Churchill now found himself in Downing Street. There was no sign of a ministerial elevation for Boothby, though, and for a while he suspected he had been overlooked yet again. But then Lord Beaverbrook called to assure him that this was not the case. Boothby hoped he might go in as Beaverbrook's Parliamentary Secretary at the Ministry of Aircraft Production. Then came the summons from Churchill on 15 May. In Boothby's own words:

Churchill received me somewhat grumpily, and gave me one of his Graham Sutherland looks [a reference to an infamous portrait of Churchill that Clemmie would ultimately destroy]. 'I would have offered you Scotland,' he said, 'but I was advised that your divorce made that impossible.' (This was nonsense.) 'As it is, I can offer you the post of Parliamentary

Secretary to the Minister of Food. Your Minister will be in the House of Lords, so you will be in charge in the House of Commons, and we will see how you get on.'[20]

It was hardly the most bountiful prize that Boothby could have hoped for but he accepted it and took on the new job with admirable gusto. He got on well with his minister, Lord Woolton – a much respected department store boss who had been earlier given his ministerial posting by Chamberlain. It was the ministry's job to ensure that the nation was fed nutritiously in the face of rationing and threats to the food supply lines. Woolton became a household name as a regular on the wireless, where he dispensed homely advice as part of the Kitchen Front campaign, and gave his name to a vegetable pie that came to epitomise Home Front cuisine. Boothby got his chance to take to the airwaves, too, gaining priceless experience ahead of his post-war career, and became a popular figure in his own right when he spearheaded an initiative guaranteeing milk for poor children and nursing mothers.

But his relationship with Churchill continued to falter. When Boothby made pretty harmless comments criticising luxury eating in hotels and restaurants at a time of rationing, Churchill took offence and complained. What was wrong, he demanded to know, with those who could afford it eating well to keep up their spirits? Churchill, it ought to be said, had not himself noticeably reined in his appetites as most of the population had been forced to.

More seriously, early in his stint at the ministry Boothby invited Lloyd George for lunch to discuss the question of food production. Churchill was aware that there was at that moment some disappointment among anti-appeasement campaigners like Boothby that many of the arch appeasers – including Chamberlain – remained in the Cabinet. When word of Boothby's meeting got back to him, Churchill was convinced it was part of a conspiracy designed to replace him with Lloyd George. Boothby hardly helped matters when a few days later he sent the Prime Minister a letter minutely detailing how he believed the government should forthwith operate. He called for a Committee of Public Safety with 'absolute and omnipotent powers' to replace the Cabinet, a declaration of martial law and a much-reduced role for Parliament. He then proceeded to denigrate the administration for its age, lack of energy and imagination, while claiming that he was not interested in specific questions of personnel, with the exception of Lloyd George.[21] For Churchill, still nervously finding his feet, it was too much. He summoned Boothby to Downing Street, where he dismantled the note line by line, before urging Boothby to return to his ministry and focus on the job he had been charged with doing.

Here was an example of the 'folly' to which Boothby would in due course own up. It was folly, too, that left him dangerously exposed when a new scandal hit – one that stemmed from an introduction on the London Stock Exchange many years earlier to a Czech businessman named Richard Weininger. Weininger was born not far from Vienna in 1887, the son of a noted goldsmith. By 1905, barely 18 years old, he found himself in New York, a paper millionaire thanks to some wily investments. However, the fortune was soon lost, only to be won again when he returned to Austria and began manufacturing a folding typewriter that became hugely popular. More riches followed as he repeatedly proved his credentials as an entrepreneurial adventurer. In the 1920s he took Czech citizenship and split his time between Czechoslovakia and Germany. Then, unable to ignore the threat of Hitler any more, he fled with his family to England. In the rush to get out, much of their wealth remained stored in Czech banks.

After Germany began its occupation of Czechoslovakia in March 1939, it became virtually impossible for nationals abroad to access their assets. Boothby, meanwhile, had come to be regarded as an important friend of Czechoslovakia for his outspoken criticism of the Munich Agreement that had allowed Hitler to annex the Czech Sudetenland the previous year. In 1939, the British authorities arranged for Czech assets held in Britain to be frozen so as to protect them from falling into Nazi hands. Without realising the government was already set on this path, Boothby independently lobbied for such a move. Weininger, meanwhile, had asked for Boothby's help in getting recompense for the sizeable assets belonging to his wife and daughters that were held in Czech banks. There was an informal understanding between the pair that Boothby would receive a 10 per cent cut of any assets returned to the Weiningers.

It was an appealing offer, especially as in the summer of 1938 Boothby had taken out a £5,000 loan from a fellow MP, Sir Alfred Butt. Butt now wanted repayment and was heavily pressurising Boothby, threatening to publicly shame him with a court action. However, Boothby made a serious error. He did not alert the government to his potential stake in the recovered Czech assets, even after he was appointed to lead a commission representing a number of other Czech claimants. Worse still, in a House of Commons debate, he made an appeal on the claimants' behalf, asking that a fund be set up from the Czech assets in London from which those who had lost assets in Czechoslovakia might be paid. Specifically, he asked that priority be given to the sort of assets held by the Weiningers. Of itself, this should have posed no great problem. The scheme was broadly in line with the thinking of both the government and the Bank of England. But MPs worked in a troubling grey area when it came to declaring financial interests related to any questions they might ask in the House. By making no such declaration, Boothby put himself in a perilous situation.

Given his varied business interests and links to Germany, Weininger was already a person of significant interest to the British authorities. On 16 September 1940, he was arrested at Boothby's flat under the Emergency Powers (Defence) Act, although there was an absence of evidence to suggest that Weininger posed any security threat. The police demanded that his personal papers be handed over, to which Boothby, having been charged with their care, assented. Boothby later cited this as hardly the actions of a man who felt he had something to hide. Nonetheless, there was growing concern in government circles about the relationship between the pair and Churchill called a meeting with Boothby and the Attorney General. As a result, the Prime Minister convened a select committee to look into the matter of the Czech assets, with Boothby suspended from his ministerial duties in the meantime.

He conducted his own defence in what he described as a 'trial for my life'.[22] But he found the committee hostile, its chairman the ageing Colonel Gretton, a pro-Chamberlainite who had supported the Munich deal. But Boothby was ultimately undone by the evidence of the Chancellor of the Exchequer, John Simon – a man with whom Boothby did not have an especially good relationship – that Boothby had not been candid with him about the arrangement he had with the claimants. Peter Carey, Boothby's cousin, would claim years later that when he asked him what had gone on over the Czech assets, Boothby told him: 'I fibbed to Sir John Simon.' When asked why, he replied: 'Oh, I couldn't stand Sir John Simon.'[23]

The committee found that 'the promise to pay him such a considerable sum of money was given on the understanding that Mr Boothby would render services in return'.[24] His fate sealed, Boothby resigned from the Ministry of Food but remained on the back benches, brooding over how little effort Churchill had made to look out for him. He also joined the RAF, where he was able to 'do his bit' for the war effort – Churchill's acerbic advice was that he should 'join a bomb squad'.[25] He completed his pilot's training and achieved the rank of flight lieutenant in a bomber squadron. But he was soon itching to be back on the political frontline to which his skills were more suited.

Many in Westminster relished Boothby's demise. The decadent, gambling adulterer who had alienated a large part of his own party in the preceding decade had been caught up with at last. Few, however, believed that the crime for which he was paying so dearly was particularly bad. Boothby probably ought to have declared his interest, but he would likely have made the same case for the Czech claimants whether he had a financial interest or not, and it was moot as to whether that financial interest had ever been formally agreed anyway. *The Times* captured the tone best when it described the affair as 'a stern warning of the scrupulous care and candour which public life demands'.[26] It was a lesson Boothby failed to heed.

The Other Side of the Tracks

In the months before the ignominious end to his stint at the Ministry of Food, Boothby had become a regular visitor to the East End of London. The East End had borne the brunt of the Blitz in 1940 and 1941, enduring aerial bombardment from the German air force for days and weeks at a time. The area's citizens became famed for their resilience and good-natured fortitude – what would come to be referred to in quasi-mythical terms as the 'Blitz spirit', and was acknowledged all the way up through society. After the bombing of Buckingham Palace in 1940, Queen Elizabeth, wife of George VI, famously commented: 'I'm glad we have been bombed. Now I can look the East End in the face.'

Boothby, like Elizabeth, was impressed by the character of the people he met time and again on his visits. He wondered at their eagerness to get on with things as they picked through the rubble after yet another night of Luftwaffe bombing. Ever the natural communicator, he spoke attentively to them to see what might be done to make an awful situation at least a little more bearable. Just as this Eton-and-Oxford scion of the wealthy and titled had managed to win over the straight-talking, down-to-earth men and women of Aberdeen, so he repeated the trick with swathes of East Enders in their darkest hour.

For all that Boothby enjoyed the high life – and he most certainly did – he was also fascinated by those who inhabited the social strata beneath him, too. What counted as the 'ordinary' for the working classes glistened with the aura of the exotic to him. Take his recollection of one of his trips to the East End. The people were, he reported:

> … warm, affectionate, gay, rather reckless, and almost incredibly brave. Sometimes the language was pretty rough, but it was so natural and innocent that it never jarred. One day I came across a small boy crying. I asked him what the matter was, and he said: 'They burnt my mother yesterday.' Thinking it was in an air raid, I said: 'Was she badly burned?' He looked up at me and said, through his tears: 'Oh yes. They don't fuck about in a crematorium.' I loved them, and I am glad to have been close to them in their hour of need.[1]

No corner of the East End suffered worse than Bethnal Green, which even in peacetime counted among the very poorest of London's neighbourhoods. It is reckoned that 80 tons of bombs fell on this one compact district alone, killing 550 people, seriously injuring another 400, destroying or rendering unliveable more than 3,000 homes and damaging a further 22,000. In 1943, it was also the scene of the single worst British civilian tragedy of the entire war, when 173 people – mostly women and children – were crushed to death as they attempted to enter the air raid shelter at the Bethnal Green Underground Station.

Amid a blackout, a woman and young child fell as they were going down the stairs, causing an elderly gentleman behind them to trip as well. A bottleneck quickly developed, which turned to disaster as crowds behind flooded on to the staircase only to find their route forward blocked and waves more people backing up behind them. Horrifically, the buzzing, whirring noises that many residents had taken to be confirmation that the enemy was once more on the attack were, in fact, the sounds of London's own new anti-aircraft guns. There was no German attack that night. The story was kept a virtual secret from the rest of the country so as not to damage morale or spur on the German propagandists, leaving the locals to deal with the aftermath virtually alone.

But the people of Bethnal Green were rarely cowed regardless of the trials they faced. When a building was knocked down, a specially convened Bombed Sites Association looked to clear the ground and use it to provide amenities or else grow food for the Dig for Victory campaign. About the time that Boothby was giving his resignation speech to the House of Commons, the BBC was reporting how Bethnal Green locals were digging up the concrete playground of a bombed school to make it ready to cultivate vegetables. The Queen would in due course visit, her lady-in-waiting writing that 'The Queen will never forget the good work that Her Majesty saw being done ...' The Duke of Norfolk, Parliamentary Secretary to the Ministry of Agriculture, commented:

> Here we have a group of people who have suffered an ordeal more terrible than had ever been endured before by the civilian population in this country. Yet in spite of this you have turned devastation to good account by sheer dint of hard work and determination. This is a story that will live for a very long time.[2]

Not everyone, however, was equally committed to the war effort. At 178 Vallance Road lived Charles Kray, who had absconded from military service. He spent most of the war attempting to outrun the army and the police, spending much of his time at a safe house in south London, with only very occasional visits back to the family home in Bethnal Green. Nor was he the only man avoiding his wartime duties in the vicinity. There were so many others that Vallance Road and the surrounding streets earned the nickname of 'Deserters' Corner'.

With Charles Kray absent, 178 Vallance Road became the dominion of his wife, Violet, her eldest son (Charlie) and her two twins, Ronald and Reginald (born in October 1933). All three of the boys were tearaways, earning reputations as brawlers from a very young age, especially the twins. But Violet adored them and would not hear a word said against them.

Without an earning man about the place, the war years were especially tough for Violet. Before the war, Charles had been a glorified rag-and-bone man, making money by trading this and that on a route that went from London down to the West Country and back again. With the black market booming as wartime rationing kicked in, it was all but inevitable that what small income the family did generate came from dodgy deals and low-level crime. Moreover, on those rare occasions when Charles stayed at Vallance

Road, he was often the worse for wear and abusive to Violet. As a result, Ronnie in particular had little affection for his father.

Life for the twins at this time was a curious mix. On the one hand, domestic life was based around a matriarchal system, with Violet at its head and supported by her sister Rose, the twins' beloved aunt. Beyond the front door, though, Deserters' Corner was dominated by hard-drinking, rough-fighting men making a living however they must. From a young age, Ronnie and Reggie were hero-worshipping local villains including Wasle Newman and Dodger Mullins – heads of local empires who ruled through fear and violence. Fists, bicycle chains and knives were the currency of intimidation.

Then there was the everyday uncertainty as to whether tonight would be your street's turn to be bombed. The twins carried memories of many evenings at the air raid shelter under the railway arches. The sound of the wailing air raid sirens, the searchlights scanning the sky for enemy aircraft, the distinctive drone of the bombers as they flew into range, then the noise of their bombs dropping and shrapnel falling from the sky. And when at last it was all over, the clatter of the trains overhead as they began their journeys again. Violence and the threat of it was a constant in their young lives.

It was not long before they became agents of violence themselves, although the first experience of killing that either had was accidental. In 1941, Reggie was out on the streets with a friend called Alf. They had an understanding with a local baker's driver that they could keep an eye on his van while he hopped out to make deliveries. As Reggie told it, Alf was playing around with the gears when the van suddenly jolted backwards. There was an air raid shelter behind the vehicle and, in between, a 6-year-old boy. As they got out of the van, they saw the child on the ground, his skull crushed. With a crowd gathering, the two boys ran off. Reggie and Alf were warned by the van driver never to let on what had happened or else he would lose his job. Reggie gave evidence to the inquest at Poplar Town Hall that Alf had fiddled with the gears but denied that the van had moved as a result. A verdict of accidental death was recorded. Brutality and death had already stalked Ronnie and Reggie in their short lives, but this was different. Reggie had played a direct role, albeit accidentally, in an act of extreme violence. And he had got away with it. He lied and was believed.

The incident laid down a blueprint that would serve the Krays for another quarter of a century.[3]

Reggie was also the first to have a serious run-in with the police when, aged 12, he was arrested for firing a slug gun out of the window of a train. On that occasion, he got off with nothing more than a warning, a local vicar having spoken up in his defence. Four years later, Ronnie and Reggie found themselves in court together, charged with grievous bodily harm after a fight between rival teen gangs outside a dancehall in Hackney. They were acquitted for lack of evidence but they were starting to establish a reputation for themselves – as up-and-coming toughs among the villains of Bethnal Green, and as serious troublemakers in the eyes of the police. Even Aunt Rose had her suspicions about the boys, telling Ronnie that she believed his heavy brow was an indicator that he was 'meant to hang'.

Their growing notoriety was burnished by their skill in the boxing ring. Reggie was particularly gifted, a London Schools champion who might have made it in the professional ranks. Ronnie was slightly taller and significantly heavier but lacked Reggie's discipline and ring craft. On his day, though, he was a highly efficient slugger who sent plenty of opponents crashing to the canvas. In 1950 his pugilist instincts saw him punching a policeman in the face, after he took offence when the officer tried to move on Ronnie and some friends from outside a café on the Bethnal Green Road. Ronnie had little time for the authority of men in uniform, not least because he had grown to loathe the sight of police officers arriving at Vallance Road in search of his father. A few minutes after committing the assault, Ronnie was hauled into the back of a passing police car and taken to the local station. Reggie, who had been with him and did not like the way the arresting officers had manhandled his brother, promptly sought out the original policeman and gave him another thump. The twins each received a probationary sentence for the offences.

Despite their broad rejection of authority, the boys initially chose not to follow their father's path of desertion, instead intending to see out their national service when they were called up in 1952. However, their co-operation was conditional on the army using them as physical training instructors. When the twins turned up for duty at the Tower of London (where the Royal Fusiliers were based), they met a corporal who suggested in forceful terms that rather than calling the shots, they ought instead to do as they were told. Ronnie responded predictably, punching the corporal before he and Reggie fled the Tower and went home. They were soon picked up and charged with striking an officer and being absent without leave, earning them a week's custody in the guardroom at the Tower. The Krays thus earned the unenviable honour of being the last prisoners to be held in the Tower of London.

On their release, Ronnie and Reggie took off once more to the East End and began a two-year phase of cat-and-mouse with the authorities as they attempted to bring in the deserters. In 1953, the brothers served a month's imprisonment in Wormwood Scrubs for assaulting a police officer who attempted to apprehend them. For the offence of desertion itself, they were eventually detained for nine months at Shepton Mallet Prison in Somerset.

Civilians once more by 1954, they now began to build their business empire, starting with the Regal Billiard Hall in Mile End. The previous owners sold up, having grown tired of escalating trouble at the hall. Many suspected the upsurge in violence had been choreographed by the twins themselves. The next few years saw rapid expansion by the Krays. They added drinking and gambling clubs to their portfolio, making the step from the East End to the West when they took a stake in a club called Stragglers in Soho – all underpinned by a thriving protection racket that gave them interests in countless more businesses. The twins had a 'nipping list' for those businesses that paid for protection (and the Krays' goodwill) by gifting goods as and when the brothers saw fit (donating a crate of champagne, say), and a 'pension list' for what they considered were more lucrative businesses that would make a regular cash payment.

All the while, the violence ramped up. In 1955, Ronnie shot a man for the first time. The victim had been attempting to muscle in on a garage that was already paying protection to the Krays so Ronnie shot him in the leg. The twins then visited him in prison to persuade him not to take matters further with the police, making a financial payment to his wife to the same end. As they hoped, Ronnie never faced charges over the incident. However, his luck ran out the following year when he received a three-year sentence for grievous bodily harm against members of a rival gang.

He started his sentence at Wandsworth, where he took his place among the ranks of hardened criminals and established himself as a tobacco baron. With tobacco the most important currency among the prison population, he made a small fortune trading it, which in turn secured him a comfortable standard of life behind bars. So satisfactory was it that he felt little need to kick against the system. But this came with unforeseen consequences. As he approached the latter stages of his sentence, his 'good behaviour' ensured he was transferred to the lower security Camp Hill prison on the Isle of Wight. It was in the more relaxed atmosphere there that his mental wellbeing went into free fall. With a freer schedule and regime, a far less clear hierarchy of power and a prison population that included fewer of the hard-bitten, career criminals around whom he felt most at home, he lapsed into sustained bouts of paranoia. Isolated and convinced there was a grand conspiracy ranged against him, he was moved to the psychiatric ward of Winchester Gaol, where he was formally certified insane. He was then transferred to Long Grove Hospital in Epsom, Surrey, and diagnosed with schizophrenia, a doctor's report noting that he was a 'simple man of low intelligence, poorly in touch with the outside world'.[4]

Kray was heavily medicated, which helped to alleviate the worst of his symptoms, but he would battle to keep his mental health on an even keel for the rest of his life. He had always been the more combustible and volatile of the twins but now violence threatened to erupt from him without warning at any moment. Cordial conversations might be interrupted with a sudden savage beating for a perceived slight or a harboured grudge. Spontaneous displays of aggression punctuated his social interactions and left even those closest to him wary of when the next explosion might come. Nonetheless, having absconded from Long Grove he later handed himself back to the authorities, a legal technicality allowing him to serve out the remainder of his sentence and re-enter the mainstream of society without any ongoing supervision of his mental health.

While Ronnie was in prison, Reggie opened a new club on the Bow Road called the Double R – named in honour of themselves. With a roster of live music, it was an immediate success and boasted a celebrity clientele including Barbara Windsor, Jackie Collins and George Sewell. Then, in 1962, the twins opened the Kentucky on the Mile End Road, which outdid the Double R in its aspirations to give a taste of the West End in the East End. The place was decked out with long mirrors, velvet wallpaper and plush red carpets, the furniture was gold-sprayed and chandeliers hung from the ceiling. Bow tie-clad waiters served drinks to customers done up to the nines. Reggie later acknowledged that the club was altogether a bit on the gaudy side, before adding:

> But the Kentucky was right for the time and, more especially, right for
> the toffs who wanted to come over from the West End and see a bit of
> the seamy side of life without having to get themselves dirty or put them-
> selves in any danger. They loved it. It was exciting, it was exhilarating.
> They could kid themselves it was dangerous because there were plenty of
> evil-looking gangsters around. But they were actually as safe as houses.[5]

Perhaps, but only up to a point. Much as Reggie ran the club tightly, his brother's demons ensured that the danger of violence was an almost perma-nent spectre at the Kentucky feast.

There was a further complicating factor that contributed to Ronnie's complex psychological make-up. From a relatively early age, he was openly bisexual, although with a clear preference for males. For a man who traded on his reputation as a ruthless hard man, his willingness to publicly acknowledge his sexuality was nothing less than extraordinary in an era when homosexuals were routinely portrayed as both effete and abnormal. Kray, of course, had little respect for the law so the threat of criminal pros-ecution for acting on his sexual desires was perhaps less oppressive to him than for many others. However, the code of the streets was of vital impor-tance to his identity and the East End was assuredly not a place that overtly embraced homosexuality in the 1950s and '60s.

According to the Krays' chronicler, John Pearson, it was not only Ronnie who was bisexual – Reggie was, too. In their adolescence, Pearson reported Ronnie telling him, both were sufficiently concerned about revealing this aspect of their personalities that they maintained secrecy by having sexual relations only with one another.[6] However, it was not long before Ronnie – by nature the more flamboyant of the pair and less keen to keep a low profile – disclosed his orientation to his wider family and circle of friends. While his mother was accepting, his father was predictably not, compounding the distinctly Oedipal aspect of Ronnie that saw him venerate his mother and despise his father. (Indeed, in his view his mother, along with Auntie Rose, inhabited a separate realm to other women, whom he generally regarded as smelly, dirty creatures and, most unacceptable of all, a threat to the integral fraternal bond he shared with his brother.)

By the time the twins were beginning to build their empire in their early twenties, Ronnie was doing little to conceal his taste for good looking males in their late teens or a little older. He took to paying local lads in lieu of services rendered, and operated an East End equivalent of Sherlock Holmes's Baker Street Irregulars – a posse of boys in their late teens who were on hand to carry out fieldwork for the brothers' criminal enterprises but also to act as a billiard-hall court to King Ronnie. He was seemingly unconcerned that his sexual orientation was soon common knowledge not only among those he counted as friends but among his foes, too. However, he was adamant on one point – he was utterly comfortable as a homosexual but he should be labelled neither 'a pansy' nor 'a poof'. In other words, he was who he was and he just so happened to prefer male to female company, but he was not to be considered in anyway effeminate. In an age when much of straight Britain struggled to consider gays in anything more than stereotypical terms – Hugh Paddick and Kenneth Williams' camp creations, Sandy and Julian, came to define homosexuality for much of the nation – Ronnie was at once both homosexual and uber-macho. His emergence from the closet was less a gesture of liberal self-acceptance than an aggressive challenge to anyone who dared not accept him on his terms. (However, whether Kray himself entirely came to terms with his sexuality is moot. Ahead of the Krays' murder trial in 1969, the police took a statement from a bookmaker called Charles Clark. Ronnie had lived with Clark and his wife for some nine months from the end of 1964, and according to Clark's statement: 'He [Ronnie] once told me the tragedy of his life was that he was the twin who was born the wrong way round sexually.')[7]

By 1963, the planets had aligned such that Boothby's world was set on a collision course with that of the Krays. The Kentucky was, as Reggie would later note, a magnet for characters like Boothby intent on exploring the less salubrious corners of the capital. Meanwhile, Esmerelda's – the twins' high-end Kensington hang-out – allowed Boothby to mix with underworld figures in the sort of more upmarket setting that he was used to, with the extra appeal of hitting the gambling tables. And in Ronnie, he found the most unexpected of hosts – a *bona fide* villain who just so happened to share his taste for young males and felt little compunction to hide the fact.

As for Ronnie, here was a well-connected toff of whom the twins might make use. But more than that, Ronnie – by then known as the Colonel to the members of his Firm (as his gang of henchmen came to be called) – was, perhaps against his will, drawn to those he considered genuinely upper class. While he could not abide the petty bourgeoisie – especially anyone who relied upon a uniform in order to wield power over those lower down the social scale – persons of genuinely elevated social status had the ability to turn his head. For instance, while he and Reggie were running amok at Canterbury barracks as they awaited their military court martial, only a single Sandhurst-esque officer had any success in putting a brake on them. Making them aware that he knew what they were up to, the officer insisted, 'But for God's sake, *do* stop making such a bloody row. You'll frighten the horses.'[8] It was the type of line only a man of certain breeding could naturally deliver and it had its effect. Ronnie also counted among his icons Lawrence of Arabia and General Gordon, hero of the nineteenth-century Siege of Khartoum – gentlemen of action, and both of them rumoured to have been gay as well. While Boothby did not share the same enthusiasm for Lawrence of Arabia – a man he regarded as a fraud – he too was just the sort of gent to appeal to Ronnie Kray's sensibilities.

Boothby and Kray were an odd couple. So odd, in fact, that when Boothby set out to discredit those who alleged an association, few in the country disbelieved his rebuttals. The very idea of the peer and the gangster was too ridiculous to believe. But somehow, the pair were made for each other. '… warm, affectionate, gay, rather reckless, and almost incredibly brave.' That was the impression Boothby had of the people of the East End during the war. Two decades later, though, and he was playing with a different type of East Ender altogether.

8

Recalibration

In August 1948 Boothby found himself in a hotel room in the south of France, a tray of dry martinis before him. He was there with the Conservative MP Malcolm Bullock, along with the Churchills – Winston and Clemmie, their daughter, Mary, and her husband, Christopher Soames. Winston was decked out in a blue siren suit. 'Ah,' he said, addressing Boothby, 'red trousers. Very nice. They match your tie.'

So begins Boothby's account of what he described as 'an astonishing afternoon'. An account, he said, that 'makes no claim to be more than a snapshot taken on a sunny afternoon … I cannot even vouch for its accuracy. I was very tired when I wrote it. But at least it was written the same evening, when the memory was still fresh.'[1]

There followed a narrative of the great war leader and his old comrade, chewing over the bones of the war during a lunch of langouste mayonnaise, soufflé, a couple of bottles of champagne, one of Volnay and a deal of brandy besides. Then it was off to Les-Baux, its dramatic ruined castle on a rocky outcrop tempting Churchill to arrange a painting expedition. He changed out of his siren suit for the trip, opting instead for a get-up that included snakeskin shoes and a sombrero.

Beneath the French sun three years after the war's end, Boothby and Churchill were men in search of roles in a new world order. Churchill was treading water, his Herculean wartime efforts having won him the eternal gratitude of his nation but not the right to head a government in peacetime – not for now anyway. By the time he returned to Downing Street in 1950, it was more in the guise of a national figurehead than as a political dynamo, his energies visibly dwindling in old age. Boothby, meanwhile – still in middle age – retained some hope of further political advancement but realised it was now more of an outside chance than the assured prize it had once seemed. In due course, neither Churchill nor Macmillan saw fit to give him a ministerial role. Fortunately for him, Boothby was already turning his attention to other arenas that he might conquer.

Perhaps the most remarkable feature of their post-war French get-together was that it happened at all. Theirs was a classic love–hate relationship, their political visions frequently (though not by any means always) in tune but their personalities too often out of kilter. Part of the problem was that they were so similar in key respects – as *bon viveurs*, as skilled orators and, most damagingly, as attention-seekers. They encroached on each other's territory. Neither, too, was inclined to edit his pronouncements about the other.

Churchill was riled by Boothby's ability to charm and win popular affection, although Churchill commanded affection enough of his own. In turn, Boothby did not have the good sense to play down his popularity. For example, when he emerged from the 1945 election with a hefty majority in his Aberdeen constituency, Churchill wondered how he had managed to do it. 'Because they like me in the north of Scotland,' Boothby blurted out, 'whereas, although they know you saved them in 1940, they never liked you.'[2] As he entered his own old age, Boothby became even more outspoken about his former boss. He claimed never to have truly liked him, accusing Churchill of possessing a 'streak of cruelty in his nature' and an egotism that prevented him from brooking any challenge to his authority. 'I once told him that he was a bully by nature, but that he could never bully me; and then slammed the door in his face,' wrote Boothby. 'No wonder he sometimes tried to break me.'[3] Nor could Boothby ever truly forgive him what he considered his treachery during the Weininger scandal.

Yet during their afternoon together in that summer of '48 there were moments of seemingly genuine fondness between them, as well as flashes of personal insight. Boothby, for instance, confided that 'one of the troubles of my life was that I was always right about public affairs, and always wrong about my private affairs'. Churchill considered the statement for a moment, then said: 'No. Sometimes wrong about public affairs, and sometimes right about private affairs. That would be a fairer statement of the case.'[4] It is difficult not to think that Boothby's take was the more accurate.

After the Czech assets debacle, the pair had little to do with each other for the rest of the war, save for the odd moment when Churchill needed a friend. At the beginning of July 1942, for instance, he was at arguably his lowest point, facing an unhappy Commons set to debate a no-confidence motion after Rommel's Axis forces had got the better of the Allies at Tobruk. Churchill had not spoken to Boothby since his resignation but when Boothby encountered the Prime Minister sitting alone in a corner of the Commons dining room, Churchill ushered him over. Churchill warned him that the debate was critical for the government and he asked if he could still count on his support. Boothby told him that he could and Churchill immediately arranged for him to speak in the government's defence. Churchill won the vote and afterwards toasted Boothby in the Commons smoking room, praising 'the Pegasus wings of Bob's oratory'.[5] There then followed another year of silence between the two.

Despite his difficulties, Boothby fought hard to remain politically relevant. He fostered close relations with the Free French government-in-exile, and in 1943 he published *The New Economy* – a political treatise outlining his radical vision for post-war Britain. Then, in 1946, his career took him in a new direction when he made his debut appearance on *The Brains Trust*, a BBC radio programme in which an expert panel answered audience questions. It was a phenomenon, winning audiences of up to 12 million and making its panellists (and Boothby perhaps most of all) stars. The show also provided his gateway into television when it transferred from the wireless in 1950. For a while, Boothby had been unsure whether to take up the BBC's invitation but Lord Woolton had advised him he should:

You will never be happy in the corridors of political power. You are no good at intrigue; and you are incapable of keeping your mouth shut. My advice to you is to stay in Parliament for as long as you wish, and say what you think. They won't turn you out, because they know that they can't.

But make your career on the media – journalism, the radio and television for which you have a vocation. And never underestimate their power.[6]

By the turn of the 1950s, Boothby had transformed his fortunes so that he was on as firm a footing as he ever had been. He now had his rented flat in Eaton Square and, after his mother died in 1949, he inherited sufficient money to alleviate his financial worries. He was still appallingly ill-disciplined when it came to finance, on one occasion buying four cars in a single morning to gift to friends.[7] But he had his MP's salary and income from his newspaper, radio and television work. In 1950 he was there for the debut of another TV show, *In the News*. One of its regular guests, Labour MP Tom Driberg, recounted his impressions of Boothby in a diary entry of 9 May 1952:

> Bob Boothby is that unusual phenomenon, an extrovert and an intro-vert rolled into one ample person: sometimes he sits back watching us cynically through half-closed eyes, his only contribution an occasional deep, lascivious-sounding chuckle; sometimes the folly of some statesman, usually on his own side of the House, will have excited him to almost classically rotund and uninhibited invective.[8]

Boothby retained his Aberdeen seat at the 1951 general election and was under the impression that the Ministry of Labour might be his in the new administration, but his hopes were dashed again. The stain of the Czech assets, in Churchill's view at least, ruled out an appointment. Boothby's animosity towards the old man was cemented – despite the bestowing of a knighthood on him in 1953 – but he was at least now free to cast himself as the rebel maverick that he perceived himself to be. Passionately pro-European – he was appointed to the Council of United Europe in 1948 – he fought hard for Britain's entry into the European Economic Community. Then, in 1956, the Suez Crisis gave him his last serious opportunity to flex his muscles in the Commons, and secure his reputation for being, in political terms, a politician who could locate the right side of history.

A noted supporter of Israel and an arch anti-appeaser in the 1930s, Boothby nonetheless came out strongly against Britain's decision to use military might against Egypt. He was no fan of Nasser, nor of the Egyptian leader's seizing of the Suez Canal, but he warned against the folly of unprovoked aggression. He wrote in the *News of the World* on 9 September 1956: 'Surely our course is clear. We must take care not to put ourselves in the wrong in the eyes of world opinion … Economic sanctions against Egypt are, in the circumstances, fully justified. They have been used against us. But force should only be used against force.'[9] The Commons debate on Suez on 1 November was particularly fiery, worse than after the Munich agreement according to some of the lobby press. MPs discussed whether Britain had got itself involved in an 'international conspiracy'.[10] The government narrowly won the day, but Boothby was among those Conservatives – eight in total – who voted against it.

For some in his own party, it was further confirmation of his treachery. Even his constituency party gave him a rough time over Suez. When Eden fell in January 1957 and Macmillan took over in his place, Boothby was in Monte Carlo. His absence probably made no difference, but Macmillan's decision to leave him out in the cold once more represented a virtual full stop to Boothby's long Commons career. By now, he counted pep pills among his many vices and the signs that he was getting no younger were becoming more evident. In the July he suffered a heart attack. The old Boothby was still alive and kicking – as the doctors consulted, he was said to have been watching the Goodwood races on a television and laying some bets. And when interviewed after his release from London's King Edward VII Hospital, he claimed his consultant had told him that to fully recover he should 'drink like a fish'[11] – a comment of such mischief that he was later forced to apologise for it. But despite the face he managed to put on things, Boothby himself knew that time was at last catching up with him.

Brazen as ever, he wrote to Macmillan to suggest that he might be considered for a life peerage. The letter found its way to Macmillan's private secretary, John Wyndham, who feared how the new Prime Minister would respond. In the event, Macmillan agreed, to the astonishment of many of those with knowledge of their personal entanglement. It may have been Macmillan's way of confirming that he had long since risen above Boothby and Dorothy's adultery, or perhaps even a gesture to please his wife. Macmillan gave no indication. Boothby readily accepted and made his last major speech in the Commons in a debate on the economic situation on 30 October 1957. He used the occasion to refer back to another of his orations from twenty years before. 'One bats away and does one's stuff,' he said wearily, 'and everybody says, "Jolly good speech" and stands one a drink; but nothing much happens. That is the depressing thing about politics. Here I am again, saying exactly the same thing. However, I never give in, and I am not giving in now.'[12]

Boothby had written to thank Macmillan for his ennoblement, and in his reply the Prime Minister noted: 'Life has, as you say, many ups and downs … It is curious, but true, that I think we have always agreed in politics. I hope you will believe me when I say how glad I am to have your good wishes.'[13] Their bond was as strange as ever, notable for the apparent absence of personal rancour. This despite Boothby and Dorothy still being immersed in their love affair – although by now denuded of much of its original heat and passion – and the impact it had on Macmillan's daughter, Sarah, in particular. In 1947, she had been told that Boothby was her real father by a drunken suitor at a party, one of several contributing factors to what would turn out to be a turbulent and tragic adulthood. Yet Boothby and Macmillan's friendship – a word that just about qualifies as a description of their relationship – endured for years after Boothby went up to the Lords, the men corresponding often on the matters of politics that had brought them together in the first place.

In August 1958, Boothby assumed the title of Baron Boothby of Buchan and Rattray Head. He was also offered the freedom of four burghs within his constituency (Peterhead, Fraserburgh, Turriff and Rosehearty) – a gesture that delighted him. 'Fancy,' he told a reporter, 'four Freedoms in one morning, isn't that wonderful? I'm jolly pleased. I value them much more than my barony. I am told that I cannot be arrested in any of the Burghs if I am drunk, whatever state I am in. I am just delighted.'[14] Meanwhile, he was seen on television as much as ever. In 1959 he appeared on John Freeman's landmark interview series, *Face to Face*. Despite the pair being friends, Freeman was unflinchingly honest in his introduction:

I think he is one of the most gifted and idealistic and truthful men anywhere in public life. He is also lazy and self-indulgent and over-generous.

All these qualities mixed up together have resulted in the comparative failure of his public life, and the total success of his personal friendships. He has usually backed the right political horses; but when, in the end, they gallop home, Bob seldom shares the winnings. He is either in disgrace for having blurted out something indiscreet, or he is off playing baccarat at Deauville.[15]

In 1958, he appeared on another programme to discuss 'the Establishment'. A fellow guest was Violet Bonham Carter, an old friend and the daughter of the former Prime Minister, Herbert Asquith. Boothby was characteristically undiplomatic, attacking the Establishment as sinister, wrong-headed and having held back his own career. Bonham Carter, though, affectionately took him to task for his hypocrisy, teasing him as a figure of the Establishment playing at being an iconoclast. In fact, she was highlighting a tension within him that never entirely resolved itself. 'Why, there he is plastered with decorations,' she said. 'Titles, knighthoods and life peerages rain down on him. He emerges drenched and dripping from the Fount of Honour and then shakes himself like a dog getting out of dirty water.'[16]

In his newspaper columns and appearances over the airwaves, Boothby regularly indulged his love of the polemical. The greater a controversialist he was, the more his stock rose, or so it seemed for a time. In the background, meanwhile, his personal life was as involved as ever. The Macmillans aside, there were other love affairs to bolster his reputation as a lady's man, as well as the encounters with young men that were kept out of public view. Despite the burden of needing to hide a significant part of his life, Boothby became only more reckless. He repeatedly baited, for instance, his frequent Fleet Street protector, Lord Beaverbrook.

The Boothby–Beaverbrook association was frequently uneasy. Over many important issues of state across the years, they had not seen eye-to-eye. Boothby often found himself under political attack from Beaverbrook's newspapers. Yet, Beaverbrook had an underlying respect for him, so that at various moments of political and personal crisis, he had seen to it that his titles went easier on him than they might otherwise have done. A letter from Boothby to Beaverbrook dated 8 January 1953 captures the essence of the association:

You have given me some hard knocks in the course of my somewhat erratic political career – most of them, I do not doubt, well deserved. But I never forget that whenever the sea became so rough that it looked like drowning me you were the first to throw a life-belt; and the conscious-ness of your friendship, at the deepest level, has been one of my most valued possessions through nearly 30 years of stormy political life.[17]

Yet as the 1950s passed into the '60s, their amity became more strained. In 1958, for example, Boothby was incensed when the editorial staff at the *Express* suggested a moderate overhaul of some articles he had been com-missioned to write. 'I don't know,' he wrote to the proprietor, 'whether you have instructed the Editors of the *Daily Express* to humiliate and insult me; but that is what they have been doing, in a very big way.' When Beaverbrook took issue with Boothby's tone, Boothby climbed down. 'I had no intention of being offensive to you,' he explained. 'I am not, by nature, an offensive chap. But whenever I have dealings with those who exercise great power, something seems to go wrong; and I do, say, or write things which cause offence … I think there must be a muddy and rebellious imp in my subcon-scious who wants to squirt ink at great – and successful – men of action.'[18]

The detente was only temporary, though. In 1962 came Boothby's noto-rious televised attack against Beaverbrook and other selected Canadians who, he said, had 'done nothing but damage to this country'. In the same programme, he had condemned the *Express* as 'bloody awful' and 'packed with lies'.[19] No sooner had that unfortunate episode been smoothed over than Boothby was at it again. Having made an apology to Beaverbrook and thus narrowly avoided a law suit, Boothby appeared on a show called *Dinner Time*. 'It is true. We are mealy-mouthed,' he declared on air. 'Terribly mealy-mouthed. And I think that the laws of libel are far too tough in this country … But why the devil should not you say almost anything you like.'[20]

Worse was to come in December 1963, when he wrote to the *Sunday Express*'s editor, John Junor, about an editorial Beaverbrook had written in praise of Churchill. Boothby was scathing:

But who was the great champion and supporter of Neville Chamberlain before the war? Beaverbrook. Who supported the shameful Munich

Agreement – against Churchill? Beaverbrook. Who supported the filthy Nazi regime? Beaverbrook. Who wrote, day after day, 'THERE WILL BE NO WAR'? Beaverbrook. So the tribute is not only moving. It is also nauseating.[21]

Even by Boothby's standards, it was an extraordinary attack. Junor sent it to his boss with a note: 'We have received the attached letter from Boothby. I think he must be out of his mind.' Beaverbrook was incandescent. It was, he said to his legal adviser, 'stupid of me to accept all these insults'. 'I think it might be quite interesting to go after this fellow again,' he added, 'and this time to bankrupt him if I can.'[22] In the event, Beaverbrook would be dead within a few months and Boothby was not excessively damaged by the episode. He might well have been, though, had Beaverbrook the inclination and time to exact a full-scale revenge. The incident, nonetheless, demonstrates Boothby's relentlessly kamikaze lifestyle.

In his post-war phase of recalibration, Boothby proved nothing if not his remarkable tenacity. His heart was in politics but his prospects of making his mark in high office had evidently dissolved. Yet through the development of his media persona, he maintained a degree of influence that would otherwise have surely been lost to him. His tendency towards self-destruction was ever present, though. Reviewing Boothby's 1947 memoirs, *I Fight to Live*, Richard Crossman gave a penetrating summation of the man:

Mr Boothby is that comparatively rare thing in England – a pure politician. He lives for the game, and, like the true gambler, he loves it whether he wins or loses. Mostly, as he reminds us, he has lost; but he retains his zest, and combines with it a streak of recklessness based on an inner despair.[23]

9

A Fearful Stigma

In April 1954, Boothby rose from his seat in the Commons to address his fellow MPs. 'I think,' he said, 'that homosexuality in this country is more prevalent than we are apt to admit and that it is tending to increase at the present time. In most of our great cities, there is a homosexual underground which is a constant menace to youth; and we ought to bear that always in mind.'[1]

With the benefit of hindsight, it might seem a curious speech. Boothby couched it in terms of homosexuality as a social ill, the objective 'of all of us' being to 'limit the incidence of homosexuality and to mitigate its evil effects'. This chimed with a widely reported speech he had given earlier in the year to the Hardwicke Society, the debating society of Middle Temple, on a proposition against the prohibition of homosexual relations between consenting male adults. Drawing on what he described as 'modern psychology', he argued that an individual's mature form of sexuality derives from 'primitive infantile elements', hereditary factors, upbringing and environment, and that 'sub-conscious bi-sexuality' is a component part of everyone. That being so, he continued, 'the majority of males pass through a homosexual period at one period of their lives'. He then moved his focus to 'congenital homosexuals', whom he characterised as often being endowed with creative or artistic gifts but seldom enjoying happiness. Homosexuality, he concluded, should be seen as both a physical and mental disability, which may or may not be curable – 'a biological and pathological condition for which the victim is only to a small degree responsible'.[2]

For those searching for a new language of social progressiveness, there was little to get the pulse racing. He might even have been accused of abject hypocrisy by anyone acquainted with the details of his own private life. But there was more going on behind his words than first impressions revealed. Boothby, of course, was never going to come out of the closet in the midst of a Commons debate, rising from the green leather to burst into a chorus of 'The Man that Got Away', which Judy Garland was just then popularising in *A Star is Born*. For the sake of his liberty, his social position and his livelihood, he could not admit to having homosexual relationships of his own, nor even leave room for such speculation. And even though the so-called age of permissiveness was just around the corner, nor was British society yet ready for one of its most beloved elder statesmen to advocate homosexuality as a desirable way of life. Here was a country where even the unambiguous expression of heterosexuality – let alone homosexuality – was still mostly kept behind closed doors. Where the pop charts were still a couple of years away from the hip-swivelling raw energy of a Bill Haley or an Elvis, and were instead dominated by the likes of Doris Day's 'Secret Love' and Norman Wisdom pleading 'Don't Laugh at Me ('Cause I'm a Fool)'. Where passion was personified by the brooding heterosexual intensity of a Rhett Butler and Scarlett O'Hara, or perhaps an Ilsa and Rick in *Casablanca*. Where it was a full six years before *Lady Chatterley's Lover* would overcome accusations of obscenity in the law courts even as the chief prosecutor, Mervyn Griffith-Jones, pondered if it were the kind of book 'you would wish your wife or servants to read'.[3] When, in fact, it would still be another year before the word 'homosexual' was even uttered for the first time on the BBC, during an edition of *Woman's Hour*.[4]

It was against this unforgiving backdrop that Boothby at least raised his head above the parapet in a bid to improve the conditions of gay, British men – perhaps with himself in mind, too. His speech to Parliament was a sincere plea to review the way homosexuality was policed in the country. Police campaigns against homosexuals were, he argued, often accompanied by 'methods of great dubiety' that 'do nothing, in my opinion, towards its eradication. On the contrary, they intensify the squalor by which it is surrounded, and widen the areas in which the underground flourishes.'[5] He referred to such tactics as police honeytraps. Homosexual acts committed in private between consenting adults, he said, created no injured party and where there are witnesses to such acts, their subsequent testimony was driven either by greed, jealousy or fear. The law as it stood made the field of homosexuality a hunting ground for blackmailers.

As long as the law protected against violence, prohibited sexual engagement with minors and ensured public decency, Boothby declared that what consenting adults did in privacy ought to be 'a moral issue between them and their Maker' but 'not a legal issue between them and the State'. Besides, he added almost as an after-thought, sending a homosexual to prison in the hope of 'curing' him was akin to trying to 'rehabilitate a chronic alcoholic by giving him occupational therapy in a brewery'.[6]

Boothby was asking for a radical overhaul of the law but framing it in the traditional vocabulary of homosexuality as an ill, an evil, a disorder – with those afflicted to be pitied. He was using the words of the oppressor but in the cause of the oppressed. Years later, in *Recollections of a Rebel*, he was still pronouncing theories on homosexuality that might at best be described as unscientific. It was, he suggested, not 'indigenous' to Britain (unlike 'Germany, Scandinavia and the Arab countries') but the British education system – which for so long had encouraged gender segregation between the ages of 10 and 22 – fostered it. This was especially when coupled with 'the pervading influence of ancient Greece', which he pointed out 'provided intellectual and aesthetic enjoyment' to many who studied at university. And while most undergraduates 'got through' their 'homosexual phase', he estimated some 10 per cent did not and that it was 'more prevalent than most people wish to believe'. From a young age, he wrote, he had harboured the ambition that should he ever go into public life, he would 'do something practical to remove the fear and misery in which many of our most gifted citizens were then compelled to live'.[7] That was the context of his speech in the Commons in 1954. An early salvo in a long campaign for judicial change.

At the end of 1953, he had sent a memorandum to the Home Secretary, David Maxwell Fyfe, asking for a government inquiry into homosexuality and the law, writing:

By attaching so fearful a stigma to homosexuality as such, you put a very large number of otherwise law-abiding and useful citizens on the other side of the fence which divides the good citizen from the bad. By making them feel that, instead of unfortunates they are social pariahs, you drive them into squalor – perhaps into crime; and produce that very 'underground' which it is so clearly in the public interest to eradicate.[8]

They were powerful words, drawn inevitably from personal experience.

It was true, too, that even as Britain stood on the brink of a revolution in sexual mores, the 1950s were a peculiarly forbidding decade in which to be gay. In fact, reported instances of indictable homosexual offences rose almost continuously from the outbreak of war in 1939 to a peak in 1963. Part of the reason for the surge in the 1950s was espionage. In 1951, Guy Burgess and Donald Maclean – members of the notorious Cambridge spy ring – defected to the Soviet Union. Both were gay and, although there was little evidence to suggest they were unwilling spies, their treachery confirmed for some that homosexuals posed a particular threat to national security by being at heightened risk of blackmail. It was an idea that permeated throughout society, not least to Maxwell Fyfe. He urged the police to take a hard line against those who fell foul of the so-called Labouchere Amendment of 1895, which had made 'gross indecency' (essentially, any sexual act that fell short of penetration) a crime. It was this amendment that did for Oscar Wilde and also for Alan Turing, the computing genius who had contributed so much to deciphering the German Enigma code in the Second World War and who accepted the punishment of chemical castration for his contravention in 1952.

Maxwell Fyfe demanded nothing less than 'a new drive against male vice' that would 'rid England of this plague'.[9] In 1949, the *Sunday Pictorial* (later renamed the *Sunday Mirror*) had published the results of a Mass Observation research project into English sexual attitudes and according to that data, some 12 per cent of men had experienced 'homosexual relations' and a further 8 per cent milder same-sex contact.[10] Maxwell Fyfe thus theoretically had about one in five of the adult male population in his sights. In 1939 there had been 1,276 prosecutions relating to homosexual acts. In 1952, a year after Maxwell Fyfe became Home Secretary, the number was 5,443.[11]

The following years were marked by a slew of high-profile cases. In 1953, the Labour MP William Field resigned his seat after being fined £15 for 'soliciting or importuning for immoral purposes'. Around the same time, the writer Rupert Croft-Cooke was given a six-month prison sentence for indecency and in the same year, John Gielgud was arrested for cruising in a public lavatory in Chelsea. When he appeared in court, he gave his name as it appeared on his birth certificate (Arthur John Gielgud) and his occupation as clerk. He received a fine but his real punishment was for the case to be reported by an *Evening Standard* journalist, who from the press gallery had worked out his real identity. Gielgud feared the episode would end his career. In the event it did not, but no thanks to Earl Winterton, a Conservative peer, who recommended that Gielgud be stripped of his knighthood and horsewhipped in the street.

Then, in 1954, the bisexual Lord Montagu of Beaulieu found himself thrust into the spotlight when he was sent to prison for a year for 'conspiracy to incite certain male persons to commit serious offences with male persons'. He was found guilty of gross indecency with an RAF serviceman during a party in a beach hut on his estate, a charge that he denied and which he held was the product of a witch-hunt. His co-defendants were Michael Pitt-Rivers and a journalist, Peter Wildeblood, both sentenced to eighteen months. During the trial, Wildeblood – who admitted to being homosexual in court – managed to smuggle a letter to his mother: 'Whatever they decide, I do not want you to be ashamed of anything I have done. Be glad, rather, that at last a little light has been cast on this dark territory in which, through no fault of their own, many thousands of other men are condemned to live, in loneliness and fear …'[12]

Maxwell Fyfe's response to Boothby's plea for a government inquiry was disappointing but expected. 'I am not going down in history as the man who made sodomy legal,' the Home Secretary told him.[13] But against all expectations, in 1954 he agreed to the establishment of a committee to look into the subjects of homosexual offences and prostitution. As the Earl of Arran would in due course acknowledge, without Boothby there would have been no such inquiry.[14] It was headed by John Wolfenden – a former headmaster and the vice-chancellor of Reading University – and began its work in August that year, just four months after Boothby's Commons speech. Wolfenden's own son, it was little known at the time, was himself gay. Peter Wildeblood was one of only three openly homosexual men to give evidence.

When the Wolfenden Report appeared in September 1957, it caused a minor earthquake. Concluding that 'there must remain a realm of private morality and immorality which is, in brief and crude terms, not the law's business', it recommended that 'homosexual behaviour between consenting adults [over the age of 21; the heterosexual age of consent was, by comparison, 16] in private be no longer a criminal offence'.[15]

There was a ferocious response from those in the Commons and Lords opposed to the recommendation. A foretaste of what was to come had been provided by Lord Winterton back in May 1954 when introducing a debate on homosexual crime. It was, he proclaimed, a 'nauseating subject' and while 'fornication and adultery are evils', he had to 'completely contest the view that they are more evil and more harmful to the individual and the community than the filthy, disgusting, unnatural vice of homosexuality'. It is not recorded how he felt about the fact that immediately preceding the debate, the Lords had passed the Wankie Colliery Bill.[16]

In the Commons debate on Wolfenden held in November 1957, William Shepherd, the Conservative MP for Cheadle, declared that, 'Incest is a much more natural act than homosexuality' while his colleague, James Dance, MP for Bromsgrove, gave his historical perspective: 'It was the condoning of this sort of offence which led to the downfall of the Roman Empire. I feel that it was the condoning of these offences which led to the fall of Nazi Germany.' The House at least had the good grace to snigger at the latter assertion.[17] Lord Denning in the Upper House added his thoughts, saying that homosexuality was an 'unnatural vice' that threatened 'the integrity of the human race'. While bemoaning his belief that, 'Hell Fire and eternal damnation hold no terrors nowadays', he ultimately took an in-between line that while the 'law should condemn this evil, for evil it is', 'the judges should be discreet in their punishment of it'.[18]

None of which is to say that Wolfenden did not have its high-profile supporters. In March 1958, for instance, a group of prominent individuals sent a letter to *The Times* urging acceptance of the committee's proposals for decriminalisation. Boothby was among the signatories, along with Clement Attlee, J.B. Priestly, Bertrand Russell, A.J.P. Taylor and Dame Veronica Wedgwood.[19] But moves to enact the recommendations into law were rejected in 1958, 1960 and 1962, and were not debated again until a good while after the 'Peer and the Gangster' scandal had played out. Only in 1967 were homosexual acts between consenting adults at last decriminalised. 'Lord Wolfenden ... once said to me,' Boothby would later boast, '"I have only one grudge against you. You have ensured that, for the rest of my life, my name will be associated with homosexuality."'[20]

In the meantime, though, there were still more notable individuals brought low for the crime of being homosexual. Among them was Ian Harvey, the Conservative MP for Harrow East, who was prosecuted in 1958 for having sexual relations with a 19-year-old Household Cavalry Guardsman in St James's Park. Ironically, Harvey had earlier served on a Commons Select Committee that advised strict punishments for members of the armed services found to have engaged in homosexual acts. With the gross indecency charges dropped, both Harvey and the guardsman were fined £5 for the lesser crime of breaking park regulations but the incident ended Harvey's promising political career. He resigned as Parliamentary Under-Secretary of State at the Foreign Office (the Foreign Office seeking to avoid further scandal by replacing him with one John Profumo) and gave up his Commons seat too, along with his various London club memberships. He was also threatened with a dishonourable discharge from the Territorial Army, despite a distinguished war record. Prior to getting caught, he later admitted, he had regularly engaged in risky encounters (often with guardsmen) over several years. But following his conviction he was, he said in his memoirs, destined for a tortuous period in social 'purgatory'.[21]

His painful downfall was no doubt vivid in Boothby's memory as he was confronted with the *Sunday Mirror*'s allegations six years later. In many ways, he had much further to fall, too. The hope that the Wolfenden Report had brought must have seemed a distant promise just then. Arrests of homosexuals had recently hit their peak and gay men were ripe for media attack. As Kenneth Williams – star of the *Carry On* films and a man who struggled to reconcile himself to his own homosexuality – recorded in his diary on 14 January 1963: 'The papers are full of the Vassall inquiry. The reporters giving evidence all talk about homosexual intrigue & hint at dark secrets in high places. All the muck raking is going on. To no advantage. Homosexuality in itself is no vice, a law which makes it one is evil.'[22]

As Boothby went into battle with the *Sunday Mirror* in 1964, decriminalisation was still three years away. But even if the Wolfenden recommendation had been in place, he would have had other concerns. Back in 1954, just as the Wolfenden Committee was getting down to work, Lord Hailsham wrote: 'No doubt homosexual acts between mature males do take place … but the normal attraction of the adult male homosexual is to the young male adolescent or young male adult to the exclusion of others.'[23] It was the kind of comment that wafted around at the time; subjective opinion with little or no evidential basis parading as scientific fact. It was the sort of thing that 'right-thinking' people ought to accept, according to those who were convinced that there was only 'right thinking' (which coincided with their world view) and 'wrong thinking' (which did not).

In Boothby's case, though, it just so happened to be apposite. His preference for male adolescents and young adults cast him into a murky universe of grey areas. His tastes veered towards those barely above the heterosexual age of consent, let alone the proposed homosexual age. That he also liked lads from working-class backgrounds added to the complexity. How can the issue of consent be truly judged when the negotiation is between an older man of elite education, social and political influence and significant wealth, and a younger, less educated male without anything approaching a comparable level of social, political or economic power? Throw in a mobster who believes that the law is there to be trampled over anyway, and the picture grows darker still.

10

The Gambler and the Boxer

Robert Bevan was 17 years old when, in the summer of 1959, he found himself on board a train from London to Edinburgh. It was not a journey he made from choice. Just convicted of theft at Marlborough Street Magistrates Court, he had been sentenced to twelve months' probation and the judge ordered him to return to his native Scotland. The victim of his crime was Lord Boothby, from whom Bevan had stolen a gold watch, chain and coin, together valued at £50. Boothby declared to the press how disappointed he was by the turn of events. 'He is one of several hundred people I have tried to help,' he explained, 'and only the second one to let me down. He is very young – I think the temptation was too great.'[1]

The court had heard how Bevan, an unemployed waiter, was the son of former constituents of Boothby. He had come to London, it was said, and rung Boothby several times to ask for his help in finding a job. On the weekend of the theft, Boothby's manservant, Gordon Goodfellow, was away so Boothby asked Bevan to come and help him in the flat. The boy spent the Saturday cooking and cleaning before leaving on the Sunday, along with his haul of purloined items. When local police spotted the youth on the street, a half-drunk bottle of champagne in his hand, their suspicions were aroused. Then they discovered Boothby's trinkets and took Bevan into custody.

However, when John Junor – then editor of the *Sunday Express* – sent one of his reporters to track down Bevan in Scotland, a rather different version of events emerged. According to Junor, Bevan related how he had been wined and dined by Boothby, including a meal at the exclusive Soho restaurant, Quo Vadis. They then went on to a West End club called the Pelican, he explained, before a late-night showing of *Gigi* and then back to Eaton Square. He was also adamant that the objects found in his possession had been gifted to him by Boothby, and it was Junor's understanding that they were a payment in kind for sexual services rendered.[2] But who was Bevan to cast doubt on the account given by a peer of the realm?

News that Boothby was hosting such youthful acquaintances in his home would be bound to prompt a certain amount of eyebrow raising should it ever enter into public knowledge. Yet he refused to conceal the pleasure he found in the company of young people. In 1958, for instance, he was appointed Rector of St Andrew's University and threw himself into the role. On his formal arrival at the university, he gleefully allowed himself to be 'kidnapped' by a gang of students and driven around in the car of a female undergraduate – the sort of behaviour that had the university magazine proclaiming him as 'possibly the gayest and most ebullient Rector that the University has had for many years'.[3]

Later that evening he gave a candid address to an audience of students. He told them:

> My advice to you today for what it is worth, is to make the most of life. It won't last long. As Robert Louis Stevenson said, we all sail in leaky bottoms on great and perilous waters, we have heard the mermaidens singing, and know that we shall never see dry land again. 'Old and young, we are all on our last cruise. If there is a fill of tobacco among the crew, for God's sake pass it round, and let us have a pipe before we go!' Therefore, I say to you, enjoy yourselves, and be gay. By doing so, you will obey the will to live, and fulfil the only divine orders we know of. Beware of those who talk of salvation rather than happiness. What kind of a God is he that creates a world from which we have to be saved? Above all, beware of those who spend their time nosing out the alleged sins of other people, in order to punish them. They are mad, bad and dangerous to know.[4]

But Boothby's insistence on keeping youthful company ensured a succession of uncomfortable episodes. Linda Mallard, for example, recalled a disconcerting encounter with him, probably on the occasion of his 70th birthday. Linda – who would become a Metropolitan Police officer in adulthood – was 10 or 11 at the time and a member of the Horse Rangers Association based at Hampton Court. Boothby was a friend of the association's founder, Raymond Gordon, and Gordon arranged for a contingent of his Rangers – all young girls as far as Linda could recall – to be minibussed to Eaton Square to deliver birthday wishes. Nothing expressly untoward happened at the flat but Linda recalled the experience as 'creepy' and 'uncomfortable', the ageing Boothby sitting in his armchair as the girls wondered quite who he was and why they were there. The future police officer noted: 'I always had and still have good instincts for when something is a bit off and the whole memory of that incident has never gone away.'[5]

In his speech to those St Andrew's students in 1958, Boothby took the opportunity to praise Charles James Fox, a Whig statesman of the late-eighteenth and early-nineteenth centuries and one of the great political characters of his age. In a piece of self-mythologising, Boothby presented himself as Fox's spiritual descendant – a maverick for the modern age. 'Here was a man after my own heart,' Boothby said, 'who could lose £16,000 in one night, speak in the House of Commons on the Thirty-Nine Articles [relating to the doctrines and practices of the Church of England], sit up drinking for the rest of the night at White's, and win £6,000 before leaving for Newmarket.' Boothby was enthusiastically buying into a tradition of the rake-politician whose company people could not resist. Fox was known too as an arch womaniser and Boothby extolled the way he 'fiercely resented any interference with his private life'.[6]

Boothby shared this fierce resentment, which helps to explain an angry exchange of letters he had the following year with both Junor and his proprietor, Lord Beaverbrook, regarding what he felt was their skewed coverage of the Bevan case. While happy to propagate the idea that he was a woman-chaser in the mould of Fox – there could be few more powerful pre-emptive defences against rumours of his homosexuality – Boothby was rather less keen on what he considered to be the insinuating tone of the *Sunday Express*. He wrote to Junor to express his displeasure at, essentially, being 'done over' by the paper. One of Junor's journalists, John Gordon, had written an article based on an interview with Bevan, who had, it should be said, expressed his continued 'high opinion of Lord Boothby'. There was a paragraph, though, that Boothby said implied – at least among 'sophisti-cated readers' – that he had rewarded the youth for services rendered. He had, Boothby insisted, 'had quite a rough time over it'. In response, Junor claimed Boothby's letter grieved him and he expressly denied that 'we have been implying you are a homosexual' (a denial rather undermined by those memoirs he published some thirty or more years later). Beaverbrook also assured him that there was no vendetta against him from the paper, nor could he expect anything other than a square deal from the rest of his titles.[7] And there the matter lay. For the time being at least.

Then, in March 1963 there was another court case that exposed Boothby's vulnerability. Again, it centred around a 17-year-old boy – James Buckley, a greengrocer's assistant by trade. He turned up at a bank in Chelsea and tried to cash a cheque for £1,600 bearing Boothby's signature. The boy claimed to have been sent by Boothby but the manager soon established that this was not the case and that the signature was a forgery. Buckley was arrested and found himself up before the judge at Marlborough Street Magistrates, in an echo of the Bevan case. Buckley admitted to the attempted fraud, saying he had discovered Boothby's chequebook on the street. Once he had extracted the single cheque he needed, Buckley said, he had thrown the book away down a drain. But when the police came to investigate, they found the chequebook was safely locked up in Boothby's Eaton Square home. Buckley then changed his story, saying that he had lied about that detail but everything else was as he'd described it. He refused to elaborate further on just how he had come into possession of the cheque. Found guilty, he was sentenced to a spell in borstal. The *Daily Express* felt there was more to the case than met the eye. 'Riddle of cheque lost by peer' ran a headline on page 4 in the edition of Tuesday, 7 May. How, wondered the paper, had the cheque come into the possession of Buckley, 'a cloakroom attendant at Esmeralda's Barn, Belgravia'? It was a mystery that, as the pros-ecuting barrister John Mathew noted at trial, 'remains still unsolved'.[8]

To those who knew Boothby well, though, there was not much of a mystery. Boothby was a regular at Esmerelda's – a club and casino on Wilton Place in Knightsbridge that was owned by the Krays. For a man of Boothby's tastes, there was much of what he liked best to be found there, starting with gambling. Like Charles James Fox, Boothby's reputa-tion for gaming – a passion he pursued across Europe – was legendary.

Since the 1950s he had been part of the John Aspinall set that included the likes of Lord Lucan, Lord Derby and the Duke of Devonshire. Here were men who nonchalantly won and lost thousands in an evening, most usually playing Chemin de Fer (a card game derived from baccarat). Indeed, it was in part the antics of this group that convinced the government to legislate the gambling business more closely. The 1960 Betting and Gaming Act paved the way for the establishment of new, legally accountable casinos, the most famous of which was Aspinall's own Clermont Club. Originally based at 44 Berkeley Square, the Clermont counted among its clientele the rich, the well connected and celebrities including Ian Fleming and Peter Sellers. The Krays saw the potential riches to be gained from the business – even if Aspinall found his takings down on the good old pre-legal days – and quickly muscled in on Esmerelda's, which had been operating as a nightclub serving West London's in-crowd for several years by then. They put Lord Effingham in charge in a gesture designed to create a veneer of respectability, even though Effingham had himself endured several serious run-ins with the law by then.

Boothby found his way to Esmerelda's in 1963, where on any given night you might bump into fashionable icons like Lucian Freud – another alumnus of the Clermont – and Francis Bacon. Then there were the boys. In accordance with his own tastes, Ronnie Kray had seen to it that Esmerelda's employed plenty of young, good-looking male staff. Among them, working in the cloakroom, was James Buckley. It is, in theory, possible that Buckley stole the notorious cheque from Boothby when he was charged with looking after the peer's coat. Boothby's carelessness as to what he carried around with him – not least, letters of a sensitive nature – was a long-term cause of concern to his friends. He was considered at high risk of finding himself hurled into scandal should he ever fall victim to a pickpocket. But Buckley and Boothby were actually involved in a sexual relationship. Buckley – whose older brother, Bobby, became one of Ronnie Kray's lovers – was a regular visitor to Eaton Square and, as John Junor would memorably phrase it, '… there were many who suspected that he had taken it [the cheque] from Bob's hip-pocket as Bob's trousers lay over his bed'.[9]

After Buckley was arrested, Boothby gave a statement that came into the possession of MI5. In it, he said that the Krays had visited him early one morning to apologise for any inconvenience caused regarding the cheque. They assured him that Buckley no longer worked for them and was unlikely to repeat his crime. Boothby also claimed they offered him the services of a chauffeur.[10] It is easy to see why Buckley, having had a 'chat' from the brothers, did not contest the charges against him nor give any evidence likely to embarrass Boothby. Boothby subsequently tried three times to visit Buckley in borstal but was each time dissuaded from doing so by Ronnie Kray.

By 1963, the Krays were actively seeking to expand their social circle to encompass as many figures of public influence as possible. It was a distinctive element of their expansionist strategy. Boothby was just the type of individual – famous, well connected and likely to get himself into unfortunate scrapes – that the brothers knew they might in time be able to manipulate to their own ends. The Metropolitan Police were already on to them in this respect. That year, the brothers had instructed their solicitors to write to the police in order to complain that they were being unfairly harassed. It was a tactic of quite outrageous audacity, given all the mischief that the police knew them to be up to. Nonetheless, they managed to get a couple of local dignitaries to sign their names to supporting statements. A recent mayor of Bethnal Green and a local parish priest (who was, according to police sources, suspected of being homosexual) both testified that Ronnie and Reggie were good lads who ought to be left alone to get on with their lives and to pursue their legitimate business interests. The police were predictably dismissive of the complaint and in a private memo of 1 March 1963 it was noted: 'Now they are associating themselves with persons who on the surface bear a semblance of respectability such as the two witnesses now put forward to substantiate their complaint of victimisation.'[11]

The twins had their eye on bigger fish than local dignitaries, though. They were building a network of contacts that came to embrace the worlds of sport and entertainment and ranged from glamorous up-and-coming British celebrities to *bona fide* A-list global superstars. There was Barbara Windsor and Diana Dors, Joan Littlewood and some of her gang, Francis Bacon and Lucian Freud, but also a host of big American names, among them the former world heavyweight champions Joe Louis and Sonny Liston, not to mention Judy Garland. Politicians were harder to snare but Boothby must have seemed like a godsend – one of the most famous political figures in the country, constantly on the television and radio and writing in the newspapers; a man who might open up the corridors of power. In truth, they probably overestimated his reach. Boothby could not claim to have much access to the real levers of power in those days. But for the Krays, Boothby was – although not the only political figure in their sights – about as close to the heart of government as they could hope for just then.

Key to the genesis of the association between Boothby and the Krays was another employee at Esmerelda's, a croupier by the name of Leslie Holt. Holt was in his mid-20s by 1963, a good looking, fair-haired, angular lad with an undeniable glint in the eye. Just the type to fit the Ronnie Kray blueprint. Exactly where and when Boothby and Holt met is not entirely clear, although it is possible that they knew each other as early as 1960. According to some accounts, their first encounter was at one of the boxing matches that Boothby sometimes liked to attend. Holt was a decent fighter who had been an Essex schools champion in his teens and in later years fought occasionally under the name of Johnnie Kidd.

He was one of nine children, the son of a dustman from Shoreditch. His first run-in with the police came when he was 8 or 9 years old. A great lover of animals, he returned to the family home one day with a large dog. His mother was unwilling to accommodate still another mouth to feed and ordered him to get rid of it. Unwillingly, he took the dog out and, along with a friend, stole a box of biscuits so that it would not go hungry. The matter ended up going to court and Holt was sent to an approved school, spending the next five years or so in and out of the approved school system. In 1950, the *Essex Chronicle* featured him as a promising schoolboy boxer, noting that 'Sturdy, dour Londoner Leslie Holt does not easily talk about himself.'[12] He was earning a reputation for winning fights by unleashing flurries of telling body blows. So damaged around the chest was one of his rivals that Holt was declared victor by technical knock-out – a rarity in boy's boxing. It was his hope, Holt explained to the newspaper, that he might eventually become a professional in the mould of Tommy Farr, a celebrated Welsh fighter who had given Joe Louis a run for his money in a bout for the world heavyweight title at New York's Yankee Stadium in 1937.

However, in a not wholly unique turn of events, Holt's ring ambitions derailed as he got older. While it became clear that he was not destined to become a world-beater, he cultivated increasingly expensive tastes and a hunger to experience all that the world had to offer. In order to fund himself, he turned to relatively low-level crime, proving himself an adept cat burglar. Holt developed a larger-than-life persona, driving expensive cars – often in the company of a couple of imposing Dobermans – and seeking out all the glamour and sensation that London in the 1960s was promising. As he did so, he embraced his bisexuality.

No doubt buoyed by a lifetime of reliable discretion from friends and the press alike, Boothby was not obviously wary in matters of his personal life by the time he met Holt. A large social circle was well aware that he sought male company generally more eagerly than female company. He happily joked with his cousin, the broadcaster Ludovic Kennedy: 'I'm not sure if I like the boys better than the girls or the girls better than the boys.'[13] He was a regular user of rent boys and was known on the scene as a hunter of 'chickens' – that is to say, young men from their late teens into their twenties.[14] Young men, in fact, just like Leslie Holt. That Holt's life encompassed a criminal element only added to the allure. In his 1978 memoirs, *Recollections of a Rebel*, Boothby wrote strikingly openly about his theories on homosexuality, although still without acknowledging the extent of his own inclinations. Homosexuality, he noted, is 'prevalent among what used to be called "the higher and lower orders"', with mutual attraction between the orders being termed 'plain sewing' (a phrase perhaps more commonly understood to mean mutual masturbation), although a comparable slang expression for a 'lower orders' sexual partner was 'rough trade'. Homosexuals, Boothby claimed, are 'addicted to blackmail, and to theft, but seldom to cruelty'. Such an extraordinarily sweeping generalisation no doubt owed at least something to the company Boothby was keeping back in the 1960s. 'My trouble,' he went on, 'is that, to a considerable extent, and much against my will, I share their general outlook on life.'[15] To put it another way, Boothby could not resist male sexual companionship in combination with underworld hazard – and Holt personified this heady mixture.

Through him, Boothby enjoyed the frisson of visiting the very edge of society. He was aware of Holt's occupation as a burglar but Holt had fingers in others pies too, an informant telling MI5 in 1964 that he had recently been living as a 'ponce' with a girl in Primrose Hill.[16] And while

Holt provided Boothby with the danger he craved, Boothby offered Holt a glimpse of the cultured life that he longed for. Boothby would take him to the opera, for example, and on one evening Holt found himself there sat between the politician on one side and the celebrated journalist and broadcaster, Bernard Levin, on the other.

Boothby also treated Holt extremely well in material terms, even paying for a Jaguar E-type. (Holt is said to have entertained locals one day by taking out a post-Profumo Christine Keeler for a spin in it.)[17] Holt worked for Boothby as his driver and this perhaps explains why Boothby told the police that the Krays had offered him the services of a chauffeur in the aftermath of the Buckley theft. Should the police have delved into Boothby's private arrangements, they would doubtless have wanted to know what one of the Krays' staff was doing in his service. But there was something more substantial to their relationship, too. According to that MI5 source – unnamed but clearly intimately embedded into the Krays' milieu – theirs was 'no fly-by-night affair' and they were 'genuinely attached' to each other.[18] A little before Christmas 1963, Boothby wrote a letter on House of Lords headed paper to Holt's parents to let them know in what high esteem he held their son and promising, 'I will do my best to keep Leslie on the straight path.'[19]

According to Holt, he was responsible for introducing Boothby to Ronnie Kray sometime in early 1963 – well over a year before the *Sunday Mirror* ran its story. It was an initiative bound to curry favour with Kray. Holt was also present at the infamous Enugu business meeting where Kray and Boothby were photographed together (Holt was in some of the photos from that day, as was another member of the twins' Firm, 'Mad' Teddy Smith). By all accounts, there was not a hint of attraction between the soon to be fabled peer and the gangster but they enjoyed each other's company and bonded over their shared taste in younger, prettier men than themselves. And what an opportunity for Kray. From the previous year's mayor of Bethnal Green to arguably the most famous peer of the realm in one easy bound. Kray, meanwhile, offered Boothby access to the ultimate 'plain sewing/rough trade' environment in which brutal, violent criminals mixed with the most famous, the most talented, the most beautiful in the land. Moreover, he was happy to keep up a supply of just the sort of men that Boothby desired – often at the erotic parties that Ronnie liked to throw at his flat in Cedra Court, Hackney.

How long was it before Boothby grasped that he was playing a game over which he had no real control? He was, he conceded, a gambler by nature but he must surely have come to realise that he was wagering his reputation with the odds stacked irredeemably against him. Even before the *Sunday Mirror* got a hint of its scandal, Junor at the *Sunday Express* was sniffing around again. In 1963, Lord Beaverbrook had employed a baby-faced history graduate, Michael Thornton, to work as the newspaper's film and theatre critic. He was, as one gossip columnist put it, 'the only critic in Fleet Street who needs an adult to accompany him into an A-feature'.[20] He got the job not least because he had been championed by Margaret, Duchess of Argyll, who had once almost married Beaverbrook's son.

Beaverbrook hoped that as well as providing reviews, Thornton might use his society connections to provide a few exclusives here and there. Boothby was among those to whom Beaverbrook introduced his cub reporter and Boothby took a shine to him. With some regularity he would call Thornton to invite him for drinks at Eaton Square. Junor saw an opportunity. Not well known for a particularly liberal attitude towards homosexuality, the Scottish-born editor increasingly seemed to have it in for Boothby – perhaps resenting what he regarded as Boothby's 'corrupting' of Scottish youth, as in the case of Robert Bevan. Whatever the reason, Junor was hopeful that Thornton would dig up some real dirt. Boothby, indiscreet as ever, seemed likely to oblige. He drank heavily – especially whisky – in Thornton's company, becoming ever more open about his personal life. Holt – whom Thornton recalled as a 'slim youth with movie star looks' – was often with them, too. 'Is he an actor?' Thornton asked Boothby early on. 'No, dear boy,' Boothby chuckled. 'He's a burglar. And I'm in love with him.'[21]

In 1962, Boothby had told Cliff Michelmore's daily current affairs show, *Tonight*: 'If I really told the full story of my private life, I think I'd make half a million pounds but I'd have to spend the rest of my life in Tahiti and I don't particularly want to do that.' By 1964, the arch gambler faced the risk that somebody else would tell the story on his behalf. It was perhaps mere fortune that saw Reg Payne at the *Sunday Mirror* get there before Junor, who may well have proved a more persistent adversary. Nonetheless, Boothby seemed to have played a hand too far.

11

Dangerous Liaisons

On 24 January 1960, the *News of the World* began its serialisation of the memoirs of Diana Dors, the British model and actress optimistically touted in the 1950s as Britain's answer to Marilyn Monroe. Dors was paid the princely sum of £36,000 for what the newspaper clearly expected to be a titillating confessional. Stafford Summerfield had recently taken the helm at the newspaper, which had dropped something like a million and a half readers over the previous two years, and he wanted proper headline-fodder in exchange for writing expensive cheques like this one. Dors did not disappoint.

The late 1950s and early '60s were the 'golden age' of what the tabloid press liked to term 'sex parties' and Dors gleefully provided revelations about the ones she had hosted at her home in respectable Sunningdale in Berkshire, alongside her husband Dennis Hamilton, who had died suddenly in 1959 from what turned out to be tertiary syphilis. 'There were no half measures at my parties,' she said. 'Off came the sweaters, bras and panties. In fact, it was a case of off with everything – except the lights ... Every night was party night.'[1] Her parties, it emerged, were attended by an array of (unnamed) celebrities, who could luxuriate in an indoor swimming pool with scantily clad bright young things or perhaps recline on a leopard–skin sofa to watch one of the blue movies that the couple played on a big-screen television. Then there was the bedroom with the two–way mirror, where anyone feeling amorous enough might be spectated upon by fellow guests.

Sunningdale, it turned out, had unwittingly provided the backdrop to a series of Bacchanalian orgies.

Dors in due course assured any concerned readers that those days were behind her and that her great hope now was to settle down, make a new, happier marriage and raise some children. But whatever veneer of moral rectitude was imposed upon the serialisation, it was the detailed recollections of her sexual shenanigans that were responsible for bolstering the newspaper's circulation. Hugh Cudlipp at the *Sunday Pictorial* had good reason to be miffed at his rival's success, having been outbid for Dors' story. The *Pictorial* responded by unearthing a couple of minor show business figures, Patrick Holt and Sandra Dorne, who had known Dennis Hamilton. The *Pictorial* was thus able to give its readers similar accounts of raunchy parties, although from a third-hand perspective (Holt and Dorne were adamant that they had not themselves participated in proceedings). Incidentally, Summerfield had replaced Cudlipp's older brother, Reginald, as editor at the *News of the World*. Several commentators felt that the Dors serialisation and rival efforts marked a new low for Fleet Street. Bernard Levin in the *Spectator* wrote that 'even by British newspaper standards – as far as pornography is concerned the most remarkable in the world', the Sunday tabloid battle recently played out was 'almost past believing'.

The Profumo affair provided additional fodder for those trading in tales of scandalous parties. The most famous of these (aside from the Cliveden gathering at which Profumo and Keeler first met) was a soirée in December 1961 that came to be known as either the 'Feast of Peacocks' or, after Lord Denning had passed comment on it in his wide-ranging inquiry, the 'Man in the Mask' party. It was hosted at a flat in Hyde Park Square, Mayfair, by Mariella Novotney – a glamorous former stripper of disputed heritage (she claimed to be the niece of the Czechoslovak president, Antonín Novotný) – and her husband, Horace 'Hod' Dibben, a club owner and antique dealer some three-and-a-half decades her senior.

Their parties were nothing short of legendary, with claims that assorted international leaders had enjoyed their hospitality at one time or another. But the Feast of the Peacocks – named for the roasted peacock that was served for dinner – would surpass them all for notoriety. The two women central to the Profumo scandal, Christine Keeler and Mandy Rice-Davies, were late-comers to the festivities, welcomed in by Stephen Ward who, according to Rice-Davies, was naked except for his socks. All the other male guests followed a similar dress code (socks optional) while the women also were 'naked except for wisps of clothing like suspender belts and stockings'.[2] Among the guests were a number of famous faces from the worlds of entertainment and politics. One, whose identity remains unconfirmed, spent the evening wearing only a black mask with slits for eyes and a small, square, lace apron of the type preferred by waitresses in provincial cafés of the day. The man, whoever he was, requested to be whipped (using a flail provided by the hosts) should his services fall below expectations. There was much talk at the height of the Profumo affair that he was a government minister. Lord Denning became convinced during the course of his subsequent inquiry that there was no evidence to substantiate the claim, although he had no doubt that 'there is a group of people who hold parties in private of a perverted nature'.[3]

Boothby, wisely, withheld public comment on the Night of the Peacock but he had written a highly critical piece for the *Sunday Dispatch* about the Dors serialisation back in 1960. Yet by 1963, Boothby and Dors had friends in common. The actress was a regular at the Double R and was warmly welcomed into the Krays' circle of celebrity pals. Boothby was also starting to attend parties at Ronnie Kray's flat, No. 8 Cedra Court, Hackney, where Kray had recently moved and where things happened that were guaranteed to make even the worldly readers of the Sunday tabloids blush. The Krays had been guests at some of the Dors' parties and had seemingly learned a thing or two.

Cedra Court was built in the 1960s but had a certain lustre of art deco style. Ronnie moved into his flat in 1962, the first time he had lived away from Valance Road as an adult (excluding those periods when he stayed as a guest at Her Majesty's pleasure). Reggie moved in the following year, taking up a tenancy at Flat 1 directly below his brother. There were other Firm acquaintances also living there, including Leslie Holt and the parents of the Teale brothers who worked for the twins.

Ronnie decorated his flat to reflect his love of North African and Eastern exoticism (Kray and Boothby both spent periods of time in Tangier), along with his taste for modern convenience. He slept in a four-poster bed with large mirrors adorning the room, while the bathroom was done up in pink and black, with yet more mirrors. The living room was entered through beaded curtains and Eastern-influenced tapestries hung from the wall. Billowing clouds of incense filled the air. There was a motley assortment of trinkets and ornaments too, including a 3ft-high ebony elephant (complete with real tusks), large curved knives in their sheaths and a display of taxidermy birds in glass cases. There was also a built-in aquarium, as well as a revolving electric fire that, at the press of a button, could retract into a wall to be replaced by a kitsch display of artificial blooms complete with a miniature waterfall.

Kray turned his flat into a social Mecca – a fusion of the twins' underworld circle along with businessmen, entertainers and politicians who had all been sucked into the vortex. As the building's head porter, Frederick Cox, would recall in a statement he gave to police in 1968 about life at the flats five years earlier, 'On Thursdays and Fridays there would be a lot of male visitors to Flat No. 8.'[4]

For Boothby, the gathering together of the high-born and low-born, the anonymous, the famous and the notorious, was not a new experience. During the 1950s, he had been a patron of the Soho scene with, on the one hand, its incongruous offering of piping hot Italian coffee from one of the new linoleum-and-Formica cafés then springing up and, on the other, the promise of hard vice overseen by the likes of mobster Bernie Silver and his criminal 'Syndicate' then building its empire in the area. In the latter part of the decade, Boothby was to be regularly found at a little basement dive on Old Compton Street called the 2is.[5]

The 2is had opened its doors as a coffee bar in 1956, run by a pair of Australian wrestlers called Paul 'Dr Death' Lincoln and Ray 'Rebel' Hunter. The competition from rival coffee bars was intense, with the Italian actress Gina Lollobrigida having sparked a flood of them when she opened her Moka Espresso Bar on Frith Street in 1953, complete with an imported Gaggia espresso coffee machine. To give the 2is an edge in the market, Lincoln and Hunter started booking musical turns. One of the first bands to appear was the skiffle-playing Vipers, whose singer was Tony Hicks. Hicks was quickly talented spotted on the 2is stage, remodelled as Tommy Steele and unleashed on the British public to become the country's first home-grown rock 'n' roll star before the end of the year.

The success of Steele put the 2is on the map until it could legitimately claim to be the epicentre of the national rock 'n' roll scene. Despite its tiny dimensions, it became overrun with a combination of musicians from all over the country in search of their big break, fans on the lookout for the next big things, and agents, impresarios and record producers promising to make dreams come true. Indeed, Steele was by no means the only success story to emerge from the 2is. The likes of Adam Faith, Marty Wilde and Cliff Richard all paid their dues there. It was a hive of beautiful young people and older men looking to make a fast buck or a new acquaintance. Boothby was among the latter group, willing to agree a *quid pro quo* now and then: sexual favours in return for promises of assistance in progressing careers of various types – political, literary and musical. An age-old trade-off of an older man's influence for a younger man's affection. Jon Vickers-Jones, who was assistant manager at the 2is for two years, recalls Boothby's unsettling presence there. 'Yeah, I remember seeing him,' he says, 'but I did not interact with him … I put him down as a weirdo so kept away from him.'[6]

When Boothby made it on to the Cedra Court guest list, what he saw there was unlikely to have shocked him even as it delighted. In the manner of the Diana Dors' parties, Kray liked to entertain his guests into the small hours with pornographic films as well as live-action sex shows. According to the unpublished memoir of Ronnie Hart, who was related to the twins through marriage, Boothby and Kray would sometimes swap boys with each other.[7] Virtually no sexual preference was off-bounds, with guests catered to by a throng of compliant young males whose presence Kray had arranged. Boothby reputedly had an interest in coprophilia, which fell within the remit of services provided. There are also echoes of the Night of the Peacock in the recollections of the Krays' criminal associate, Henry 'Buller' Ward, as related by the *Sunday Mirror*'s crime journalist, Norman Lucas. According to Ward, on several visits to Ronnie's flat, the door was opened by one of his 'boys' wearing a pinafore. 'The boy performed the complete duties of a housewife,' he said.[8]

In all of this, there was perhaps one feature that was less familiar to Boothby though, and that was the unique quality of menace that Kray brought to almost every social situation. Doubtless, some of those in attendance at the Cedra Court parties to provide 'entertainment' for guests were there of their own volition. But there is a body of evidence from various of Kray's friends and acquaintances that suggests a pattern of violent coercion in his dealings with the young men he took a fancy to. Laurie O'Leary went to primary school with the twins and rose to be the manager of Esmerelda's Barn. He told how Ronnie was particularly drawn to athletic, clean-cut boys with dark hair and fresh complexions. He had a habit of referring to any lads who took his eye as 'prospects' and a rumour built that if Ronnie put a £20 note in your top pocket, you had been marked out as someone he wanted to sleep with. 'Ron was always playing tricks on the young boys,' O'Leary wrote. 'One lad I know told me that he had heard the rumour and Ronnie put some notes into his top pocket. Panicking, he quickly took them out again and pushed them gently back into Ronnie's hand. "I'm not like that, Ron!" the boy protested. "It would be a waste of your money." As the boy hurried away as rapidly as he could, Ronnie burst out laughing at his obvious fear.'[9]

Another who witnessed this ability to induce fear was Jess Conrad, who had a string of chart hits in the early 1960s and was named 'Most Popular Male Singer' in the 1961 *New Musical Express* annual poll. Born in 1936, he was three years younger than the Krays and grew up in Brixton, south London. Having endured a childhood marked by wartime rationing and post-war austerity, he entered into adulthood hungry for some glamour in his life of the type that had hitherto only been available in short bursts at the cinema. He gravitated towards Soho, where he started mixing with the likes of Barbara Windsor and Diana Dors, as well as gangsters from across the city. He recalls the Krays in their sharp suits, drinking and smoking at the right joints, and stepping in to protect Windsor, Dors *et al.* should they start to receive unwanted attention. They were James Cagney or Spencer Tracey made flesh for the local youngsters. Conrad himself aspired to their lifestyle and ended up socialising with them at spots like Sissy Jackson's in Soho. 'Back then no one knew anyone in show business so you hung out with glamorous gangsters like the Krays,' he said. 'When they walked in it was like a film star had walked in.'

Nonetheless, it was not long before knowledge of Ronnie Kray's homosexuality filtered through. The reputation of his 'parties' spread and it was commonly understood that if you didn't want an invitation, it was best to stay off his radar altogether. 'You had to keep your wits about you if you were a young man and Ronnie really fancied you,' Conrad told the *Sunday Mirror* in 2015. 'Word used to go out that the Krays were on their way to a certain pub and all the good-looking boys used to piss off. Because otherwise if he asked you to go back to the house you had to go back and that was it. You'd make yourself scarce, unless you didn't want to make yourself scarce of course.'[10] On other occasions, Kray would ask his driver to take him to London's Piccadilly to seek out rent boys who caught his eye working the infamous 'Meat Rack' there.

Michael Thornton, the young journalist sent by John Junor at the *Sunday Express* to muck-rake on Boothby, endured his own experiences of Ronnie's violent, predatory nature. He was at Boothby's Eaton Square flat one evening in May 1964 when Leslie Holt suggested to Boothby that he ought to go and collect 'the Guv'nor'. The Guv'nor was, of course, Ronnie Kray, who soon arrived at the flat in the company of a young, blond-haired Cockney who Thornton believes was called Ted. He sported a cut lip and a bruise on one cheek. 'Go on, be nice to Lord Boothby,' Thornton quotes Kray as saying, 'or I'll give you a fucking slap.' The teenager then stood still as Boothby, already the worse for drink, kissed him on the mouth.

Kray suggested that the party should move to one of his favoured haunts, the Society Club on Jermyn Street. Here, Thornton became aware of Kray staring at him through his glasses with a dark intensity. 'It put one in mind of a dead cod on a fishmonger's hook,' he later wrote. Convinced that Ronnie had taken against him, the group, which had now been joined by Reg, made its way to Esmerelda's Barn – a short drive away, during which Thornton found himself sandwiched in the back of a car by the twins. In the club, he was taken aback to be told by Ted that 'Ron fancies you rotten'. Thornton now discovered the gangster's tendency towards predation, his demeanour becoming more menacing as Thornton attempted to duck his invitations to go home with him. According to Thornton, he would not 'take no for an answer' while Boothby urged him, 'Just play along. He's not a man to offend.' It was a position backed up by Diana Dors, who also happened to be in that night. 'Babycakes,' she said, 'you're dicing with death here. Don't get stroppy with him for God's sake.'

Reggie also made an appeal to the journalist on his brother's behalf and then, when Thornton repeated his reluctance to submit, suggested, 'Well, if you don't fancy Ron, I can look after you, you know? Make things OK.' His meaning, Thornton later wrote, was unmistakable. Nor was this the end of his discomfort for the evening. Later on, he found himself in a corridor at the club confronted by Ronnie – 'now a gargoyle of bulging-eyed fury' – who was pointing a gun at him. 'Go on then,' the rather drunk Thornton challenged him. 'That will make a great headline. Journalist gunned down in Krays' nightclub.' Ronnie promptly hit him and slammed him into the wall, before Reggie appeared and intervened, telling his brother: 'Leave it out, Ron. You can see the kid's not interested. And he's the fucking press.' Reggie then took Thornton out of the club and put him in a taxi back home.[11]

For several weeks, Ronnie made attempts to contact Thornton, which he ignored while also keeping his distance from Boothby. However, there was to be a coda to the story. One afternoon in July 1965, Thornton was walking to his home in Marylebone when he felt an arm come around his throat before he was struck on the forehead. He fell down to the ground where he received a kicking, accompanied by the admonition: 'That will teach you to show some fucking respect to Ronnie.' His injuries included a broken nose, a cracked cheekbone and a cut on his forehead that needed twenty-two stitches.

The Cedra Court parties were by no means all-male affairs. Ronnie counted several women among his sexual conquests, although an occasion when he awoke to find a partner's menstrual blood had stained the bed clothes seems to have confirmed his preference for homosexual relationships. Nonetheless, as related in the Teale brothers' account of their time with the twins, *Bringing Down the Krays*, Alfie and David Teale were present at one party where Kray took a fancy to a boyishly pretty, slim-hipped, short-haired girl. He led her to a bedroom and before long her anguished cries could be heard by the other guests. When David Teale called through the door to check that everything was alright, Kray ordered him to 'Fuck off out of it.' David was sure that he was anally raping the girl, who emerged distressed from the bedroom a little while later and immediately left the party.[12]

According to the Teales' account, David Teale would himself fall victim to Kray's predatory advances when he found himself unable to get back to his own home one evening so accepted an invitation to stay at Vallance Road. Kray insisted that he should share his bed rather than take the couch, arguing that he would be less likely to disturb his parents. Teale awoke during the night to find Kray bearing down on him. As Teale wrestled to get free, Kray used his bulk to pin him down, telling him 'Just try it' and warning him to 'shut up' when he shouted for help. Kray put his arm around Teale's neck in a bid to strangle him at one point and eventually succeeded in overpowering and raping him. Another of the Teale brothers, Bobby, had a similar experience, this time at a location on the Isle of Wight. He too was raped and, once the attack had finished, Kray kicked him to the ground.

It is hard to envisage how Boothby was able to reconcile his association with Ronnie Kray with his admonition to the Commons in the mid-1950s that they each had a duty to be conscious of 'a homosexual underground which is a constant menace to youth'. When did he judge that the frisson of danger he felt around Kray was worth the price of fear and violence that he must have known others were having to pay? At what stage did he decide his conscience could cope with kissing a youth decades his junior and under threat of a slap from Ronnie? When did it become the right thing to do to encourage a young journalist to submit to Kray's will rather than risk offence?

In December 1958, Boothby had appeared on an episode of *Frankly Speaking*, presented by the broadcaster and former Member of Parliament, John Freeman. Among Boothby's interviewers was the eminent broadcast journalist, George Scott. He asked Boothby: 'The threat of physical violence, of physical threat, does that frighten you?'

'If I saw someone bashing another chap about, with blood all over the place,' he replied, 'my instinct would be to go away, rather than to rescue somebody, 'cause I don't like the look of trouble of that sort of kind. But if my passion was aroused, my temper was aroused and I was involved in the fight for some issue then I think I would probably take part. But if I saw a row, my natural instinct, on seeing a row at the end of the street with people knocking each other around, my natural instinct would be to beat it – and get out.'[13]

Boothby's life was defined by espousing causes and contesting the intellectual battleground, not by taking on physical confrontation. Nor was there any chance that he would find himself the victim of Kray's unwanted advances. The gangster was not interested in a portly 60-something-year-old whose body evidenced a life never lived in half-measure. As Kray told his friends: 'I would rather be seen dead [*sic*] than in bed with 'im.'[14] Yet his association with Kray exposed him to a level of violence that he came implicitly to accept even as he might have been expected to rail against it. Where now was the Boothby who at Eton had vetoed the punitive beatings he so detested?

Perhaps he was merely blinded to the violence, distracted by the dazzle that the Krays gave off and which drew in so many other public figures at the time. Or maybe he could see no way of breaking off his ties with the twins once the full reality of their existence became obvious to him. At the time of the 'Peer and the Gangster' scandal, there were whispered rumours of more damaging photos in the Krays' possession than those that fell into the hands of the newspapers. There were suggestions of intimate images captured at parties, the type that no amount of talking would allow you to wriggle free of. And while there is no evidence that any such pictures ever existed, the mere suggestion that they might have done would have been enough to heap enormous pressure upon Boothby. He found himself immersed in a world far easier to enter than to leave.

Boothby maintained sufficient autonomy that he was able to turn down the Nigerian investment opportunity that Ronnie had offered him. But he likely already realised he was now a cog in the Kray machine – a man who had revealed too much of himself to engineer a retreat. And having rejected the Nigerian proposal, it was only a matter of time before he would have to say yes to something else.

12

Under Surveillance

When the revelations about Boothby's association with the Krays became a brief *cause célèbre*, they prompted a flurry of intelligence gathering from the Security Service, MI5. It was, though, only the latest chapter in the service's surveillance of Boothby, which by then spanned five separate decades.

In March 1939, Neville Chamberlain's promise of 'peace for our time' made just a few months earlier appeared increasingly empty. Czechoslovakia had fallen and Hitler showed no inclination to rein in his expansionist ambitions. In Birmingham, Chamberlain was compelled to make a speech asserting that German aggression would not go unchecked.

Boothby, meanwhile, was dining one evening that month at the Mirabeau restaurant in London. His unmistakeable tones drifted across the venue, catching the ear of a diner at a table close by who just so happened to be an operative of MI5. Although the specific content of Boothby's conversation is not recorded, the fellow diner decided to scrawl Boothby a note on the back of a sheet of the restaurant's note paper. 'If you will forgive me for saying so,' it read, 'you are talking too loud and too much.'

Boothby was having none of it, firing off a swift response: 'I certainly do not forgive such a piece of unwarranted impertinence. I happen to be a minister of the Crown, and I would have you know that we are not yet a Nazi State; that the methods of the Gestapo do not apply in this country; and that there are better ways of serving the country than writing foolish little notes in restaurants.'[1]

It was classic Boothby on a number of scores: in its eloquent rejection of unwarranted authority, but also as an example of his propensity to embroider the truth. He was not, never had been and never would be a minister of the Crown – that is, a member of the Cabinet. But that detail did not matter just now, as Boothby pulled rank to right a perceived wrong.

The very first note on Boothby that MI5 retained in its files dates from December 1928. It is innocuous enough, relating to press cuttings concerning a speech he gave in Peterhead on the subject of Russian trade relations. Then there is nothing more for over four years, until on 27 January 1933 it was noted that he appeared on a list of members of an Anti-War Committee, with the hope that he would support the anti-war movement financially. By the middle of the decade, however, Boothby had been identified by MI5 as a subject of more consistent interest to them. In 1936, for example, his attendance at a meeting in London of the Friends of Russia was recorded.[2]

His wide-ranging business contacts were also a source of some suspicion, and increasingly so when war eventually broke out. In late 1939, a Belgian called J.R. Francotte, attached to an arms-dealing firm in Liege, cited Boothby's name in a visa application to the British authorities. A memo was filed by MI5 noting: 'The name of Mr Robert Boothby does not inspire much confidence. He has in the past been associated with Mr Oliver Hoare, who at one time was mixed up with dubious arms traffickers.'[3] Francotte's firm, moreover, was suspected of being controlled by a figure with connections to German intelligence. Then, in 1940, it was recorded that Boothby was visiting Paris with a Dutch passport-holder by the name of Jacobus Smith, a man whom the French were sure was in touch with a known German spy.[4]

The early stages of the war ushered in a period when intelligence officials were tempted to see intrigues everywhere. Virtually anyone with any sort of a link to a business on the Continent might come under suspicion. Boothby's network was extensive and it was all but inevitable that at least a few of his contacts were involved in enterprises that would not pass muster with MI5. But it was also a time of official paranoia, in which the mere sound of a name or an ancestral association was enough to prompt misgivings.

In Boothby's case, the spooks' concerns were particularly inflamed by his association with Weininger, who had been on their radar for some considerable time even before the Czech assets drama. A memo from 22 June 1940 confirms as much, while conceding that despite several investigations, no subsequent action was ever taken against him.[5] A further report on the Weininger case, this one from 1 March 1941, gives a flavour of the suspicion bordering on hysteria that many foreign nationals faced. 'Richard Weininger is an unscrupulous but plausible financier,' it began, 'with both unscrupulous associates and influential friends. His outlook is international, his standards of honesty low, and his interest in personal gain considerable. A number of his contacts … have caused him to be suspected of espionage, and there is no doubt that if he was a spy he was in a position to be a very dangerous one.'[6] Another note reads: 'Since the international element is marked in him, it is likely, [words missing] that if he is a spy he is a double cross agent and willing to sell himself to the highest bidder.'[7]

The MI5 code was hardly difficult to crack. The references to an international 'outlook/element' was shorthand to mean he was Jewish. Weininger was a rich Jew with international (and specifically German) connections and so, in the eyes of MI5 at the time, a major security risk. No matter that there was not yet any evidence of wrongdoing. (Boothby would always claim that Weininger had undertaken important missions on the nation's behalf, some of them of such a sensitive nature that they could not be discussed in public.) The conclusion – that were he to be a spy, he'd be a double agent available to the highest bidder – is a dumbfounding piece of forejudging. Because of his friendship with Weininger, Boothby was, unbeknownst to him, subject to telephone surveillance and postal intercepts. There was also an understanding that anything Boothby became caught up in had potential repercussions for Macmillan. An intelligence report from October 1940 observed: 'He is, I believe, very fond of Diana Cavendish's cousin, Mrs Harold Macmillan … Harold Macmillan is therefore pretty closely concerned …'[8]

Around the time that the Czech assets affair was reaching its crescendo, Boothby found himself involved in another conflict-of-interest embarrassment at the Ministry of Food. This one involved bread – specifically, loaves produced using a flour fortified with vitamin B1 and calcium. Boothby was a great advocate of the new fortified loaf but others were more sceptical. In a parliamentary debate, it was noted that most medical professionals believed that a standard wholemeal loaf was, in fact, the healthier option.[9] But Boothby defended the government position – a significant proportion of the country simply would not embrace a wholemeal loaf, he argued, so the food ministry decided to develop an enhanced white alternative. Alongside the milk scheme he was already championing, Boothby considered this his ministry's other great nutritional breakthrough.

The enrichment process was not patent-protected but there was only one firm in the UK able to supply the synthetic vitamin B1 required, a Hertfordshire company called Roche. Until Churchill gave him his ministerial role, Boothby had been its chairman. He subsequently stood down but was given a parting gift of 5,000 shares in the company. MI5 held a copy of the note Boothby sent to express his appreciation.[10] When the conflict of interest came to light, Boothby was permitted to sell the shares at significant personal profit. However, by then the Security Service was building an impression of Boothby as something of a liability, even before the parliamentary select committee found against him for the Czech assets affair.

Another potential source of embarrassment for the government, and another area of interest for officials at MI5, was Boothby's friendship with Oswald Mosley. When the pair were first together in the Commons in the 1920s, Mosley was far removed from the path that he ultimately followed. He had entered the House in 1918 when he was barely 22 years old. His political philosophy was still evolving, although his wartime experiences had a profound and lasting influence on his desire to avoid further warfare. He began his parliamentary career as a Conservative but sat as an independent from 1922. By the time Boothby won his seat for the first time in 1924, Mosley had decided to join the Labour Party.

Politically, Boothby was deeply attracted by Mosley's ideas of a radical economic prescription based around the ideas of John Maynard Keynes. Privately, too, the pair forged strong bonds of friendship at Cliveden and other grand estates where they frequently found themselves as weekend guests. There closeness was further bolstered because Boothby adored Mosley's wife, Lady Cynthia Curzon – Cimmie – who served as a Labour MP herself from 1929 until 1931, while Mosley was Chancellor of the Duchy of Lancaster in Ramsay MacDonald's government. But it was about then that Mosley's career began its dangerous veer. (Stanley Baldwin, incidentally, was among those who was not surprised by his political change in direction, having observed: 'He is a cad and a wrong 'un and they will find it out.'[11])

Over-estimating his own popularity within the party, in 1930 Mosley issued what became known as the Mosley Memorandum – a radical economic response to the mass unemployment of the Depression based on a mixture of nationalisation, protectionism and large-scale public spending. When his programme was rejected by the party, he threatened to resign but Boothby attempted to dissuade him, writing to him:

> I care about your political future far more than about any other single factor in public affairs, because I know that you are the ONLY ONE of my generation – of the post-war school of thought – who is capable of translating into action any of the ideas in which I genuinely believe. Consequently, I can conceive no greater tragedy than that you should take a step which might wreck your chances, or at any rate postpone the opportunity of carrying through constructive work.[12]

It was no good, though. Mosley resigned in early 1931 and immediately threw his energies into launching the New Party, whose political credo was derived from its leader's earlier memorandum. Boothby was convinced it was a mistake and doomed to failure, but his protestations again fell on deaf ears. It marked the beginning of a parting of the ways, Boothby convinced that Mosley no longer greatly valued his opinion.[13]

The New Party never achieved any significant electoral breakthrough, as Boothby had predicted. It did, however, rapidly absorb a number of both fascist ideas and supporters. Mosley himself was converted after visiting Benito Mussolini in Italy in January 1932. The New Party was disbanded in the April and Mosley returned in the autumn, now as the leader of the British Union of Fascists. Boothby stayed resolutely away from it and when, in 1933, Cimmie died, his reasons to engage even socially with Mosley dissipated, too.

The BUF staged a number of spectacular public events but mass support eluded it. Mosley was a compelling orator and his rallies attracted tens of thousands at a time. But there was deep suspicion around the movement, with meetings and marches routinely disrupted – most memorably in the 1936 Battle of Cable Street, when large numbers of East Enders mobilised under the banner of anti-fascism. When war began three years later, Mosley called for a negotiated peace with Germany but public opinion quickly, and predictably, swung resolutely against him. Then, in 1943, he was interned along with his new wife, Diana Mitford, at Holloway Prison.

The decision to lock them up was a source of much public debate, between those who felt that the couple had been asking for it and others who questioned the extent of the risk they posed to national and public security. While Boothby made no public declaration on the matter, he nonetheless decided to visit his old friend – one of a very small number of Mosley's former chums who did so. Boothby could be loyal, often to a fault, and it is noticeable that he often kept up associations when others might have deemed it politic to cut certain acquaintances adrift. Weininger, for example, remained a lifelong friend despite the trouble that their association had heaped upon him. Nor was there anything to be gained by visiting Mosley, other than the sense that he was doing the right thing by a man whom he had once admired almost more highly than anyone else.

Towards the end of 1943, Mosley and Mitford were released from prison to live out the rest of the war under house arrest and police supervision. They remained objects of press fascination, too, and of public disdain. But Boothby continued his association and, in 1949, made representations on their behalf for the restoration of their passports. 'I cannot feel that it is right to deprive any British citizen of a passport, in time of peace, on political grounds,' Boothby wrote, citing the ridiculous situation in which leading members of the British Communist Party were allowed to visit the Soviet Union to make anti-British speeches, while Mosley couldn't have a holiday in the south of France for the good of his health.[14] Even with a character as unsympathetic as Mosley, Boothby was able to find an injustice to crusade against. All the while as he did so, MI5 kept a close eye on him. A note from August 1951 in his file summarised their impressions of him to date, and it is clear that his ties to Mosley had damaged him: 'Although a right wing Conservative with some fascist contacts, I do not feel that his case warrants being brought to the attention of the DG but at the same time I think the files should be retained …'[15]

There was further surveillance of Boothby's activities over the next few years but the intelligence gathered by MI5 in 1964 was of a different order to all that went before. What is striking about the information gathered until that point was just how unincriminating most of it was. Boothby kept some interesting company, most certainly, and in regard to the Weininger and Roche affairs, greater transparency would have been well advised. But there was little if anything that would have made much of a splash were the newspapers to have had unrestricted access to his files. However, with their 'Peer and the Gangster' intelligence, MI5 were sitting upon a goldmine of potential scandal. With contacts in Fleet Street and embedded within the Krays' organisation, MI5 had built a vivid picture of the 'kinky' peer who attended sex parties with Ronnie Kray, where they would 'hunt' together for young flesh.

It was the sort of stuff that was so toxic that Boothby could not hope to keep a lid on it alone.

13

Twice Bitten

In June 1963 Harold Macmillan wrote to the Queen in light of the Profumo affair then engulfing his administration. 'I had of course no idea of the strange underworld in which other people have allowed themselves to become entrapped,' he explained. 'I begin to suspect in all these wild accusations against many people, Ministers and others, something in the nature of a plot to destroy the established system.'[1]

The note reveals just how advanced was the British government's bunker mentality, developed in the aftermath of the Profumo scandal and the Vassall affair before it. Long gone was the optimistic Macmillan of 1957 enthusiastically advising the public that they had 'never had it so good', or the premier who emerged from the 1959 election with a landslide victory and a hundred-seat majority. Now he and a good many of his ministers and MPs felt assailed. The patrician ranks of both parties – but perhaps Conservatives most of all – were subject to unparalleled scrutiny from a public weary of their leaders' sexual misadventures, especially when it seemed to imperil the national interest. The press, meanwhile, had adopted an iconoclastic tone unprecedented in British history. The kind of *quid pro quo* between newspapers and public figures that had allowed, for instance, the Macmillan–Lady Dorothy–Boothby *ménage à trois* to go unreported for decades was, while not yet dead, seriously on the wane. There was a new appetite for searing satire too, exemplified by the arrival in 1962 of the David Frost-helmed *That Was the Week that Was*, which soon boasted an audience of 12 million.

Coupled to this was a lumbering economy, rampant inflation and dismal industrial relations giving the lie to that 'never had it so good' claim. After fighting two world wars, the joy of being at peace had long since dissipated and the public was growing short on patience for a ruling class that seemed content to impose on the population at large a different set of rules – economic and social – than it was prepared to adhere to itself.

For Macmillan, the rot had set in with the Vassall affair and its fallout. It was bad enough that a British civil servant had been exposed as a KGB spy. Vassall's name was added to a list of British traitors that had expanded since 1950 to include the likes of Burgess and Maclean (who scandalously defected to the Soviet Union in 1951) and the Portland Spy Ring, broken up by the British authorities in 1961. But perhaps more damaging still was how the government lost control of the investigation into Vassall in the face of a newspaper feeding frenzy. Fleet Street saw security risks everywhere, all underpinned by a homophobia rooted in the belief that the government and security services were overrun with closeted homosexuals.

A complicated case of espionage turned into something far thornier for Macmillan and his colleagues with the discovery of a number of letters sent to Vassall from Tam Galbraith, the Civil Lord of the Admiralty from 1957 to 1959. Vassall was already a valuable asset to Moscow embedded in the Naval Intelligence Division at the Admiralty when he was summoned to an interview with the recently appointed Civil Lord in 1957. Their discussion went well and Vassall was duly appointed Galbraith's assistant private secretary. Vassall's Soviet handlers were actually disappointed, according to Vassall himself. Galbraith's ministerial documents were of far less interest to them than the material to which Vassall had access in Naval Intelligence. But Vassall and Galbraith clearly enjoyed a warm relationship, and this would prove troublesome for Macmillan and his ministers a few years down the line.

In truth, there was sufficiently little evidence that it ought never to have been much of a problem for the Prime Minister. The cache of letters that Galbraith sent was innocuous enough. There was a postcard from a holiday abroad with his wife, Simone, and some other missives containing informal chatter about office carpets, stationery provisions and the like. But when the *Sunday Pictorial* got hold of the correspondence as part of a deal they had signed with Vassall, the government felt compelled to publish its own copies in a bid to stave off scandal. It was a tactic that spectacularly backfired.

Amid the poisonous climate of the time, the newspapers set about framing this paltry evidence as proof of an inappropriate – that is to say, homosexual – relationship between the treacherous civil servant and his political master. The *Daily Mail* noted with a nudge and a wink that the postcard from the holiday abroad revealed 'a friendliness which one would not expect between a clerk and a senior colleague'.[2] The *Daily Express*, on the other hand, ran a front-page story under the headline 'My Dear Vassall', as if that utterly common term of address conclusively proved an illicit love affair.[3] Vassall had also made a trip to Galbraith's Scottish home to deliver some papers on one occasion but this was interpreted not as the 'above-and-beyond' efforts of a private secretary to equip a government minister with the files he needed but as an indicator of a lovers' tryst. The implication was clear – the sexual peccadillos of a senior government figure had helped protect a Soviet spy in his ranks.

The *Sunday Pictorial* added further fuel to the fire with an article at the end of October 1962 headed 'Spy catchers name "sex risk" men'. 'Civil servants with homosexual tendencies were especially vulnerable as security risks,' reported Norman Lucas, who also asserted that 'several groups of these men have been traced and broken up in Whitehall'. A secret list, he wrote, was being prepared by detectives, naming 'homosexuals who hold top government posts. The list will be considered by the Prime Minister's committee of inquiry set up to probe the John Vassall spy case.'[4] To some observers, this was the worst of something-and-nothing reporting but it broke through to the concerns of readers. Galbraith eventually found the scrutiny to which he was being subjected unbearable and offered his resignation.

Macmillan had an inkling of how the drama would play out almost as soon as he had been made aware of Vassall's arrest in the September. At that point, Sir Theobald Mathew, the then Director of Prosecutions, had warned the recently appointed Attorney General, Sir John Hobson: 'We have arrested a spy who is a bugger, and a minister is involved.'[5] Meanwhile, Sir Roger Hollis – head of MI5 – had spoken to the Prime Minister. 'I've got this fellow – I've got him,' he said. Macmillan was notably displeased. 'When my gamekeeper shoots a fox,' he explained using a characteristically patrician analogy, 'he doesn't go and hang it up outside the master of fox-hound's drawing room. He buries it out of sight. But you can't just shoot a spy as you did in the war.' There would be, he said, 'a great public trial. Then the security services will not be praised for how efficient they are, but blamed for how hopeless they are. There will then be an inquiry. There will be a terrible row in the press. There will be a debate in the House of Commons, and the government will probably fall. Why the devil did you catch him?'[6]

Macmillan had originally intended to appoint a civil service-led inquiry into the affair but in the end was forced to establish an independent judicial one instead. It was headed by Lord Radcliffe and was charged with looking at the security implications of the case, along with the conduct of the press. Macmillan was livid on several scores – that a minister felt compelled to resign despite the lack of evidence that he had done anything wrong, that the Opposition (and particularly Labour's deputy leader, George Brown) were striving to make political capital out of the situation, and that the press had been able to stir things up so comprehensively.

On 14 November Parliament approved the Radcliffe tribunal and Macmillan used the opportunity to vent against the press. He spoke of the practice – 'although I do not think it is a very laudable one' – of popular newspapers buying 'for large sums the autobiographies of well-known criminals', as the *Sunday Pictorial* had done with Vassall. This was, Macmillan continued, a 'rather squalid form of journalism' that pandered 'to a certain demand for horror and terror which is understandable, if not particularly praiseworthy'. Rather acerbically, he added:

> So, when I read that the Vassall memoirs – if one can give such a name to such a compilation – had been purchased by one of the popular newspapers, I assumed that it was to meet a demand of the same kind. However, I now understand that this decision was taken not from any purpose of satisfying the appetite of their readers, but from a deep sense of public duty.

Indicating his belief that there was a witch-hunt in progress, he concluded: 'I have a feeling that the time has come for men of propriety and decency not to tolerate the growth of what I can only call the spirit of Titus Oates [the seventeenth-century perjurer who fabricated evidence of a Catholic plot to assassinate King Charles II] and Senator McCarthy.'[7]

When the Vassall Tribunal made its final report in April 1963, it exonerated both Galbraith and Lord Carrington, First Lord of the Admiralty, of any involvement in assisting or concealing Vassall's espionage. Knowledge of Vassall's activities had only come to light through information offered by a KGB defector, Anatoli Golitsyn, in 1962. Crucially, Lord Radcliffe put on record that: 'There was nothing improper in the relationship between Galbraith and Vassall.'[8] Moreover, the press came in for heavy criticism. Among those called to give evidence at the inquiry were two journalists, Brendan Mulholland of the *Daily Mail* and Reg Foster of the *Daily Sketch*. Mulholland had written that Vassall was known as 'Aunty' in the Admiralty, while Foster had claimed Vassall was in the habit of visiting the West End to buy women's clothes. Each was asked to reveal the sources of their information but both – in the best traditions of British journalism – declined. Mulholland argued, 'I believe I am being asked to do something that is morally wrong.'[9] Radcliffe sent them to the High Court on charges of contempt of court, and they received sentences of six and three months respectively. They were the first journalists in British legal history to be imprisoned for refusing to identify their sources.

It is true that over the preceding years much of Fleet Street had become more virulently critical of the Establishment than ever before. In 1962, Hugh Cudlipp, editor of the *Sunday Pictorial*, had given voice to the prevailing newspaperman philosophy in his book, *At Your Peril*. He urged newspapers to strive to be provocative and to cock a snook at 'the hoary traditions and pomposities of our times'.[10] When he paid £7,000 to Vassall for his 'memoirs', he could argue that he was less interested in prurience than in holding the powers-that-be to account. The subsequent imprisonment of Mulholland and Foster prompted an unbridgeable rift between Fleet Street and Macmillan's No. 10. By sending the journalists to jail, the High Court brought the full wrath of Fleet Street down upon the government. Bill Deedes had been appointed Minister without Portfolio in Macmillan's Night of the Long Knives in 1962, with a special remit to spearhead Downing Street's communications campaigns. As he noted in his memoirs: 'Fleet Street was enraged. From then on my task of winning hearts and minds in the newspaper world became immeasurably harder. In the trials which lay ahead of us, this was to have profound consequences.'[11] (Deedes' view of Boothby, meanwhile, was that he 'simply could not resist drinking from brim to dregs every cup offered him'.)

It was on 21 March 1963, during a House of Commons debate on the imprisoning of the Vassall journalists, that the question of John Profumo's conduct leapt from a matter of press tittle-tattle to an issue of national importance. Four Labour MPs, Reginald Paget, George Wigg, Barbara Castle and Richard Crossman, brought up the subject of rumours surrounding the Secretary of State for War on the basis that they might have led to a perversion of the course of justice. If the Vassall affair had been an ordeal for Macmillan, he soon realised that Profumo would be far worse. As he noted in a diary entry at the time: 'I do not remember ever having been under such a sense of personal strain. Even Suez was "clean" – about war and politics. This is all "dirt".'[12]

Profumo could have had no idea of the devastation that his brief dalliance with Keeler – commenced during a weekend stay at Lord Astor's Cliveden Estate in 1961 – would cause when he broke off the relationship sometime around the end of the same year. MI5 had got word to him to be more circumspect about the company he was keeping and he had taken the warning. But events spiralled beyond his control when two rival claimants on Keeler's affections, a Jamaican jazz singer called Aloysius 'Lucky' Gordon and an Antiguan ex-merchant seaman called Johnny Edgecombe, clashed in the latter months of 1962. Their feud saw Gordon slashed with a knife during a nightclub brawl in the October and then, in December, Edgecombe turned up at a house in Wimple Mews, Marylebone, where Keeler was staying with her friend, Mandy Rice-Davies, and unleashed a volley of gunfire when he was not allowed in.

In the weeks that followed, Keeler was unguarded in talking about the Edgecombe incident, as well as her involvement with Profumo, a Russian naval intelligence officer called Yevgeney Ivanov and their mutual friend, the society osteopath Stephen Ward. Among those to whom she told her story one evening in a nightclub was a former Labour MP called John Lewis, who happened to harbour a grudge against Ward. Lewis passed on the intelligence he had picked up to George Wigg. By now, most of Fleet

Street was aware of the rumours and Reg Payne at the *Sunday Pictorial* agreed to buy Keeler's story for £1,000, although the paper did not go on to publish for fear that it would struggle to defend a libel action on the basis of her testimony alone.

Wigg outlined the case against Profumo at a dinner hosted on 10 March 1963 by Barbara Castle and attended by Harold Wilson, Richard Crossman and Michael Foot. Wilson had become party leader just a few weeks earlier, following the death of Hugh Gaitskell. Initially the diners advised Wigg against pursuing Profumo on accusations of infidelity. The Labour hierarchy were aware that George Brown had been loose-tongued about Tam Galbraith the previous year, and with Galbraith now cleared of any wrongdoing they were nervous of fostering a reputation as salacious muckrakers. However, within a few days a new twist in the developing narrative prompted a rethink. When Jonny Edgecombe's trial began for the Wimple Mews incident, Keeler was expected to appear as the star prosecution witness. However, by then she was holed up in Spain, having bolted without warning. It is likely that she agreed to the flit in order to maximise press interest in her story, and accordingly the price they might pay for it. Nonetheless, a rumour began circulating that Profumo had squirrelled her abroad for fear of what she might say in the witness box. In light of this, the Labour leadership felt emboldened to raise the issue in Parliament to determine whether a senior government minister had perverted the course of justice.

It was at this point that the government lost all control of the narrative. It was decided that Profumo had no choice but to respond to the claims against him, which he duly did on 22 March when he made his fateful claim of 'no impropriety whatsoever' in his relationship with Keeler. He could not keep up the charade for long though, especially since Stephen Ward – by then himself the subject of an aggressive police inquiry – was making it known that he had been covering up for Profumo. At the start of June, the Secretary of State for War admitted he had lied and resigned from the government.

It was a savage blow to Macmillan. In 1962 he had allowed Galbraith to resign in the face of scurrilous rumours. A year later, and the regret this time was that he had stuck by a minister in not dissimilar circumstances.

In each case, he could not have played his hand more wrongly, appearing fickle and disloyal regarding Vassall and then gullible when it came to Profumo. Macmillan survived a parliamentary vote of confidence by the smallest of margins but his days were numbered. The Conservative MP, Nigel Birch, memorably called time on him by quoting Robert Browning's words on William Wordsworth. Never, he declared, would it be 'glad confident morning again'.[13] At the end of the month, the trial of Stephen Ward began on what are now widely regarded as trumped up charges of living off the immoral earnings of Keeler and Rice-Davies. In August, he was found guilty but by then he was unconscious in his flat from an overdose of barbiturates and would never recover. The coroner ruled he died by suicide, although rumours of third-party involvement have been aired regularly over the years.[14]

In late September, Lord Denning delivered his famous report into the Profumo affair, which found the government substantially blameless for the scandal, instead blaming the 'utterly immoral' Ward,[15] who was, of course, no longer able to defend himself. Many observers felt discomfort at the treatment of Ward, whose entry in the *Oxford Dictionary of National Biography* (authored by Richard Davenport-Hines) notes: 'Ward was in fact incidental to the Profumo episode: he was a sacrificial offering. The exorcism of scandal in high places required the façade of his conviction on vice charges.'[16]

Another to harbour concerns about his pursuit was Lord Boothby's cousin, Ludovic Kennedy, who published *The Trial of Stephen Ward* in 1964. In his preface, he wrote:

> My original intention in writing this book was, as I put it at the time, 'to make a permanent record of the last public act of the Profumo affair before the curtain comes down for the last time'. If on occasions the book is now rather more vehement than I had intended, that is because I had not bargained on seeing justice miscarry before my eyes.[17]

Meanwhile, Dick Crossman, a Labour backbencher at the time but soon to serve in Wilson's Cabinet, noted in his diaries: 'One can really say that the whole Establishment did everything possible to rally round the Profumos and to try and save them from their fate.'[18] But it was Mandy Rice-Davies who most effectively captured the sense that the Establishment had over-reached this time. During Ward's trial, she was being cross-examined concerning Lord Astor's claim that he had never met her, let alone had an affair with her, when she chirpily responded: 'Well he would, wouldn't he?' It was a devastating put-down not only of an individual but of an entire class structure. He may be a lord, went the subtext, but he (and by extension, they) are no better than the rest of us and certainly not to be trusted. Under a cloud of ill health, Macmillan resigned in October 1963, and although the high-born Douglas-Home replaced him, there was an undeniable feeling that a changing of the guard was in the offing.

Although the Conservatives had suffered the worst of the injuries from the Vassall and Profumo sagas, the extent of the political damage caused was shocking to the Labour Party, too. Among the political class, you did not need to be a Tory to feel wary of how the public might consider you. It was against this backdrop that Boothby endured his moment in the spotlight a year later.

While Boothby did not publicly stray into either the Vassall or Profumo dramas in any meaningful way, he nonetheless had tangential cameos in both scandals. Having been 'there or thereabouts' at so many vital moments in the nation's twentieth-century history, here he was again, a spectral figure floating in the background at these dishonourable feasts.

His connection to the Vassall story resulted from an association formed in Wormwood Scrubs between Vassall and a fellow prisoner, Colin Jordan. In a story of unlikely pairings, here was another. On the one hand, Vassall the homosexual spy who betrayed his country's secrets, and on the other, Jordan the homophobic, thuggish neo-fascist leader of the National Socialist Movement. In August 1963, Jordan published an article in the *National Socialist*. It began:

The sensational downfall of War Minister, Profumo, with the glimpse it has given of the private life of one democratic politician, has aroused such a degree of public disgust as to suggest that these politicians and their system could not long endure, if the people as a whole were ever allowed to know the full story of the reality of filth, fraud and folly which lies behind democracy's façade of morality, liberty and brotherhood.[19]

He explained that although he had made clear to Vassall that he 'condemned him both as a homosexual and as a spy for Russia', Vassall had nonetheless supplied him with information, which Jordan had noted down on prison toilet paper. Vassall hoped, if made public, it would serve to get him a reduced sentence. Jordan detailed one of the items of intelligence:

> An acquaintance of Vassall who kept an establishment catering for sexual perversions at an address in London, W8, numbered among his distinguished clients one of our most frequently televised peers, who used to go there to procure 'chickens' (the homosexual term for boys).[20]

MI5 documentation confirms that Boothby was the subject of this accusation and while Vassall refused to discuss the claims in greater detail with officials, he did confirm that the contents of Jordan's article were accurate, bar one exception unrelated to Boothby. From Boothby's point of view, the *National Socialist* had a pleasingly small and niche readership. His name was not dragged into the parliamentary question the article prompted, nor did the press make much of it. But it was another close shave.

As for the Profumo scandal, Boothby was, of course, familiar with the Minister for War from their dealings around Parliament, but he also knew Ward. Back in July 1960, Boothby had sat for a portrait by him – he was a talented artist as well as an osteopath to the well-to-do and famous. The picture of Boothby was one of a series by Ward to feature in the *Illustrated London News* that year, and was later shown as part of an exhibition at the Leggatt Brothers' gallery. Both Ward and Boothby were in attendance at the exhibition launch, during which Boothby was recorded talking admiringly of Ward's artistic skills. (Curiously, in a June 1963 interview with MI5 conducted at Scotland Yard, Colin Jordan claimed that Vassall learned of Boothby frequenting a West London brothel from its 'owner', a fellow inmate called Mr Ward. Stephen Ward had been arrested a few days earlier in relation to the Profumo affair but Vassall surely could not have been referring to him, since Ward was held at Brixton Prison, rather than Wormwood Scrubs where Vassall was serving his sentence. The coincidence, though, is striking.)

One of those who took note of Ward's sketches was Colin Coote, editor of the *Daily Telegraph* and Boothby's holiday companion when the 'Peer and the Gangster' scandal broke. He already knew of Ward because the osteopath had previously worked wonders on his lumbago. Now, Coote decided to commission Ward as a sketch artist to cover Adolf Eichmann's war crimes trial in Israel in 1961. Ward also harboured hopes of travelling to Moscow to make portraits of leading figures from the Politburo but was unable to secure a visa. Coote intervened, arranging a lunch at the Garrick Club (a private members' club) where he introduced Ward to someone he hoped might be a useful contact – the Soviet Embassy's naval attaché, Yevgeny Ivanov. The pair immediately hit it off and became staples in one another's social lives. Without that initial contact at the Garrick, the paths of Ivanov, Keeler and Profumo would likely never have crossed.

If this brought Boothby rather incidentally into the orbit of the Profumo affair, he ended up having a decidedly more direct effect on proceedings. Since the 1920s the political fates of Boothby and Macmillan had run in tandem as a result of the former's affair with the latter's wife. But never was the impact of Boothby and Dorothy's betrayal on public life more starkly evident than during the Profumo scandal. Not that it was the first time that the state of his marriage had impinged on Macmillan's premiership. Back in 1961, he had met with President John F. Kennedy at Key West in Florida to discuss nuclear arms policy. During a break in proceedings, Kennedy turned to Macmillan and said: 'I wonder how it is with you, Harold? If I don't have a woman for three days, I get a terrible headache.'[21] Macmillan was understandably taken aback by the comment. Kennedy was famously highly sexed and may well have been taking additional testosterone injections for a medical ailment at the time, so for the correspondingly undersexed Macmillan, it must have been a deeply uncomfortable moment.

But there was a subtext too, with Boothby at its centre. Back in 1945, Boothby had entered into a brief engagement to Inga Arvad, a Danish journalist who had once been an entrant in the Miss World contest. She had also captured the attention of Hitler in the 1930s, who described her as 'the perfect Nordic beauty'[22] and granted her a number of exclusive interviews, as well as inviting her as his guest to the 1936 Olympic Games. She in turn wrote of him: 'You immediately like him. He seems lonely. The eyes, showing a kind heart, stare right at you. They sparkle with force.'[23]

When she subsequently moved to the USA, the FBI – under the steward-ship of J. Edgar Hoover – opened a file on her, convinced that she was a German spy (despite a dearth of supporting evidence). Hoover's concern increased when word got out in 1941 that Arvad was in a relationship with a handsome young member of staff at the Office of Naval Intelligence in Washington. His name was Jack Kennedy. Fear that they were falling for each other was likely an important consideration in Kennedy's transfer to South Carolina at the start of 1942, which effectively brought the blossom-ing romance to a close.

In April 1945, it was Boothby's turn to woo her while he was covering the opening session of the United Nations in San Francisco for the *News of the World*. She swept him off his feet and after only three days together he was con-vinced they were in love and proposed to her in an orange grove. She accepted and then reality hit Boothby once more. Returning to England, he knew he would soon face the wrath of Dorothy and so he attempted to dissuade Inga from making any public declaration about their betrothal. But she could hold out only until late May, when she released a statement. Boothby, facing a tricky re-election campaign in Aberdeen, now started to panic, especially as some journalists were making the connection between his fiancée and Hitler – not a good look on the post-war campaign trail. In far from gallant language, he attempted to distance himself from her, telling one enquiring journalist: 'I can truthfully tell you that I do not know whether I am engaged or not. You had better ask the editor of the *Daily Mirror*.'[24] It was a line designed to give the impression that the story was but a bit of newspaper fluff.

The Boothby–Arvad marriage never came to pass but at that 1961 meet-ing in Key West, there was the curious situation in which the American president likely knew that his one-time lover's lover had cuckolded the British Prime Minister. In that context, Kennedy's comment to Macmillan takes on a different air. Given the curious way their romantic lives were entangled, there is every chance that Kennedy was aware of Macmillan's virtually sexless reputation. Even at the highest level of global politics, then, Macmillan could not escape the shadow of his great love rival.

So too, in the depths of the Profumo crisis. In the eye of a storm that would see one man resign his ministerial post to enter into a professional and social wilderness and the other cede his premiership, at no point did Macmillan directly confront Profumo about the allegations against him.

John Wyndham, one of Macmillan's most trusted friends and at the time his personal secretary too, would later confide that there had been basic failings in the early stages of the scandal's handling. In particular, Macmillan's reluctance to engage with his minister over questions of marital infidelity.

Given his personal experience, private sexual conduct and spousal loyalty were subjects that seemed off-bounds for the Prime Minister. Macmillan's official biographer, Alistair Horne, talked in terms of a blind spot that resulted from Boothby and Dorothy's affair that had grave consequences during the Profumo saga. As the scandal exploded, Macmillan spoke of Profumo inhabiting a 'different world'. In Horne's assessment:

> The 'different world' was the world of adulterers, to which he did not belong, but to which Profumo – and Boothby – did ... It was a world to which, for the past thirty-odd years and more, Macmillan had resolutely closed his mind as well as his ear; and it went grievously against his nature to have to open both now, over Profumo. It was here that he was perhaps overprotected by someone as close to him as John Wyndham, who, more than anyone, would have become aware of his deep vulnerability over the many years he had spent with him, from 1942 onwards. To underestimate the 'Boothby factor' in Macmillan's handling of Profumo would be as misguided as to fail to comprehend just how grievously it hit him.[25]

Just as Macmillan needed to be at his best, he could not shake off the ghost of Boothby's duplicity.

When the *Sunday Mirror* published its allegations of an improper relationship between a lord and a mobster in July 1964, Britain's political parties were still struggling to make sense of what had happened with Vassall and Profumo. The government had used two contrasting strategies in a bid to manage the affairs – cutting adrift one minister because he could not immediately prove his innocence, and standing resolutely by another – and not only had neither worked but they had failed spectacularly. With public disgruntlement at the actions of the Establishment peaking, the political firmament retreated into defensive mode. What each of the previous two years' scandals had revealed was that the playing out of such dramas in public was a risky business. So, a third – tried-and-tested – game plan was put into action instead. Keep the scandal away from the public by any means necessary.

14

Cover-up

On 21 July 1964 – two days after the second part of the *Sunday Mirror*'s 'Peer and Gangster' exposé – a high-level meeting was convened in the Home Secretary's room in the House of Commons. The group included Henry Brooke (the Home Secretary), Viscount Blakenham (Conservative Party Chairman and Deputy Leader of the Lords), Bill Deedes (Minister without Portfolio and popular former editor of the *Daily Telegraph*), Sir John Hobson (the Attorney General), Sir Peter Rawlinson (the Solicitor-General), Martin Redmayne (the Conservative Chief Whip), Sir Timothy Bligh (the Prime Minister's Principal Private Secretary) and Sir Charles Cunningham (the Home Office's most senior civil servant). This was a council of war, hand-picked to stave off looming crisis.

Notes from its meetings on 21 and 28 July, which were not made available to the public for some thirty years, reveal the extent to which the Conservative government were complicit in protecting Boothby in his run-in with the *Sunday Mirror*. By a combination of outright duplicitousness and what might generously be termed self-deception, the government allowed Boothby to mislead the public and extort a massive pay-out from the International Publishing Company. Where Boothby stated that he was not a homosexual, the government had evidence that this was untrue, and where he denied having met Ronnie Kray other than at two business meetings, they knew this to be a lie. Yet at no stage did they attempt to intervene in proceedings, instead adopting a policy of passivity and deniability.

Guiding the government's actions was an encroaching sense of doom. Its legitimate fear was that the affair would blow up into a Profumo-sized scandal, which was to be avoided at virtually any cost. For a government thirteen years in office and still barely recovered from the painful wounds inflicted by Profumo and, before that, Vassall, there was a feeling of 'Not again!' Among those who assembled in the Commons for that first meeting, not a single one had emerged from those previous scandals unscathed.

For Brooke, the Home Secretary, his tenure had been dogged by public relations disasters ever since coming to office in the Night of the Long Knives in July 1962. Within days, he found himself mired in controversy over a deportation order made against a Jamaican woman convicted of shoplifting goods to the value of £2. But much worse was to follow. There was scarcely any respite before the Vassall affair burst into life in September, and only six months later Brooke faced the conundrum of what to do about Profumo. Fearing that Stephen Ward would provide damaging stories about Profumo to the press or to members of the Opposition, Brooke ordered the criminal investigation that resulted in Ward facing trial on trumped-up charges, and which ultimately led to his suicide. By intervening in the hope of defusing a crisis, Brooke played his part in turning the affair from a political disaster into a human tragedy.

Brooke could seem dour and rather mechanical to those who met him, and he was uncomfortable when confronted with society's underbelly. In April 1964, he spoke in the Commons about a trip he had taken with the police one night to see first-hand the social problems London faced. He was, he told his parliamentary colleagues, struck by 'all that sleazy stuff' that went on. Nor was he very keen on the idea of legalising homosexuality among consenting adults or liberalising the laws on prostitution, as had been recommended by the 1957 Wolfenden Report that Boothby had championed. In an interview with *New Society* magazine in 1962, Brooke said: 'Public opinion is not prepared for a change. At this time, when a growing number of people feel free to do anything not specifically condemned by Act, we should be slow to loosen up.'[1] Faced with the prospect of yet another scandal – one involving Boothby, of all people – it was little surprise that he held his nose.

Sir Timothy Bligh, meanwhile, had been among those initially convinced by Profumo's denials of a relationship with Christine Keeler as the scandal had bubbled into the public consciousness in early 1963. Suitably assured, Bligh advised Profumo not to offer his resignation, only to find himself a few months later the recipient of Profumo's confession that he had lied. Macmillan was in Scotland at the time, so it fell to Bligh to communicate to the Prime Minister the contents of Profumo's resignation letter. It was Bligh, too, who had been asked by Ward for help in curbing the police investigations into his personal life – an act that might have saved Ward's life but a plea Bligh opted not to act upon.

The Chief Whip, Martin Redmayne – a military man suited to implementing discipline among MPs but less comfortable dealing with the subtleties of an emerging political crisis – had similarly been buffeted by the events of the Profumo saga. Viscount Blakenham, meanwhile, had counted Profumo as a close friend, while Sir John Hobson knew him when the pair were undergraduates at Oxford and then as a regimental colleague during the war. Then there was Bill Deedes, who had been just a couple of years behind Profumo at Harrow. A celebrated former editor of the *Telegraph* and a quasi-legendary Fleet Street figure – Evelyn Waugh was said to have partially based Boot, the hero of 1938's *Scoop*, upon him – Deedes was drafted into Macmillan's cabinet in 1962. He would, Macmillan hoped, bring his newspaperman-nous to bear and help restore the crumbling image of the government. Instead, he found himself among those hoodwinked by Profumo. In March 1963 he was present at the late-night meeting at which a posse of ministers worked with Profumo and his lawyers to draft the notorious statement to the Commons in which he asserted that there was 'no impropriety whatsoever in my acquaintanceship with Miss Keeler'. In the absence of anyone else with suitable secretarial skills, Deedes had even been charged with typing up the statement.

Finally, Sir Peter Rawlinson, another beneficiary of the Night of the Long Knives when he became Solicitor-General. Having been *in situ* for the Vassall affair, he had witnessed the resignation of Tam Galbraith. When it came to Profumo, he encouraged a more circumspect attitude. He was among those who interviewed Profumo and believed his initial denials, helping to draft his statement to the House. When Profumo confessed to his lies, Rawlinson was pilloried in certain quarters as a gullible dupe. 'I of course regret that we were so totally deceived,' he wrote to Redmayne at the time. 'But I utterly reject any suggestion that Profumo's claim was one which could have been obviously or readily rejected.'[2] He nonetheless offered his resignation, which Macmillan refused. This was a war council, then, that collectively and individually bore the scars of recent battle.

There was a pervading sense of paranoia among the group as they attempted to get on top of the Boothby saga. The Chief Whip, according to a note written by Bligh for the No. 10 files, said his main concern was that 'there should not be a mushroom of rumour as had happened in 1963'.[3] He believed the story stemmed from an alliance between the *Mirror* papers and certain members of the Labour Party keen to stir up trouble ahead of the impending general election. The Home Secretary added fuel to the fire by pointing to reports that Cecil King had claimed the articles were the start of a story set to 'wreck the Tory Party'.[4] This fear of worse to come was palpably a driving force in the group's discussions. There was particular concern around a persistent rumour that the press were in possession of information with which they intended to unleash a major scandal once Parliament went into recess.[5]

There was unsettling uncertainty, too, as to quite what had motivated the *Sunday Mirror* story in the first place. Was it an attack on the government *per se*, or rather on the police – whom the *Mirror* papers had been suggesting for a while were failing to get on top of the capital's organised crime – or perhaps on 'the Establishment' more broadly? The general conclusion was that the police were the primary target, not least because it was rumoured – as Lord Poole, the Conservative vice-chairman disclosed to Bligh – that members of the *Mirror* staff had themselves fallen victim to a protection racket.[6] But even if the government was only a secondary target, the group realised that 'innuendo about homosexuality in high circles' was 'useful incidental ammunition in this campaign' and posed an existential threat to Douglas-Home's administration.[7] Beset by a torrent of ifs and buts, the group decided on a plan of action. It was agreed that 'the government should rebut the allegations publicly at the earliest opportunity', while making it clear that they would support the police in looking into them. Privately, Boothby was impelled to make a statement to the police. In reality, Her Majesty's Government was intending to undermine the story without committing itself to an outright repudiation. Denials, as Profumo had shown, were best left until you were absolutely sure of your ground. Much better to simply put some distance between the government and the allegations.

Crucial to the government's strategy of self-protecting non-intervention was the statement of the Metropolitan Police Commissioner, Sir Joseph Simpson, issued on the evening of Monday, 13 July – just a day after the *Sunday Mirror* broke its story. Simpson was the product of the Met's policy in the 1930s of seeking a 'higher class' of police recruit. An elite police training college had been set up at Hendon in 1934 and Simpson was among its first graduates, passing out second in his year before taking up a position as a junior station inspector in Westminster. A high-flyer, by 1943 – aged just 33 – he became the country's youngest chief constable when he headed up the force in Northumberland. After a stint in the same role with Surrey police, he returned to the Met as Assistant Commissioner before taking the top job in 1958. A knighthood came along a year later. Although a consistently powerful advocate for rank-and-file Bobbies, the fast-tracked Simpson struggled to shake off the impression that he was an Establishment man.

The highly politicised *Sunday Mirror* story was doubtless an unwelcome distraction. Leading a force whose manpower was stretched to breaking point and whose morale he worked tirelessly to keep up, he was well aware of the growing concerns over crime in general and organised crime in particular. He understood, too, that certain sections of the public were increasingly unhappy with the performance of the police. Ethnic minorities had good reason to claim unfair treatment, while the wider, burgeoning civil liberties movement was also quick to critique police conduct. The recently swelling ranks of car owners resentful at perceived heavy-handed policing of the rules of the road had added a still further political dimension to policing the capital.

Fighting on so many fronts, Simpson was keen to keep the Home Office onside as much as possible. Whether or not he came under direct pressure from his political masters to spear the *Sunday Mirror* story is unlikely ever to be known for sure, although he was certainly in contact with the Home Secretary throughout the crisis. Regardless, the government must have been relieved by his early intervention. His statement was carefully worded, seemingly dismantling the main pillars of the allegations. Crucially, he was adamant that he had ordered no investigation to look into a homosexual relationship between a member of the House of Lords and an underworld figure. But his statement told only part of the story.

C11, the Met's secretive intelligence-gathering division, had been monitoring the activities of the Krays since the beginning of the year. Within the remit of that operation, Boothby and his association with Ronnie Kray had come on to the police radar. It is not credible that Simpson, as head of the Met, was unaware of the intelligence C11 were generating so the haste with which he went public with his statement is striking. In a catch-all disclaimer, he said he hoped that 'it will be understood by the press and the public that I am not going to disclose information about the many enquiries being conducted into various aspects of underworld life' and that 'inquiries of this kind are going on almost continuously'.[8] In one fell swoop, he managed to cast doubt on the *Sunday Mirror*'s claims while avoiding an explicit denial that the Krays (still unidentified by the newspaper, of course) were under investigation. He had merely denied commissioning an investigation specifically interested in a homosexual relationship.

It was an extraordinary statement on several levels. Firstly, with the subjects unidentified in the press, there was no compelling argument for the police to comment on the story at all – at least, not so precipitously. Secondly, for the officers who had spent months tracking the Krays and strongly suspected that there was substance to the story, it must have been dispiriting to hear their boss seemingly washing his hands of the matter. Thirdly, and perhaps most vitally, it compromised the evidence that had already been gathered. To use it in a future prosecution would have potentially caused acute political embarrassment. Simpson himself, it might be argued, would hardly want to see evidence entered into court that emanated from an inquiry that he had publicly seemed to disown. Moreover, if that evidence corroborated aspects of the *Sunday Mirror* story, questions would legitimately be asked as to why the Metropolitan Police Commissioner had given a statement that looked awfully like it was misleading.

Simpson might well have believed his statement was simply putting to bed unhelpful gossip – and in doing so, alleviating pressure on the government whose goodwill he desired – but the effect was to derail the Met's ongoing investigation. No prosecution emanated from C11's work of early

1964 despite officers believing they were close to a breakthrough. It also sent a message to the press – the police will not support you snooping into the business of the Krays. Were it not for Simpson's intervention, it is difficult to see how the cover-up that ensued could ever have happened.

So, just what did Douglas-Home and some of the most senior figures in his government know about Boothby and Kray by the time that Boothby – stewarded by Arnold Goodman – went after the *Sunday Mirror*? Rewind just under a year from the first council of war meeting, and Sir Charles Cunningham could be found in his familiar position of fire-fighting on behalf of the Home Secretary. The allegations made about the private lives of assorted public figures in Colin Jordan's incendiary magazine article had prompted a parliamentary question. In preparing the ministerial response, Cunningham had consulted with Roger Hollis, the head of MI5. Records kept by MI5 show that Jordan's allegations against Boothby were discussed, although Hollis and Cunningham agreed that the government need not be concerned with details of his private life and so should not comment on the claims specific to him.[9] But Cunningham and, by extension, the Home Secretary were aware some twelve months before the *Sunday Mirror* story that there was strong evidence that Boothby frequented male brothels.

Then there was the uncomfortable trial of James Buckley, which had taken place the month before Jordan's article was published. At the time, Boothby had given a statement in which he revealed he had received a visit from the Kray brothers. This statement was also retained in MI5's files on Boothby. Brooke and Hollis then met on the evening of 21 July 1964 to discuss the *Sunday Mirror*'s allegations. Hollis made a note of the meeting the following day, in which he stated that he had told the Home Secretary that MI5 'had heard a story which associated Lord Boothby with the Krays and, furthermore, we had heard allegations that Lord Boothby was a homosexual. I reminded the Home Secretary that Colin Jordan had written an article … I also reminded the Home Secretary that there had been a question put down to him by Mr Bellenger about a year ago on the subject of Jordan's article.'[10] Hollis would also have presumably briefed the Home Secretary on the very latest intelligence, which placed Boothby as an attendee at sex parties hosted by Kray. When the council of war met again a week after its first meeting, the Home Secretary can have been in no doubt that there was at least a strong possibility that the *Sunday Mirror* had stumbled onto something of substance.

Moreover, we know that Brooke and Commissioner Simpson were in contact as the scandal threatened to explode. Although the content of their discussions is not known, there are only two conclusions that may be drawn. Either Simpson alerted the Home Secretary to the nature of the ongoing investigation into the Krays, which included sightings of Boothby and Kray together, or else he deliberately kept the Home Secretary in the dark. If the latter, it is not clear why, other than to allow the government a route of plausible deniability.

Yet in truth, deniability was becoming increasingly implausible. On 22 July, Bligh wrote a classified note for No. 10's files in which he detailed the Home Secretary's account of the report given by the police officer sent to take a statement from Boothby.[11] A number of points had emerged that were inconsistent with the letter Boothby had written to the Home Secretary only three days earlier. The Solicitor-General went as far as to tell his colleagues that he did not think Boothby's letter to the Home Secretary was 'in the least bit plausible'.[12] It was apparent as well that Ronnie Kray had been in contact with Boothby to seek protection from the police who were, he alleged, harrying him. In fact, it is possible that this exchange took place in front of an audience of journalists. While the *Sunday Mirror*'s story was gaining momentum, John Jackson was a new reporter at the *Daily Herald* (which would be relaunched later in the year as the *Sun*). He rushed to Eaton Square to get a response from Boothby but found him to be out. 'He'll be coming round the corner any minute,' his cabbie wryly noted. 'Totally pissed and clutching the wall for support.' And so it played out, with Boothby keeping on-script to deny any knowledge of Ronnie Kray or a homosexual affair. The following day, Jackson and a colleague, Harry Arnold, were back at Eaton Square. Boothby invited them into his flat, where he repeated his denials. But while he was talking, his phone rang and he asked Arnold to answer it. A gruff voice came through the receiver: 'Tell his Lordship, it's Ronnie here.'[13]

Bligh's notes reveal that by 17 July he, as the senior civil servant closest to Douglas-Home, was aware of the story (told to the Chief Whip by two backbenchers) about Boothby importuning males at a dog track and keeping the company of 'gangs of thugs who go to the dog tracks to dispose of their money'.[14] An update on events was even sent to the head of Special Branch, that part of the police force concerned with matters of national security. The pressure was telling on everybody. Lord Poole discussed with Bligh his concerns as to whether the Home Secretary was really up to the job of fending all this off. On 22 July, the Home Secretary appeared in the Commons to reject a demand by Labour MP Marcus Lipton for a tribunal of inquiry into the growth of protection rackets. 'Contrary to your view,' Brooke said, 'the Commissioner of Police advises me that the protection racket situation is less serious in London than it has been on several occasions in the past.' And as for the *Sunday Mirror*'s claims: 'The police have no evidence to support the allegations published in this newspaper.' The die had been cast.[15]

Yet even as the government set about discrediting the allegations, there was little sign of any willingness to actively help Boothby clear his name. The Met had pooh-poohed the paper's claims and Roger Hollis privately asserted that 'as far as I could see, no security issue was involved as Lord Boothby held no official position which gave him access to Government secrets and therefore the Security Service was not concerned'.[16] The way seemed clear for government officials to come out for Boothby in his hour of need. But with senior Cabinet figures and the Prime Minister himself privy to the growing bank of incriminating evidence, there was little stomach for that particular fight.

While the Home Secretary told Hollis that he could not think there was any substance to the dog track claims, the Chief Whip was insistent that if a prosecution was pending, it should not be held up.[17] The government could not be seen to be thwarting justice. If Boothby could navigate his way through the furore, so much the better, but he would have do it on his own. In the week of 28 July, Boothby contacted Bill Deedes about the possibility of getting help in launching a legal action. After speaking to the Attorney General, Deedes told Boothby that 'there was no advice that Members of the Government could give him in this matter'.[18] No wonder Kissin had found him in such a state around this time.

One of the most disconcerting aspects of the government's conduct was its aggressive stance towards the press. With the Met repeatedly pressing Reg

Payne and Norman Lucas at the *Sunday Mirror* to hand over the evidence for their story, it looked suspiciously like an Establishment stitch-up. On 21 July, Martin Redmayne had told his colleagues that he thought it essential that the 'proper authorities' obtain the incriminating photos from the newspaper. He also argued that the government should be prepared to give immediate publicity to the fact that the police had made two approaches to the paper but had received no positive response.[19] Payne and Lucas had, it was said, 'appeared to be uncomfortable throughout' their interview with officers.[20] Sure enough, the following day Brooke pronounced that only after 'continued pressure' from the police did the newspaper agree to pass on its evidence.[21]

Reg Payne gave a furious response: 'Until the Home Secretary spoke in the House of Commons this afternoon, I was unaware that "continued pressure" or any pressure was being brought to bear on the *Sunday Mirror*.' He went on to say that the paper was anxious to help the police and that its overriding goal was to smash the protection racket. 'The *Sunday Mirror* stands by its statement that a vicious protection racket is being run,' his statement continued. 'I am surprised to hear the Home Secretary say that the police have no evidence to support this.'[22] He had met with the police on 14 July, he explained, when he gave them the names of the men behind the racket and promised to supply further evidence as the newspaper's investigation progressed. Simpson sent Payne another letter on 19 July, which he did not receive until two days later when he had agreed to supply the additional evidence requested (namely, the photograph of Kray and Boothby). This he duly did, delivering it to a senior officer shortly after Brooke made his statement on the affair on 22 July.

But it was not just the *Mirror* titles that were drawing the interest of the council of war. Deedes was charged with using his Fleet Street connections to see what was afoot elsewhere. He picked up on suspicions that the *Mirror* had passed its evidence to an investigative team at the *People*, a rumour that had reached Bligh's ears by 21 July. In a minute for the No. 10 files the next day, Bligh wrote: 'After some discussion as to the wisdom of taking an initiative with the *People*, it was felt that the right thing might be to send a policeman round on Friday to make the same sort of enquiries … as had been made of the *Sunday Mirror* …'[23] By 28 July, according to the council of war's own minutes, the police had done 'as ministers had asked' but the *People* denied being in possession of any relevant information.[24]

It was shocking enough that government ministers were urging police officers to interrogate journalists but such heavy-handedness had a still more sinister aspect. Memories were still fresh concerning the imprisonment of journalists Brendan Mulholland and Reg Foster for refusing to give up their sources at the Radcliffe inquiry into the Vassall affair. With the police now bringing fairly intense pressure to bear on reporters in relation to Boothby, it was no wonder that Payne and Lucas seemed uncomfortable in their dealings with officers, and so too the staff of the *People*. Nor could the government have been insensitive to the impact of these police interventions, since, as Attorney General, Sir John Hobson had questioned both Mullholland and Foster at the Radcliffe inquiry and thus played a pivotal role in their downfall.

With the acquiescence of the Metropolitan Police and MI5, a government cabal that included the Prime Minister and the Home Secretary set out to diffuse a potentially shattering scandal by a mixture of withholding information and intimidating the press. When Boothby published his denials of being a homosexual or of having anything other than the most cursory business relationship with Ronnie Kray, the Conservative Party hierarchy – all the way to No. 10 – knew that he was lying. When, based on those false denials, Boothby secured a huge financial pay-off from the *Mirror* and received an unqualified apology on the grounds that 'any imputation of an improper nature against Lord Boothby is completely unjustified',[25] the government surely had a moral duty to intercede. Instead, there was only silence.

15

Cross-Party Co-operation

Some five years after the 'Peer and the Gangster' scandal briefly seemed set to put a match to the British political Establishment, the journalist and author John Pearson asked Boothby who was responsible for the crucial intervention of his crack legal pairing, Goodman and Gardiner. These two, after all, were responsible for overseeing Boothby's impossibly successful counteroffensive against the *Sunday Mirror* at a moment when all had seemed lost.

'It was the little man,' Boothby told Pearson.

'Little man? What little man?'

'Who d'you think I mean? The little man. Harold Wilson.'[1]

When Pearson probed further, Boothby clammed up and changed the subject. What did he mean that 'the little man' had come to his rescue? In the summer of 1964, Wilson had his eye fixed on the ultimate prize – the keys to No. 10. Under the uninspiring hand of Douglas-Home, the feeling pervaded that the Conservatives were coming to the natural end of their stint in government. So, why would the Labour leader step in to save the reputation of a Tory grandee so long pursued by rumours of impropriety? Why send his most reliable legal advisers to help out his political enemy? Especially when the Conservatives seemed reluctant to overstretch themselves on his behalf for fear of imperilling themselves. Why not, to put it bluntly, stick in the sword to see off the dragon once and for all? Boothby's claim seemed extraordinary, a conundrum to be unpicked.

***

Arnold Goodman was fiercely independent in all things. He was cultured and good company when in the mood, but happy to rough it up with the best of them in his professional life. Unmarried, he threw himself into his career with a ferocious vigour and will to win but also a steely pragmatism. Highly strategic, he constantly calculated when to go in hard for his clients and when passivity was the better strategy. Credited as perhaps the finest media lawyer of his age, he advised many clients to take perceived slanders and libels on the chin rather than expose themselves to the unfettered scrutiny of the courts, while in other instances – such as in Boothby's case – he pursued actions with intense aggression. The rightness or wrongness of any individual claim tended to be a secondary consideration, behind the likelihood of a court finding in the client's favour (and at what cost to their public image).

In 1965 Wilson made him Baron Goodman of the City of Westminster, and he spent his years in the Lords sitting as a cross-bencher. In his memoirs, he would suggest that his peerage 'could properly have been attributed to many services that I had given to the government – of both colours.'[2] It is true that he represented prominent figures from all of the main parties – Boothby most famously for the Conservatives, and Jeremy Thorpe for the Liberal Party. (Boothby and Thorpe were themselves well known to each other. It was Thorpe's father who had acted as Weininger's solicitor during the Czech assets hearings, with the three men staying close afterwards. In 1971, Boothby and Jeremy Thorpe threw a lunch for the Weiningers in the Palace of Westminster, and seven years later Weininger would contribute to Jeremy's defence costs for his Old Bailey trial.)

But at heart, Goodman was a Labour man despite making a point of never holding party membership. He had met George Wigg, a future Paymaster-General, when they both served in the army during the Second World War. Wigg was then elected to Parliament in the 1945 election and from the 1950s introduced Goodman into a circle of left-wing politicians centred on Nye Bevan. However, it was many years before he first encountered Wilson.

His association with Labour was cemented by his part in the 1957 libel action against the *Spectator* on behalf of Bevan, Richard Crossman and Morgan Phillips. Hugh Gaitskell, by then the party's leader, increasingly turned to him for advice on what Goodman called 'quasi-political' matters, although he never achieved quite the status of trusted confidant as he did once Wilson replaced Gaitskell in 1963. By then, though, he had played a significant part in the Vassall saga.

Lord Radcliffe's tribunal in 1962, charged with looking into the Vassall affair, should have been a boon to the Labour Party, with the conduct of the Conservative government and the civil service set to come under the spotlight. However, it soon became apparent that Radcliffe's remit included an investigation not only into Vassall's conduct but also into the rumours that had swirled around him ever since the story had broken – in particular, those speculations concerning his sex life. Unfortunately for Labour, one of the principal sources of some of the darkest innuendo was George Brown, the party's deputy leader. He had made unguarded comments at a private dinner party that suggested the involvement of several more Conservatives in the affair besides Tam Galbraith. Should Brown be called to give evidence, as was likely, there was concern within the Labour ranks that his testimony would reflect badly on them. Rather than highlighting the incompetence of the government, there was a legitimate fear that Labour would appear to be engaged in an unseemly conspiracy to smear Tories – a lose–lose scenario in which attention would be deflected from Macmillan's administration and directed towards Gaitskell's stewardship.

Goodman knew Brown socially, although the two were not on particularly close terms. But Goodman had no desire to see him publicly humiliated, nor for Labour to be thrown on to the back foot just when they should be able to sit back and watch the tribunal land its blows on the Conservatives. Goodman's solution was to come up with a procedural ruse that would prevent Radcliffe from calling Brown. To achieve it, he called on Gerald Gardiner, whose public profile had risen since he defended the publisher, Penguin, against accusations of obscenity in the *Lady Chatterley* trial of 1960. The pair decided that the best course of action was for Labour to request that Gardiner appear for the party – with which he was closely affiliated – at the tribunal. Gardiner would then make his representations before informing Radcliffe that the party had no additional witnesses to call. They calculated that Radcliffe would not want to discount Gardiner's evidence by then calling Brown, thus likely sparing Brown the ordeal of testifying. That is exactly what happened, with the Labour Party effectively withdrawing from the tribunal's proceedings once Gardiner had completed his evidence.

When Wilson succeeded Gaitskell as party leader after the latter's sudden death in January 1963, he was eager to bring Goodman, with all his wiliness, into his inner circle. He had clearly been impressed by what he had seen the lawyer achieve for his predecessor, although according to Goodman, he only met Wilson for the first time in February 1963. On that occasion, Wilson consulted him on what to do about a persistent leak from the National Executive to what was then still called the *Manchester Guardian*. Characteristically, while Wilson was keen to weed out the mole, Goodman counselled caution, believing that the hunt for the source might prove more damaging than the content of the leaks themselves.

Wilson rapidly came to rely on the solicitor as an important sounding board for his ideas, although Goodman felt that while he enjoyed Wilson's 'undivided trust', the politician generally rejected his political advice. Wilson undoubtedly remained his own man and sometimes went his own way, but Goodman's voice was an important one in his decision making. Having won Wilson's complete trust – 'I never breached that trust,' Goodman would later recall, 'assuming that I had any information of a sufficiently intriguing character to make it worthwhile betraying a friend' – he was called on to help other party figures too. 'My activities had no goal and no aspiration,' he would claim, 'and I had no competitors, which meant that I rapidly acquired the confidence of the leadership of the Labour Party. Through my office door there flowed an increasing number of Labour politicians seeking professional and personal advice on a score of topics.'[3] Goodman was by now the party's recognised 'Mr Fixit'.

When the Profumo affair exploded a short time into Wilson's tenure as Labour leader, Goodman was naturally called upon for advice, although he considered that it went largely unheeded. It was his old friend, George Wigg, who initially consulted him. Wigg harboured a deep-seated animosity to Profumo as he believed the War Minister had lied in a response to a question he had raised in 1962 about British troops overseas. As the flames of scandal now licked around Profumo's feet, Wigg saw his opportunity for swift and decisive revenge. Goodman's advice, which he later communicated to Wilson, was that the demand for an inquiry into Profumo's private life could only be justified if there was a reasonable belief that he had acted in such a way that national security was compromised. Goodman was uncertain that such a belief was indeed justified in the circumstances, and he warned Wigg that to pursue Profumo to satisfy a personal agenda would in the long run be to Labour's detriment.

Wigg would not give up on his quarry, though, and was a prominent figure – as we have already seen – in the subsequent assault on Profumo's reputation. 'Wigg did not believe in the doctrine that you did not kick a man when he was down,' Goodman wrote in his memoirs. 'On the contrary, he considered this an exceptionally valuable opportunity for enabling you to kick him more robustly and with least personal danger.'[4]

Having preached a policy of restraint on the part of Labour, Goodman was appalled when Macmillan set up an inquiry into the affair headed by Lord Denning. The parameters of it were so loose, in Goodman's opinion, that Denning could turn his gaze on virtually any public figure and examine their conduct on the basis of little more than whispered innuendo. He advised Wigg to urge Wilson to contact the Prime Minister and express his opposition to the inquiry, even drafting a letter for Wilson to send. But Wilson refused to do so, probably conscious that whoever might deign to stand in the way of Denning's investigation might themselves be suspected of having something to hide. Given the climate of the time, he was probably right, too.

When Denning published his final report, there was no 'smoking gun' that Labour could seize upon as evidence of the Conservatives' unsuitability to hold power. Moreover, the whole process had been enormously damaging to the political firmament as a whole. Profumo had been ruined and there were plenty on all sides of the House who must have thought, 'There but for the grace of God go I.' Macmillan was effectively finished as Prime Minister, and there can have been few politicians of any persuasion who did not shudder at the way in which the affair had so rapidly taken on a life of its own. The whole saga was hugely distasteful to Goodman, who believed that public figures had a right to private lives as long as their conduct did not impinge on their public duties. Of Profumo he said: 'It is rather terrible to think how unforgiving the world can be and how willing to inflict continuous torture on account of a single piece of behaviour that without

the political element and the adventitious addition of one or two other elements would have faded into obscurity in no time at all.'[5]

When the Boothby allegations reared their head the following year, little
surprise then that Wilson – under the influence of Goodman – might be
somewhat circumspect. True, the allegations might just have been sufficient
to kill the Conservatives' last hopes for the general election expected in the
next few months. But what if the affair took flight as Profumo had, escap-
ing beyond the control of Wilson and his team? What if the public would
not countenance another episode of political blood-letting? Boothby was
beloved by large swathes of the population and was sufficiently distant now
from the front line of government. What if the public turned their resentment towards those throwing the mud? Might Labour be perceived as being
on a homosexual witch-hunt, which would hardly chime with the message
of social progressiveness that Wilson was hoping to communicate?

Then there was that phrase again: 'There but for the grace of God go I.'
Reflecting in his memoirs on the likelihood that Wilson did not oppose the
Denning inquiry for fear of appearing to have something to hide, Goodman
wrote: 'While I have no reason to believe that this was the case in respect
of Wilson, or indeed any senior member of the Labour Party, I can understand why such a person would be reluctant to try to abort the inquiry.'[6]
Whether or not Wilson did harbour the secret of a private indiscretion,
he was acutely conscious of the widespread rumours attached to him and
which he must have feared might yet spike his own path to Downing Street.

In 1955 Marcia Williams, later to become Lady Falkender, began working for Morgan Phillips, then Labour's general secretary. A year later, she met
Wilson for the first time, at an infamous dinner where Soviet leader Nikita
Khrushchev and Wilson's future foreign secretary, George Brown, engaged
in a shouting match. Before the year was out, Wilson invited Williams –
some sixteen years his junior – to work in his private office. She would
run his office for the next twenty-seven years and came to be regarded as
the single most influential figure within his staff. He trusted her implicitly
and she coupled an astute political brain with high ambition. But she was
also immensely divisive. She could be aloof and imperious, prone to bouts
of unpredictability and tigerishly protective of her boss. Goodman was
one among many of those close to Wilson who were nervous of her clout

with him. As he got more comfortable in his own relationship with Wilson, he even suggested that the by-then Prime Minister might find a way of dispensing with her services. As Goodman told it, Wilson did not deem it possible. She was difficult enough at the best of times, he suggested to the solicitor, and 'matters might be worse' were he to attempt to dismiss her.[7]

Many others who encountered them over the years shared an impression that Wilson felt unable to stand up to her. This inevitably led to speculation about the nature of their relationship. Did she have some sort of hold over him? Were they, perhaps, lovers? Goodman was reasonably certain on the question. 'I do not believe,' he said, 'that at any time, and certainly not at any time when I knew them, there was any emotional relationship between Harold Wilson and Marcia Williams.'[8] But even he left some room for doubt.

Others were less cautious in their assumptions. In 1967, the rock band *The Move* – the first band to have a chart single played on Radio One – ended up in court when they publicised one of their singles with a postcard depicting Wilson and Williams together in bed. But allusions to their relationship had been doing the rounds much longer than that. In March 1964, just a few months before the Boothby revelations, there had been a public meeting at the Mid Herts College, Welwyn Garden City, where Barbara McCorquodale (better known as the romantic novelist, Barbara Cartland) was speaking in support of a prospective candidate. She declared to the audience that Wilson had entertained a mistress for many years, that it was his secretary and that the relationship was common knowledge among members of the House of Commons.[9] The speech was subsequently reported in coded terms in the *Daily Telegraph*. Wilson turned to Goodman and Gardiner to see whether some sort of legal action was possible. They advised against, citing the difficulty in proving exactly what damage he had suffered as a result.[10] Goodman was also well aware that to sue would likely turn the story from a coded footnote into a front-page scandal.

The insinuations continued, however, albeit in heavily guarded terms. In October 1964, just before Douglas-Home called the general election, Quintin Hogg – then serving as Secretary of State for Education and Science – attended a public meeting in Plymouth. Hogg rebuked Wilson for saying that Macmillan had 'debauched' public life but was heckled with the accusing cry of 'What about Profumo?' 'If you can tell me,' he hit back, 'there are no adulterers on the front bench of the Labour Party you can talk to me about Profumo.'[11] When word got back to Marcia Williams about Hogg's outburst she was incandescent. Goodman, she insisted, must issue a writ against the Conservative. Again, Goodman counselled against it, wary of stoking the fires of intrigue. On this occasion, he was able to talk Wilson around despite Williams' contrary view, and the incident cemented the animosity between the solicitor and the secretary.

Three years earlier, Goodman had assisted Williams in her divorce from Ed Williams, whom she had married in 1955. For a while there were rumours that Wilson might be cited as a co-respondent although that never came to pass. But speculation as to the exact status of their relationship would hang over them for the rest of their lives. Williams was adamant that it was never sexual in nature, and as recently as 2006 successfully sued the BBC for airing a drama that suggested it was. But Joe Haines, Wilson's influential Downing Street press secretary, insists that in 1972 Williams told Wilson's wife, Mary, that Harold had indeed been her lover back in 1956, that she had slept with him some half a dozen times and that the experience had been 'unsatisfactory'.[12]

Whatever the truth, the McCorquodale and Hogg incidents provide ample evidence that Wilson knew he was vulnerable to accusations about his private life. In a climate where the electorate were becoming only too accustomed to revelations of private indiscretions by public figures, and with a Fleet Street pack emboldened to call the powerful to account like never before, the temptation to squash a potential scandal must have been high. The *Sunday Mirror* was one of the newspapers for Labour, so its readership would likely assume that Labour was in on the revelations about Boothby. If the Conservatives also suspected that the gloves were now off, Wilson could expect attacks far more ferocious than those he had already endured.

Yet even against this background, the decision to unleash Goodman and Gardiner to save Boothby was confounding. It is one thing not to kick a man when he is down, quite another to send your best men to drag him from the floor and then fight off his assailants. For Gardiner, though, it was also an opportunity to prove his credentials after an approach the year before to gauge his enthusiasm for taking on a senior role in the prospective Labour government. A few months earlier, he had been summoned to dinner at Goodman's Portland Place flat. When he arrived, Wilson and George Wigg were there too, and Wilson asked Gardiner how he would feel about going into the House of Lords with a view to becoming Lord Chancellor. After a period of reflection, Gardiner decided it was too good an opportunity to turn down. Now Boothby's predicament offered a chance to show that their faith in him was not misplaced.

Gardiner and Goodman worked well together despite strikingly different characters. Where Goodman enjoyed good living, Gardiner – an Old Harrovian – was a dedicated socialist with a streak of puritan austerity. Goodman would in due course speculate as to 'whether he ever enjoyed anything at all'. 'I never took a meal with him,' he noted, 'but I should be surprised to find that he ate with a good appetite. He would have regarded mastication as a terrible waste of time.'[13] He also suspected, as he expressed in rather scathing terms, that Gardiner was teetotal. But Goodman did recognise his strengths as a lawyer, particularly in contract law and libel, even if he considered the extent of his expertise somewhat limited. (Wilson seems to have had a much higher opinion and inscribed a copy of *The Labour Government, 1964–1970* to Gardiner with the words, 'For Gerald in friendship, with recollections of great days and the contributions thereto of the greatest Lord Chancellor of this century …')

Whether it was known to Goodman and Wilson is unrecorded, but Gardiner also had some personal history with Boothby. They had been contemporaries at Magdalen, when Gardiner had harboured hopes of perhaps forging a career on the stage rather than in the courtroom. Boothby was also active in the university's drama circles, but more pertinently the pair shared a suite of rooms in their third year. Despite Gardiner's reputed puritanism and his largely conventional lifestyle, it could hardly have escaped his notice that he was cohabiting with a flamboyant young man whose sexual exploits had earned him the nickname of 'the Palladium'. How awkward, then, must have been the meeting at which Gardiner and Goodman demanded confirmation from Boothby, prior to acting for him, that he was not a homosexual nor had had any homosexual relationships in the previous ten years. That ten-year caveat at least offered Gardiner something of a get-out clause should it come to light that he had any knowledge of his client's historical homosexual life. It must be assumed, too, that neither Goodman nor Gardiner knew that Boothby had been driven to that assignation by his lover (and Kray associate), Leslie Holt.

Indeed, in due course Gardiner would even apologise to Boothby for the tough treatment they meted out to him. Gardiner wrote to 'Dear Bob' from the Hotel Cipriani in Venice on 10 August 1964, less than a week after the *Sunday Mirror* issued its apology and paid Boothby his £40,000. 'I half expected that with your ill-gotten gains you would fly here!' Gardiner wrote. 'I do realise that you must have had an awful 6 days and have felt that we were being very tough with you but that sort of thing requires a great deal of thought and some very careful handling.' Meanwhile, Gardiner described Goodman as 'one of the shrewdest bargainers in the business' and said that Boothby was 'lucky in having [his] help'. 'It is, I think,' Gardiner concluded, 'the fastest and largest settlement of the kind ever made. So it should have been.'[14] Whether Gardiner – writing months before becoming the Crown's senior officer in charge of the functioning and independence of the courts – believed the result was an expression of justice at work or an example of 'ill-gotten gains' is uncertain.

If Wilson had believed that it would be politically damaging to allow Goodman and Gardiner to represent Boothby, they surely would not have done so. Despite its counter-intuitiveness, there must have been a sense that the move was somehow to Labour's advantage. Wilson might have decided to save the country from another 'Profumo', or perhaps feared for himself if politicians were no longer permitted a few indiscretions in their private lives. But there is a further intriguing possibility as to why the Little Man came to the old Tory's rescue. The reason is buried deep in a series of letters swapped between Wilson and Harry Kissin, the entrepreneur who ostensibly put Boothby in touch with Goodman. It would seem that for a little over a year before Boothby's troubles, Kissin had been coordinating some kind of interaction between Boothby and Wilson. To what end it is impossible to tell, but it is clear that efforts were made over a prolonged period to ensure the pair met.

As early as 7 May 1963, Kissin wrote to Wilson: 'Bob B is coming back from his holiday about the 18th June. I would love to arrange an evening at the house, when your wife could join us. What about Friday, June 21st?'

Another letter from Kissin, this one dated 23 November 1963, reads: 'I enjoyed our evening together very much – and Bob has told me that he hopes we will have an early opportunity of repeating it.' A third from Kissin to Wilson, dated 15 January 1964, says: 'Regarding the evening with Bob (I know that he has written to you) but I suggested it because I thought you said it might be useful at this stage.'[15] In what way might it have been useful? It is possible, given Kissin's background and Boothby's extensive business contacts throughout Europe, that there might have been a commercial imperative. Alternatively, with a general election pending, Wilson was perhaps keen to nurture a friendship with a 'tame' member from the other side, especially one who was known to be free and easy with gossip when in his cups.

Regardless, by the time that the *Sunday Mirror* was on Boothby's trail, Boothby and Wilson must be assumed to have been on better personal terms than has previously been suspected. This would also help to explain a remarkable letter Boothby sent to the recently confirmed new Prime Minister on 12 November 1964:

> My Dear Prime Minister,
> I am down with bronchitis for the fifth year running and my doctor says it is no longer funny. He added yesterday that although there is no immediate reason for alarm, if it continues it can be a killer. He has therefore ordered me to the Caribbean for a minimum period of two months, and I am leaving for Barbados next week. In many ways it is a great relief.
>
> One final word, if I may. If it is not an impertinence for me to say so, after forty years of unbroken public service in parliament I have not got what I ought to have.
>
> This, I know, means little or nothing to the public. But if, at any time, you could see your way to put it right, it would give very great satisfaction to, Yours very sincerely, Bob Boothby[16]

Having been saved from ruin only three months earlier, Boothby's effrontery in complaining about not having 'what I ought to have' is jaw-dropping. Boothby delivered a memo to Kissin around the same time, asking him to put in a good word for him with the Prime Minister. Much of the memo echoes the letter but additionally reveals that Boothby does not desire a job or a GCMG (the Knight Grand Cross of the Order of St Michael and St George – an honour usually accompanying a posting as a governor-general overseas) 'and would only accept one if the Prime Minister told me it was my clear duty to take it'. Instead, Boothby implied he desired membership of the Privy Council, an accolade that had hitherto eluded him. Furthermore, he suggested, it was an honour Churchill had intended to bestow upon him at an earlier date. In the event, there was no such gift forthcoming from Wilson but that Boothby asked at all suggests that – Goodman and Gardiner's contribution to the maintenance of his good name and his bank balance aside – he considered there was still a debt of honour due to him from the new Prime Minister.

Their friendship continued for years to come. In April 1969, during a particularly stormy period of his premiership, Boothby sent Wilson a letter intended to express 'encouragement, admiration and gratitude from an old parliamentary hand' at a time when 'the sea is rough'. 'I have been wanting to write to you for some time,' it began, 'but have hesitated to do so because I was afraid you would think I was after an honour – which I am not.'[17] In the October of that year, Wilson was among a group of friends to throw a private dinner in honour of Boothby.

The Little Man's decision to grant Boothby the expertise of his most trusted legal advisers in 1964 was seemingly justified on several counts. Fear of an open season on the reputations of politicians and some sense of personal loyalty or indebtedness to Boothby were among them. But there was yet another compelling reason for Labour to want to see the 'Peer and the Gangster' story buried every bit as much as the Conservatives – the knowledge that within their party ranks dwelt a man named Tom Driberg.

16

Thin Ice

Henry Fortescue had always suppressed his homosexuality in pursuit of his dreams of high political office. But as his hopes of a Cabinet post receded, he decided the time to deny his sexual self was over. It was during the Second World War that he was discovered in Glasgow by a police officer partaking in an unspecified act of public indecency. Facing the threat of shameful, career-ending exposure, Fortescue attempted to throw himself upon the mercy of the police officer. 'What good will it do the country if you charge me with what you are going to charge me?' he pleaded.

'You should have thought of that before you did what you did, Mr Fortescue,' the officer responded unpromisingly.

'Which naturally I should deny,' shot back Fortescue. 'But whether you were successful or not in establishing a case against me it would cause a nasty scandal for a man in my position to get such unpleasant publicity … one does silly things sometimes.'

The policeman seemed unlikely to waver until Fortescue played his ace. By charging a public figure with a crime such as this, the officer would be delivering a coup to Lord Haw-Haw. That reviled British traitor would be bound to use the story as fuel for his hateful Nazi propaganda. This, he would gloat, is how British politicians behave. And so the patriotic police-man, having extracted a promise from Fortescue that he would return straight to his hotel and stay out of trouble until he left the city the next day, relented.[1]

Fortescue was, in fact, a fictional creation, the lead character in Compton Mackenzie's 1956 novel, *Thin Ice*. But his experiences in Glasgow were rooted in a story told to Mackenzie by his old friend, Bob Boothby. Boothby, in turn, was repeating an anecdote about his parliamentary colleague, Tom Driberg. According to Driberg, he was walking along Princes Street in Edinburgh one night in 1942 in the midst of a wartime blackout. He had recently won the seat of Maldon in Essex as an independent in a by-election, and he was up in Scotland to support the campaign of another fellow independent. Making his way home after giving a speech, and somewhat the worse for wear, he bumped into a man in uniform walking towards him down the street. He was, it turned out, a member of the Norwegian army and Driberg promptly led the willing soldier to a nearby air raid shelter where he proceeded to fellate him until they were interrupted by a policeman on his beat. 'Och, ye bastards – ye dirty pair o' hores,' the officer roared at them.

Driberg, though, was quick to try to retrieve the situation. He handed the officer his card, which showed him to be not only a Member of Parliament but also the author of a popular gossip column in the *Daily Express*. The policeman was, it turned out, an avid reader of Driberg's celebrated *William Hickey* column. The officer promptly dismissed the special constable out on duty with him and sent the Norwegian away with a flea in his ear. Driberg then made his case to be let off just this once. Promising – through gritted teeth – never to repeat the offence again, he also appealed to the officer's sense of national duty. What mileage might Lord Haw-Haw and Goebbels make from Driberg's shaming? The policeman took the point and agreed to let Driberg off this time. In fact, the pair struck up an unlikely friendship that was carried across a series of letters over the ensuing weeks and months.[2]

Driberg and Boothby came from contrasting political positions. For all his independent spirit, social liberalism and early penchant for Keynesian economics, Boothby was, as far as the public were concerned at least, a broadly conventional Conservative. Driberg, by contrast, was a dyed-in-the-wool left-wing radical, a former member of the Communist Party of Great Britain who only came to the Labour Party after a stint as an independent in Parliament. Where Boothby might have become a party grandee of the highest magnitude with a little more considered career management, Driberg was a notorious loose cannon who was never seriously in danger of getting a major job in government. But for all their differences, the pair were kindred spirits. Both came to regard themselves as Westminster outsiders, their political philosophies rendering them rebels to the mainstream. They also bonded over the fact that their private lives were irreconcilable with their careers in the public sphere. Every bit as much as Boothby, Driberg enjoyed the sexual company of young, pretty males, and whereas Boothby to some extent flitted between men and women, Driberg was exclusively male-only.

Their unlikely friendship is perhaps the single most important key to unlocking the mystery of Arnold Goodman and Gerald Gardiner's involvement in Boothby's wrangle with the *Sunday Mirror*. For Tom Driberg was up to his neck in it with the Krays every bit as much as Boothby. He was 'the other man' in those backbenchers' reports of Boothby's visits to White City dog racing meetings, where the pair socialised with criminals and procured the sexual services of young men. Should the story blow up into a full-blown scandal, the Labour Party would suffer the same sort of political damage that threatened the Conservatives. Driberg's association with the twins likely pre-dated Boothby's by a few weeks or months. Over his lifetime, Driberg forged very few enduring relationships with women – he found physical contact with the opposite sex repulsive in general – but one of the few women to command his affections was the theatre director Joan Littlewood. He had first met her shortly after the end of the Second World War and became one of her greatest supporters as she developed the experimental Theatre Workshop. Littlewood's ability to meld high art and social radicalism appealed to Driberg the poet–politician, and her far-Left sympathies closely mirrored his own. From 1953, the Theatre Workshop was based at the Theatre Royal Stratford East and so Littlewood and her company became fixtures of the east London social scene. In 1959, Barbara Windsor joined the company for a production of *Fings Ain't What They Used to Be*. It marked the start of a fruitful if fiery association that reached its zenith in 1963, when Windsor took the starring role in Littlewood's first foray into film, *Sparrows Can't Sing*. By then, the actress was in a relationship with Ronnie Knight, a friend of the Krays. When Littlewood said she wanted to film a scene in an authentic East End club, Windsor called in her contacts and the twins agreed to supply the venue. As a result, Littlewood became a regular visitor to the Double R, which was where she first introduced Driberg to the brothers.

The Krays were intrigued to learn how he might be useful to them. They probed him about his political influence and he gave the impression that all sorts of things might be possible. How about, for instance, helping an old friend banged up in Dartmoor secure a transfer to a London prison? (The prisoner in question was Frank 'Mad Axeman' Mitchell, whom the twins would bust out of prison several years later.) Driberg told the Krays he would do his best for them. The twins always had more than an inkling that friends in high places helped you get things done and keep trouble away from your doorstep. What luck to have just such a friend stroll into your nightclub! And all the more so when he started bringing *his* friends too. When enough fun had been had in East London, it was off up West to Esmerelda's – the twins' gambling club – where Driberg and Boothby laid down their chips together.

Soon Ronnie was pointing in their direction a succession of the type of men they all commonly craved – young, good-looking toughs. Then came the parties at Cedra Court. In addition, Driberg has long been rumoured to have been in something approaching a relationship (by his standards anyway) with Firm member Teddy Smith. Smith, in turn, is alleged to have been a sometimes-lover of Ronnie Kray.[3] How quickly things moved. One minute, Boothby and Driberg were ageing politicos enjoying the danger-ous frisson of fraternising and flirting with up-and-coming gangsters. The next minute, they were old fools giving ruthless criminals all the possible ammunition to keep them in their power for evermore. Recklessness had decisively spilled over into irretrievable self-sabotage.

★★★

Driberg, five years Boothby's junior, was born in Sussex to a father – a retired colonial administrator – already in his mid-60s and a mother fast approach-ing 40. His brothers were both the best part of a generation older than him so that he was effectively raised an only child in a household he found cold and distant. Like Boothby, he considered school a trial, not least as he sought to express his sexuality that, by his own account, blossomed from a remarkably early age. According to his posthumously published autobiography, he was only 2 or 3 years old when he experienced 'the first authentic sexual thrill of my life'. On that occasion, he was crawling on the floor when he looked up and saw a hole in the crotch of his brother's trousers. Two years later, he found himself asking the 40-year-old family gardener to drop his trousers for reasons that his child's mind could not quite fathom.[4]

From the age of 8, he attended the Grange School in Crowborough as a day-boy, where his natural rebelliousness developed in line with a distrust of authority. A defining experience was the punishment he received for sketching a caricature of one of the masters on to a blackboard. He was subjected to a 'school mobbing', whereby the headmaster authorised what was essentially a gang beating by fellow pupils, a frightening experience that lasted until the master saw fit to call off the dogs. His later years at the Grange evolved into a period of concerted sexual exploration, with Driberg recalling a habit of comparing genital development with fellow pupils behind the raised lids of their desks as an unwitting teacher lectured them from the front of the class.

When he was 13, Driberg moved on to the prestigious Lancing College, where his personal development continued in what A.J.P. Taylor would later describe as 'the strange one-sexed system of education at public schools and universities' that 'had always run to homosexuality'.[5] From his earliest teens, Driberg took to cottaging – cruising for sexual partners in public lavatories. He recalled, for instance, an old tramp who 'was induced to masturbate me in an underground lavatory at Tunbridge Wells'. Nonetheless, he rose to become deputy captain of the school, only for his last year to end ignominiously when he made what he called 'nocturnal overtures' to two of the boys in his dormitory. A complaint was made to the housemaster and, under normal circumstances, Driberg might have expected immediate expulsion. However, there were concerns for his mother's health should news of her son's behaviour reach her, so an alternative plan was put in place. In essence, Driberg was quarantined from other pupils for the remainder of term, at which point he left, ostensibly so he could receive intensive private tuition in order to achieve an Oxford scholarship.

Driberg duly did enough to win a place at Christ Church. He admitted to feeling a certain *schadenfreude* when, not long afterwards, he heard that Rev. H.T. Bowlby – the head of Lancing who had overseen Driberg's dismissal from the school – was up on charges of molesting two young girls on a train. At Oxford, meanwhile, Driberg developed a rather foppish persona, sporting the Oxford bags look that Boothby had helped champion just a few years earlier. Driberg struck up a friendship with Evelyn Waugh – even introducing him to the works of T.S. Eliot that would prove so influential on Waugh's writing – and circulated among the aesthetes who came to be characterised as the Bright Young Things. He wrote poetry, enjoyed a succession of spontaneous homosexual encounters and barely found the time to study, leaving Oxford degree-less. Nonetheless, he was increasingly certain of his own ideas and beliefs, which manifested themselves in what he suggested were three mutually irreconcilable compulsions: 'deviant' (in other words, gay) sex, 'exotic' religion (specifically High Anglicanism) and left-wing politics (he was the Communist candidate for the presidency of the Oxford Union).[6]

For all that Driberg fluttered among the Bright Young Things and read poetry with Evelyn Waugh, his Oxford life was far from all *Brideshead Revisited*. Such were his lack of financial resources, for example, that he sporadically accepted payment from sexual partners. After university, he moved to London where money was even tighter. He sold the few items of value he had – among them a gold cigarette lighter given to him by his mother on his 21st birthday – and for a while worked in a Soho café. There he encountered a clientele that he described as a 'rough and villainous lot' but one which he rather liked and respected. It was, he said, 'one of the most undilutedly happy periods of my life'.[7] Driberg already knew that he had a thing for tough, working-class men – especially those in whom he detected intelligence as well. Like Boothby, he was a fan of rough trade (that is to say, paying rough- or tough-looking men for sex), although it was not an exclusive interest. He was open to partners of varying ages and different classes when caught up in the thrill of the moment, which was commonly seized in public – in doorways, public toilets, phone boxes and the like.

The disparate strands of Driberg's life always competed against each other. While effectively down and out in London, he still enjoyed the patronage

Bob Boothby, wearing a top hat and carrying a cane, accompanies then Chancellor of the Exchequer Winston Churchill, as he makes his way to Parliament to deliver the 1928 budget. Boothby was his Parliamentary Private Secretary and tipped by many as a future Conservative Party leader and perhaps even Prime Minister. The Boothby–Churchill relationship was always combustible but the friendship between the 'coming man' and the aging statesman was probably at its strongest in this period. (Fremantle/Alamy Stock Photo)

Boothby (second from right) seen here just before Christmas 1957 at a social engagement with the journalist and Labour politician, Tom Driberg (second from left). Driberg had recently become the chairman of the Labour Party. A character of exotic tastes, Driberg knew Boothby well by this time and would come to play a significant role in 'the Peer and the Gangster' drama that followed. (Photo by Evening Standard/Hulton Archive/Getty Images)

Ronnie and Reggie Kray in their 1960s heyday. The East London twins built an underworld empire that saw them become the most recognised criminals in the country. Their social network encompassed the rich, powerful and famous. Boothby was one of the political contacts they sought to nurture. (Chronicle/Alamy Stock Photo)

Harold Wilson, who was poised to take over as Prime Minister at the time of Boothby's troubles. Why did Wilson's trusted lieutenants race to the rescue of such a prominent figure from the opposition? (Trinity Mirror/Mirrorpix/Alamy Stock Photo)

Born in 1879, Max Aitken – who was made Lord Beaverbrook in 1917 – was perhaps the single most powerful newspaperman of the twentieth century. He was a political force too, serving as an MP from 1910 to 1916 and as a government minister in both world wars. Despite sporadic political and personal differences, he demonstrated notable loyalty to Boothby over the years. (From the archives of Press Portrait Service; formerly Press Portrait Bureau.) (David Cole/Alamy Stock Photo)

Stephen Ward's portrait of Boothby, which was one of several featured in *The Illustrated London News* in July 1960. As an osteopath, Ward counted many notable figures among his clients. His 1960 collection of portraits included Labour leader Hugh Gaitskell, and Prime Minister Harold Macmillan. The year before 'the Peer and the Gangster', Ward would be recast as a central player in the Profumo affair that reconfigured the political landscape. (© Illustrated London News Ltd/ Mary Evans)

Arnold Goodman, the Labour Party's 'Mr Fixit', on his way to a meeting in the early 1960s. The greatest media lawyer of the age, his involvement in the Kray–Boothby affair has raised many questions over the years. (Alamy Stock Photo)

John Vassall, a mid-level civil servant, caused a media frenzy in 1962 on being exposed as a Soviet spy. He is seen here leaving Wormwood Scrubs (where he was serving an eighteen year sentence) to appear at the Radcliffe Tribunal, set up to investigate the affair. The Vassall case would prove highly damaging to the political firmament. (Keystone Press/Alamy Stock Photo)

Cedra Court in Hackney, a nondescript block of North London flats that became home to both the Kray twins and several of their associates in the early 1960s. Ronnie's flat, No. 8 (on the 1st floor and to the left in this image), earned a reputation for the wild parties he liked to host. (Clive Jones/Alamy Stock Photo)

Gerald Gardiner, who partnered with Arnold Goodman to advise Boothby on his action against the *Mirror* newspapers. Within months of the affair, Gardiner was appointed Lord Chancellor in Harold Wilson's government. (Photo by Central Press/Hulton Archive/Getty Images)

As Commissioner of the Metropolitan Police, Sir Joseph Simpson (pictured here in his Scotland Yard office in 1967) was the most powerful police officer in the country. His intervention in the Boothby–Kray saga proved pivotal. (Photo by Loomis Dean/ The LIFE Picture Collection via Getty Images)

Cecil King (left) faces off with Hugh Cudlipp at the annual meeting of the International Publishing Corporation in July 1968. After many years working together, Cudlipp had replaced King as chairman of the Corporation, which published the *Sunday Mirror* and the *Mirror*. King had given the go-ahead to print 'the Peer and the Gangster' allegations four years earlier in Cudlipp's absence. (Keystone Press/Alamy Stock Photo)

Sir Alec Douglas-Home was the patrician leader of the Conservative Party who replaced Harold Macmillan in Downing Street in 1963. Macmillan's tenure had started with high hopes and ended dripping in salacious scandal. Douglas-Home was the man many expected to return the ship to an even keel. (Trinity Mirror/Mirrorpix/Alamy Stock Photo)

of Edith Sitwell, who considered him to be nothing less than the great hope of British poetry. Aleister Crowley – the notorious British occultist – was another to become beguiled by him, to the point of seemingly anointing Driberg as his spiritual successor. Certainly, Crowley's philosophy, the essence of which he summarised as to 'discover your own true will and do it',[8] fitted neatly with Driberg's own world view.

In 1928, Driberg got one of the great breaks of his life. Sitwell helped him secure a job with the *Daily Express*. It was an extraordinary coup. Driberg, a member of the British Communist Party, managed to utterly charm the paper's distinctly non-left-leaning owner, Lord Beaverbrook. It was the beginning of a relationship that was often tempestuous – there would be some serious fallings out – but marked by a respect and fondness that ultimately held strong. After a couple of months working as a reporter, Driberg was put to work co-writing a column known as 'The Talk of London' – a job in which he could use his social contacts. Then, in 1932, Driberg was given sole charge of a new column to replace 'The Talk of London'. Beaverbrook wanted something that was harder hitting, a column that didn't worry so much about what Lady So-and-so had worn at Henley but focused more on the real movers and shakers who were getting things done in society. A column headed 'These names make news …' was born, with Driberg adopting Bill Hickey as his pseudonym.

Initially kept on a tight leash by Beaverbrook, over time Driberg enjoyed growing autonomy. He developed a winning concoction of tittle-tattle and seriousness, with the column being, in his own words, '… an intimate biographical column about … men and women who matter. Artists, statesmen, airmen, writers, financiers, explorers …' All the while, his personal life remained a roller coaster of spontaneous sexual encounters. He was, he explained, a follower of Mary Magdalen's credo: '*deliciae meae sunt apud filios hominum*' ('my delights are with the sons of men').[9] As Boothby would reveal in his memoirs: 'Tom Driberg once told me that sex was only enjoyable with someone you had never met before, and would never meet again.'[10]

But in 1935, his world threatened to fall apart. The hotshot Fleet Street columnist found himself up at the Old Bailey on charges of indecent assault. His alleged victims were two Scottish miners – one about the same age as the 30-year-old Driberg and the other considerably younger. According to Driberg's version of events, he bumped into the pair (who had recently arrived in London) on a street corner quite by chance as he walked home one night. They were, he learned, trying to find somewhere cheap and decent to stay. Driberg had recently written a series of articles on the miseries being caused by unemployment in the Welsh valleys. He had been mulling over writing something similar in relation to Scotland's coalfields. Now fate had seemingly availed him of two characters around whom he could build his narrative.

He invited them to stay at his lodgings, despite the fact that it contained only a single bed little over 3½ft wide. By the time the unlikely trio arrived at the property, there was a growing air of mutual distrust. Driberg had a few valuables in the living room and was unwilling to leave the strangers to their own devices for fear they would rob him. Neither of the miners, on the other hand, was keen to bunk up with Driberg, of whose motives they were still uncertain. The unsatisfactory solution was that all three men ended up in the bed together, with Driberg the filling in the sandwich.

The idea that, wedged between two fairly robust mine workers, Driberg launched a full-scale sexual attack pushes the bounds of credibility. It was surely too risky even for his tastes and he would have been sure to be overpowered were his advances unwanted. But it seems likely that, within his own terms of reference, he gently tested the waters to see if at least one of the men was keen to get more closely acquainted. Whatever he did, he received an unequivocal response. In the early hours of the morning, the visitors sprang out of bed and accused him of assault. An argument ensued, during which Driberg apparently sought an answer as to how he could make things right. No answer was forthcoming but if it had all been a set-up to extort money from him, it was not a very good one. It is usual in cases of blackmail to leave a threat hanging over the potential victim until they decide their only choice is to submit to the blackmailer's terms. The miners, though, headed straight for the local police station and lodged a complaint. What might go in Driberg's London was clearly way out of kilter with acceptable behaviour among the mining communities of Scotland.

A hearing at West London Magistrates saw the case sent up to the Old Bailey. The intervening weeks were a period of intense worry for Driberg and he saw no other option than to explain the full extent of his predicament to his editor at the *Daily Express*, Arthur Christiansen. Christiansen escalated it to Beaverbrook, whose unhappiness at the turn of events was inferior to his affection for one of his star writers. He not only agreed to ensure that none of the newspapers under his control, nor belonging to any proprietors who wished to remain on his right side, would report on the case. He also put up the cash for Driberg's defence. Driberg had to make a personal call only to the editor of the *News of the World*, upon whose mercy he fell. By the time the case came to trial, the only mention in the newspapers was in *The Times'* list of hearings. Among the small part of the population who realised that William Hickey and Tom Driberg were one and the same man, fewer still made the association that he was the Driberg (identified by initials only) due in the Old Bailey dock.

Between the hearings, Driberg struck up a friendship of sorts with the arresting detective sergeant, hosting the officer at the *Express* headquarters. It emerged that the two Scotsmen had been politely advised to go away and consider their complaint when they had first arrived at the station. But, the detective sergeant explained to Driberg, had he and his colleagues known then that the accused was a leading columnist on a national newspaper, the advice would have been reframed in much ruder terms. Beaverbrook, meanwhile, was discussing the case with the Lord Chief Justice, Lord Hewart, who intimated that he considered it had all been a mistake. For the first time in his life, but not the last, the cloak of Establishment protection was gathering around Driberg's shoulders. Writing about the events in later life, he was candid. While the comments made in his favour by the Lord Chief Justice and the arresting officer were, he said, 'disturbing' in an abstract sense, his wish to escape the threatened ordeal trumped his concerns about the abuse of due process. As for Beaverbrook's intervention: 'In theory and in principle, I deplore such suppression of news, if what is kept out is newsworthy (which my trial perhaps, just marginally, was); but I am bound to admit that when it is something which concerns one personally, the suppression is jolly welcome.'[11]

Come the time of the trial, Driberg was acquitted. He was convinced that the tide turned decisively in his favour thanks to the intervention of two aristocratic figures – the Hon. Wilfred Egerton (brother of Lord

Ellesmere) and Lord Sysonby. Both stood in the witness box and testified to Driberg's unimpeachable reputation. The whole sorry misadventure was thus brought to a rapid close. The defendant walked free, his name unblemished, the episode almost completely unremarked upon in public. Only the *World's Press News*, a trade paper, made a wry acknowledgement of what had taken place. Playfully adapting William Hickey's tagline, it reported: 'That was a curious case that Fleet Street was talking about last week. Not all names make news.' Speaking many years later, Driberg's fellow Labour MP, Woodrow Wyatt, claimed that Driberg admitted to him that he had lied in court.[12] Regardless, the great and the good had discreetly saved one of their own from public shame. And having experienced the beneficence of the Establishment, it would come to his rescue again – and Boothby's – in 1964.

17

The Tightrope Walker

Despite the scare of his Old Bailey appearance, it was not long before Driberg resumed his risky sexual escapades. In 1937, for example, he made an extended trip to the USA, during which he was robbed in a brothel. Then there was the wartime incident in Edinburgh, not to mention an episode at Jockey's Fields in central London. On that occasion, Driberg was cottaging when he was apprehended by two police officers, one of whom had acted as *agent provocateur*. Driberg once more pulled the 'Don't you know who I am?' trick, while reminding the officers that many magistrates took a dim view of police evidence that could not be corroborated. Sure enough, no charges were brought against him.

Driberg was summarily dismissed from the Communist Party in 1941 for reasons he apparently could not fathom. It was, though, perhaps a stroke of luck. The following year he entered Parliament as an independent for the Essex constituency of Maldon, a by-election he would not likely have won had he been a card-carrying Communist. By the time of the 1945 election, he was a member of the Labour Party, regaining the constituency and holding it for a further decade. His political life effectively made it impossible to continue as a columnist for the right-leaning *Express* and so he migrated to *Reynolds News*, where he remained a heralded and much-read journalist. His journalistic skills were key to him finding passage with a parliamentary team to Buchenwald in 1945, where he was among the first civilians to see first-hand the unspeakable horror of that prison camp. By then he had proved his chops as a war correspondent reporting on the Normandy landings and in due course he would be embedded with British troops fighting in Korea.

A trip to the US for *Reynold's News* in 1946 resulted in him coming to the attention of the FBI. When he appeared at the public relations office of the Eleventh Naval District in San Diego, stating he wanted to do a story on the American Navy, the official he spoke to was struck by his unkempt appearance and lack of credentials. The local FBI office was notified and they in turn contacted the federal office to enquire about him for fear that someone was impersonating the real Driberg. The federal office's response reads: '[REDACTED] stated that Driberg is a very unsavoury individual, being generally known as a homosexual. He has been in constant trouble with the Government and is considered a very irresponsible person. REDACTED stated that the Embassy was cognisant of his presence in the United States but was in no way sanctioning his activities.'[1] Trouble had a tendency to follow Driberg about.

Politically, he was a maverick, although he became an established figure on Labour's National Executive Committee. Utterly committed to his constituents, at least in the early part of his parliamentary career, he espoused numerous causes, notably a socialist 'fair deal', anti-racism, anti-colonialism, penal reform and nuclear disarmament. Socially, he could be charming and highly entertaining, but rather too fond of a tipple and prone to indiscretion, which was all good and well when the indiscretion was not at your expense. He could also be prickly, snobbish and unkind. His socialist sense of comradeship, for instance, often did not extend to waiting staff, to whom he could be astoundingly rude (when he wasn't trying to seduce them for a quickie in the toilets).

He knew, too, that his personal life effectively ruled out a serious run at any of the big jobs in government. He described himself in these terms: 'A journalist when I might have been a poet, and a backbench MP – the lowest form of parliamentary life – with no hope, under the prevailing heterosexual dictatorship, of ministerial office.'[2] While he did everything possible to ensure that his homosexuality did not become public knowledge – given that exposure would represent professional and social suicide and quite possibly criminal conviction – he was nonetheless admirably unrepentant. And, of course, dangerously reckless. Few who navigated the same social and professional spheres were under any misapprehension as to his proclivities. He would note:

> The usual shallow sneer at homosexuals in any sort of public life ... is that they are hypocrites. Except in the sense that the Greek word 'hypocrite' means 'actor', and that, especially in an intolerant society, all of us have to do a certain amount of protective or comedic role-playing, the charge is false. In my own case, the two interests were parallel and simultaneous, and I was not a hypocrite: whether functioning as an acolyte in the sanctuary, or practising fellatio in some hotel bedroom or station W.C., I was doing what I most wanted to do at that moment, and doing it with complete sincerity.[3]

(There was undoubtedly a hint of this considered role-playing in 1963 when Driberg gave a talk on 'Christians in Politics'. Of the Profumo affair he said: 'The whole thing is terrible, tragic and sordid. You can't generalise about the whole government from this sort of thing. You can't conclude that the whole government is involved in sexual irregularities.')[4]

In 1951, he married a widow, Ena Binfield. All the evidence suggests neither entered into the partnership believing it would be a traditional marriage. Instead, they seem to have had a rather optimistic idea that it would be a union of companionship and shared interests – political and otherwise. In practice, it was nothing short of a nightmare dragged out over more than twenty years until she at last left him. If he had hoped she might serve as a 'beard' (a partner whose role is to make a gay man seem heterosexual), it was surely not worth all the pain. He treated her abominably from very early on, and the marriage was certainly not consummated. If he had behaved hypocritically to enter into the relationship in the first place, it was a façade he could not carry for long. But he was a realist. As he once reflected on his original passage into Parliament: 'If I had thought the electors entitled to such intelligence when I first stood for Parliament, I should have had to put "Homosexual, promiscuous", and I don't think there would have been many votes in that.'[5]

But winning Maldon only really emboldened him in his sexual adventures. Although the Old Bailey affair had calmed him down for a brief while, 'fear of the consequences, penal or even medical, does not long deter the incorrigible practising homosexual, any more than fear of the rope deterred the average murderer. If anything, I became more promiscuous after my election to Parliament, relying on my new status to get me out of tight corners.'[6] There was one occasion when he claimed that he encountered a uniformed officer on Hungerford Bridge and, after a nod of ascent, proceeded to perform oral sex on him. Perhaps most notoriously of all, Driberg told a select few of his inner circle that he once treated Nye Bevan the same way in his Commons office after a particularly boozy lunch – a tale whose truth has never been verified.[7]

All this risk taking pales when set against his involvement with the Krays, though. For many years, it was assumed that Driberg had been the one who introduced Boothby to the twins, although it now seems possible that Boothby had already come to their attention (perhaps initially observed as a guest at Leslie Holt's flat) and that Driberg merely provided an additional avenue through which he might be accessed. Regardless, at Ronnie's Cedra Court nights, in the words of Driberg's biographer Francis Wheen, 'rough but compliant East End lads were served like so many canapes'.[8] How could Driberg have been expected to resist?

The fact that his pleasures were not taken in private stolen moments but in the company (and on the home territory) of serious criminals seems not to have bothered him for a moment, just as it did not obviously worry Boothby. While they may have had no reason to believe Cedra Court was under police surveillance, it seems astonishing that neither entertained the thought that their hosts might endeavour to record their participation at the parties in some form or another. That was undoubtedly a consideration for Harold Wilson and the Labour leadership as they realised that Boothby's problems were theirs, too.

There is evidence that knowledge of Driberg and Boothby's association, although not widespread, was growing that summer of 1964. Certainly, the two backbench MPs who had reported Boothby's visit to the dog track knew exactly who his parliamentary companion was that night. The backbenchers were both Conservatives, Brigadier Terence Clarke, the member for Portsmouth West, and Burnaby Drayson, the member for Skipton. Clarke in particular held no candle for either Boothby (against whom he had been deeply opposed over Suez) or Driberg, who represented what he considered to be the unacceptable far left of the Labour Party. Whether either party's leadership would be able to keep a lid on what the pair might reveal in light of further revelations in the press was uncertain. Moreover, Douglas-Home had been informed that Boothby and Driberg's indiscretions at the dog track were also known to an unnamed Chief Constable who had so far taken no official action but who, ominously, was apparently prepared to sell his knowledge to MPs.[9]

Another Conservative MP, William Rees-Davies from the Isle of Thanet, was confiding to colleagues his belief that Driberg knew the Krays, although he claimed no evidence that the association was 'discreditable'.[10] Incidentally, Rees-Davies, a barrister by trade, had the previous year found himself immersed in the Profumo scandal when Stephen Ward and Lord Astor chose to consult him in light of Christine Keeler's decision to sell her story to the *Sunday Pictorial*. Rees-Davies later shared the intelligence he gathered with Sir Peter Rawlinson, the Solicitor-General. Meanwhile, over at MI5, a mole considered credible had also pointed the finger at Driberg in relation to Boothby and the Krays, going as far as to speculate 'whether some of the Labour people mightn't be going to burn their fingers if they tried to make much out of it all for their own purposes ...'[11]

It should not be presumed that Wilson felt any great personal compulsion to extract Driberg from a mess so starkly of his own making. Joe Haines, Wilson's press secretary in Downing Street, recalls that Wilson 'had no regard for Driberg – whose proclivities were well known at Westminster at a time when they were illegal'.[12] But it was, needless to say, not merely Driberg's neck on the line, but that of the party as a whole. How word of Driberg's involvement made it to Labour's upper ranks is not clear, although there are several viable alternatives.

It may have been that Driberg approached Wilson directly. Just as Boothby's panic levels would have risen on first seeing the *Sunday Mirror's* headline, so must Driberg's. The two men were quickly communicating with each other over the matter and Driberg might have decided that the quickest way to fix the problem was to get Wilson to exert some pressure on the newspaper that was customarily his greatest cheerleader. But if he chose not to approach Wilson directly, there is another credible avenue that he may have used – one that would directly implicate a third Prime Minister, alongside Douglas-Home and Wilson, in covering up the scandal. According to one source, in the 1950s Driberg had a direct line to the Cardiff MP, Jim Callaghan – who served as Prime Minister from 1976 until 1979 – when he ran into problems with the police. At the time of the Boothby saga, Callaghan was shadow Chancellor and would have been an obvious port of call for an old colleague in distress.

The link between Driberg and Callaghan was alleged in the self-published memoirs of the enigmatic John Symonds, a figure whose own career was chequered to say the least and whose life has been marked by outrageous claim and counter-claim. Symonds joined the Metropolitan Police Force in 1956 and rose through the ranks to become a detective sergeant. However, in 1969 he was one of three officers identified as guilty of corruption in an investigation by *The Times* newspaper. Facing trial in 1972, he skipped bail and fled to Morocco, where he initially worked as a mercenary. However, his willingness to share his knowledge of corruption within the British police force brought him to the attention of the KGB, the Soviet state security agency.

Symonds returned to Britain in 1981 and approached the authorities to confess that he had spent eight years as a Soviet spy. He had been used, he claimed, as a so-called 'Romeo spy', charged with extracting secrets by seducing female employees of Western embassies. But neither the British police nor the security agencies took his claims seriously. He appeared occasionally in the pages of the British tabloids but his story seemed too extraordinary to be credible. But then, in 1992, one Major Vasili Mitrokhin defected from the Soviet Union to the UK, bringing with him a huge archive of KGB files. They corroborated Symonds' story that he had been a Soviet agent.

According to Symonds, in 1957 he was a probationary police constable at Bow Street Station when one day he brought in two prisoners to present to the desk sergeant. He had arrested the pair for outraging public decency at a public urinal near Covent Garden Market. One was an actor while the other (whom Symonds described as a 'small pompous man') said he was a Member of Parliament and demanded to speak to the chief superintendent. It was Driberg. Symonds then claimed he was sent to the canteen to write up his notes while the superintendent was summoned from his flat above the police station. When he was called back to the front office, Symonds witnessed Driberg 'in a friendly huddle' with the superintendent and the newly arrived Callaghan, who had been summoned to the station in a phone call from Driberg.

Symonds had lived in Cardiff during and after the war and recognised Callaghan as his former local MP – one his father considered a 'Bolshie Rabble Rouser' and a 'bugger' who had 'his nose into everything'. At the time of the incident with Driberg, Callaghan was parliamentary adviser to the Police Federation and as such had close contacts within the force. Symonds was told to put his pocket book away and return to his patrol while Driberg left the station, free to take up the chairmanship of the Labour Party a few weeks later.[13]

It is impossible to corroborate Symonds' story now but Callaghan's friend and head of policy research, Bernard Donoughue, would recall that Callaghan claimed to have been entirely unaware of homosexuality until well into adulthood, and that it was 'the notorious behaviour of the Labour queer Tom Driberg that brought it to his knowledge'.[14] If Driberg did indeed turn to Callaghan before anyone else after his arrest in 1957, there is no reason to think that he wouldn't have maintained the line of communication through to 1964.

Alternatively, it is possible that the Labour hierarchy got wind of Driberg's involvement before Driberg himself ever made contact. With senior government figures scrabbling to establish truth from fiction in the days and weeks following the *Sunday Mirror* exposés, a certain degree of cross-party communication could have been expected, particularly as it became clear that the scandal was not as clearly partisan as it first appeared. By 22 July, Sir Timothy Bligh had noted that Boothby had brought up Driberg's name in his private statement about the affair 'without any prompting'.[15] Given Driberg's reputation at Westminster, this may well have acted as a hint that Driberg's involvement should be scrutinised. Boothby would have known that his own chances of surviving the tumult would be increased if Labour and its Fleet Street mouthpieces had reason to hold back on their attack. Boothby would not have known at the time that Clarke, Drayson and MI5 had all done their bit to focus attention on Driberg, too.

There was also a very clear channel of potential communication between the secret meetings of the Conservative war council and the Labour ranks. The Solicitor-General, Sir Peter Rawlinson, was a member of Gerald Gardiner's chambers. The relationship between the pair was such that when Wilson replaced Douglas-Home at the end of 1964, and Rawlinson ceased his tenure as Solicitor-General as Gardiner began his as Lord Chancellor, Rawlinson replaced Gardiner as head of chambers. There can rarely have been a more useful time to make use of such a cross-party conduit, as it emerged that both teams were in dire trouble … unless they might find a way to work together.

Like Boothby, Driberg had become accustomed to getting away with personal indiscretions for most of his adult life. This promoted a trait in each of them whereby they tended to bite the hand that fed them. In particular, both came to take for granted the press protection they enjoyed as a result of Lord Beaverbrook's patronage. There were a couple of particularly notable instances in Driberg's case. The first came in 1946, when he and Michael Foot had successfully pushed for the establishment of a Royal Commission to look into the power and influence of newspaper proprietors. In the Commons debate on the motion, Driberg argued:

> Personally, although I may deprecate him as public figure, I do, and always shall, regard Lord Beaverbrook with considerable affection, with great affection and respect – personally, I have found him a very good employer to work for, and a very good employer to be sacked by. [Driberg had departed the *Express* in 1943.][16]

He then proceeded to denigrate the British newspaper business as one dominated by advertisers and shareholders such that the papers could not carry out their primary function as outlets for news, comment and entertainment. Then, when giving evidence to the commission itself, Driberg revealed that Beaverbrook operated a 'white list' of individuals who were not to be mentioned in either the *Express* papers or the *Evening Standard*.[17] It was revealed that Stanley Baldwin made it on to the list even when he was Prime Minister but with the caveat that while it would be impossible to avoid all mention, he should not receive undue coverage or any sort of publicity not checked in advance with the editor.

It is surprising enough that Driberg went after the press baron not much more than a decade after Beaverbrook had bankrolled his Old Bailey acquittal and effectively silenced reporting of the story. More shocking still was that Beaverbrook – not a man known for a gentleness of spirit when it came to personal or public conflict – soon overlooked the attack. 'I expected no better from that fellow Driberg,' he was recorded as saying, sounding more like an exasperated uncle than a furious maker and breaker of countless individuals.[18]

The next test of the friendship came a few years later when Driberg – every bit as unwise with money as Boothby – agreed to arrest the decline in his finances by writing a biography of Beaverbrook. Beaverbrook even signed up serialisation rights with the *Sunday Express* to boost Driberg's coffers. But the project soon descended into vitriol. Determined to avoid the peril of writing an elongated puff piece, Driberg produced a text that did not hold back in critiquing its subject. When Beaverbrook read it, he was appalled and told friends: 'Man has been falling ever since the birth of Adam. But never in the whole course of human history has any man fallen quite so low as that fellow Driberg.' It was duly communicated to Driberg that Beaverbrook considered the book was driven by hate, a claim to which Driberg responded in a letter: 'I have no "hatred" for you; how could I have?'[19] As Beaverbrook continued his protests, insisting on numerous amendments and cuts, Driberg became more defensive. He suggested that Beaverbrook was taking the complimentary strands of the text for granted and honing in on those sections that were more critical. Why not let Bob Boothby cast an independent eye over it, he suggested? Beaverbrook rebuffed the offer, being in the middle of one of his intermittent feuds with Boothby at the time – a fact Driberg had thoughtlessly overlooked.

The frostiness between Driberg and Beaverbrook took a long time to thaw, but it nonetheless did. A warmly worded telegram to acknowledge Beaverbrook's 80th birthday in 1959 did the trick, followed by a personal reunion the same year at a lunch hosted by Beaverbrook for the former *Express* editor, Arthur Christiansen. Beaverbrook sent Driberg a case of champagne afterwards, a sign that relations had been normalised. It was a situation that maintained until Beaverbrook's death at the end of May 1964, a few weeks before the 'Peer and the Gangster' drama began to unfold. It is difficult to imagine just what Driberg needed to do to lose the baron's faith.

Driberg's up and down relationship with Beaverbrook fits with his broader tendency to push boundaries even at the risk of self-destruction. With all the near misses he survived, he maintained an extraordinary sense that he would always find a way to get through. And for all the calamitous events that peppered his life, it did at times feel like he wore some invisible cloak of protection. In fact, this ostensibly most anti-Establishment of figures enjoyed a level of Establishment protection that few guessed at during his lifetime.

The clues were there as early as 1941 when he was thrown out of the British Communist Party. The path to his dismissal began in 1934 when a near neighbour, the occult and thriller writer Dennis Wheatley, invited Driberg to join a club he had established for authors, critics and publishers that met at the Cheshire Cheese pub in Fleet Street. There, Driberg hit it off with another writer of thrillers called Maxwell Knight. Knight was virulently anti-communist and anti-homosexual yet the pair enjoyed each other's company enormously, particularly their shared love of gossip. As that rare beast – a communist on the *Daily Express* – Driberg did a fine line in chatter involving figures from both the left and right. What he did not know at the time was that Captain Maxwell Knight headed up the counter-subversion section of MI5. Knight had found not only a new friend but an intelligence asset as well. By 1941, Harry Pollitt, the Communist Party's General-Secretary, had received word that Driberg was a (perhaps unwitting) MI5 agent, hence his removal from the party.

Others have noted that Driberg had all the attributes of a terrible spy. Here was a gossip who constantly brought attention to himself and struggled to keep a secret. Nonetheless, for a while at least, MI5 were able to take advantage of his loose lips. Moreover, he became a double agent when he was caught up in a sting operation while cottaging in Moscow during a visit to interview the spy Guy Burgess in 1956 for what turned out to be a highly profitable series of articles and a book. The Mitrokhin archive confirmed as much.[20] How long Driberg supplied intelligence of any real quality to

MI5 is unclear. However, at the time of the Boothby affair, the Director-General of MI5 was Roger Hollis, who had been a friend of Driberg's and a fellow left-winger at Oxford. (In later years, he was also a golfing partner of Boothby's old friend, *Telegraph* editor Colin Coote). Chapman Pincher, an investigative journalist who led Fleet Street in knowledge of the intelligence world, became convinced that Hollis was a KGB mole, although other experts (including Dr Christopher Andrew, author of *The Defence of the Realm. The Authorised History of MI5*) have made convincing attempts to debunk the theory.[21] Chapman, though, also claimed that Driberg enjoyed lifelong protection from the organisation, a vital factor in his avoiding criminal conviction. Driberg is known to have boasted privately that he was immune from prosecution because he knew too much. He alluded, for example, to unspecified dark secrets of Macmillan's Chancellor of the Exchequer, Deryk Heathcote Amory.[22] It is certainly not beyond the realms of possibility that MI5 did keep an eye out for its asset, regardless of how long he had outlived his usefulness, and that Hollis decided to alert Driberg's Labour bosses to his predicament when he knew that the Conservatives were trying to work out how to manage Boothby's troubles.[23]

In a March 1982 edition of the *Spectator*, the Labour MP Leo Abse, who had done so much to secure the implementation of the Wolfenden Report's recommendations, wrote: 'Driberg walked all his life on a tightrope and gained his thrills in public and private by a never ending series of adventures, courageously and foolhardily oscillating from one role to another almost every day of his life.'[24] His lifestyle was sufficiently chaotic that he pulled figures from across the social echelons into his orbit, which made him a dangerous character for those who wished to distance themselves from his world. A man who carries the secrets of others and threatens guilt by mere association is a threatening presence in the corridors of power. His reputation doubtless served him – and Boothby – well in July of 1964. For Harold Wilson and his team anticipating soon going into government, the cost of not digging him out of yet another hole was too great to countenance.

18

Over-Mighty Barons

On 8 May 1968 there occurred a meeting at 2, Kinnerton Street, SW1, that might conceivably have changed the course of British history. The location was the London address of Louis Mountbatten, 1st Earl Mountbatten of Burma, cousin of the Queen, uncle of the Duke of Edinburgh, Supreme Allied Commander (South East Asia Command) during the Second World War, last Viceroy of India, first Governor-General of independent India, a former First Sea Lord and Chief of the Defence Staff. In attendance at the meeting alongside Mountbatten were Hugh Cudlipp, Cecil Harmsworth King and Sir Solly Zuckerman, then chief scientific adviser to the government having made his name as a key military strategist during the war.

Cudlipp had arranged the gathering at the request of King, who was growing increasingly agitated at the conduct of the Wilson government. Having taken a large slice of the credit for getting Wilson through the doors of Downing Street in the election of 1964, King had subsequently become disillusioned with his political protégé. Some of those closest to him, like Cudlipp, suspected that King's disillusionment was turning into something rather more sinister, akin to a paranoid fixation. King became convinced that the nation was careering towards an economic precipice and feared that a crisis would bring about social turmoil and bloodshed on the streets.

When all the attendees had arrived at Kinnerton Street, King outlined his concerns. For somewhile he had been conjuring with the notion of an emergency government, one that would call on the talents of men like himself and others from the commercial world who – though unelected – could steady the economic ship, backed by a compliant military. As to who might head such an administration, it had to be a unifying figure, an individual of standing and widespread public recognition. A figure, King proffered, like Mountbatten.

Cudlipp detected signs of acute discomfort in Mountbatten and Zuckerman as they listened to King's scheme. In the end, it was Zuckerman who reacted first, condemning the idea as 'rank treachery'. 'All this talk of machine guns at street corners is appalling,' he said as he urged Mountbatten to have nothing to do with it. Within moments the meeting broke up and with it were extinguished King's hopes of a bloodless coup.[1]

Cudlipp and his colleagues at the *Mirror* papers had spent several months working hard to keep their editorial free from the boss's more extreme views, but now King broke cover. Two days after the meeting with Mountbatten, he published an article in the *Mirror* under the headline, 'Enough is Enough'. 'Mr Wilson and his government have lost all credit,' he wrote, 'and we are now threatened with the greatest financial crisis in history. It is not to be resolved by lies about our reserves but only by a fresh start under a fresh leader.'[2]

King, who resigned as a part-time director of the Bank of England only the night before publication, sent the pound into a tailspin. Wilson and the Labour Party were, predictably, appalled at the turn of events, as were the board of the IPC, who demanded King's resignation and, when that wasn't forthcoming, dismissed him. One of the great press barons of mid-century Britain shuffled off from Fleet Street into quasi-retirement, an isolated figure who had gravely misjudged the extent of his power and the mood of the country. Cudlipp took up the reins as chair of the IPC in his place.

The conventional theory goes that the seeds of King's animosity towards Wilson were sown early in the Prime Minister's term of office. King expected to be a significant power behind the throne, nudging and cajoling the government to do his bidding. But almost as soon as Wilson was inside No. 10, it was apparent that this was not how events would play out. While Wilson understood the importance of King's support,[3] he was not prepared to be a newspaperman's puppet and treated King's voice as merely one of many that he needed to consider. Things got off to a bad start, too, when

Wilson offered King only a life peerage rather than the earldom he had been hoping for. King rejected it outright, as well as the suggestion that he might serve as a Minister of State. Before long, his newspapers that had championed Wilson's ascent to the premiership were openly critiquing him and his government.

It was a startlingly quick turnaround in King's feelings toward Wilson, but it becomes less startling if the process of jettisoning support had started earlier – at the time of the 'Peer and the Gangster' scandal. Here was a story that was supposed to cement the union between the two. King had personally authorised publication in the expectation that the Conservative administration would crumple under the weight of further dishonour. The election was being delivered on a platter to the Labour Party with his best wishes. Instead, he found himself cornered into a humiliating climb down (for the newspaper, the company and himself personally) and forced to hand over a huge sum of money – all orchestrated by Wilson's closest legal advisers. It cannot have failed to rankle. And when Wilson then declined to provide the rewards to which King felt entitled a few months later, the writing was on the wall.

★★★

The 'Peer and the Gangster' episode was a calamity for all those working on the *Mirror* papers – a chance for journalistic glory quickly turned into excruciating professional embarrassment. At least Goodman tied up the legalities so tightly that no one dared speak of it again for years to come.

Along with King, it was especially a moment to forget for Norman Lucas, the story's author. Lucas was nobody's fool. His contacts within the police – especially the murder squad – and the criminal underworld were unparalleled, a network of informants built up over many years. Most weekends he would entertain one murder squad detective or another at his home, treating them to a home-cooked family lunch and in return guaranteeing that he would be first with the latest tip-off. Such was his closeness to many of the Met's most senior detectives that in due course he would enjoy a nice sideline ghosting their biographies.

He had encountered the Krays already, too. He was hearing about their activities from as early as 1960 but had not reported on them for fear of a libel action. Then, a little later, he received a visit from the brothers, offering to sell him their story for a cool £25,000. The paper declined the proposal but Lucas was left with the impression that they had hoped he and the *Sunday Mirror* would boost their public profile. Their narrative, he recalled, was that of decent lads from the East End made good. Lucas, though, was a hard-nosed journalist in whom cynicism was hard-wired and he had little interest in writing underworld PR copy.

But when it came to Boothby and the Krays, his story was just not quite tight enough. It seemed inexplicable. His chief source was as reliable as ever – an officer with the Met's intelligence arm, C11. Although his identity has never been established (Lucas refused to ever divulge it), it was almost certainly not the team's Chief Superintendent, John Cummings. Nonetheless, Lucas got a look at the team's intelligence report based on months of surveillance that took in the twins' various criminal enterprises, their liberal use of violence and Ronnie's penchant for hooking up with young men in the company of well-known public figures.

Lucas may have put two and two together and arrived at the wrong answer when he noted that Ronnie and Boothby had been seen fraternising. In an interview he gave several years after the events, he suggested that he had been told by sources within the Met that they were in no doubt of the relationship between them but could not gather the evidence to prove it.[4] Certainly, C11 had not caught the pair in flagrante and so it represented quite a leap to take the proof of their association as evidence of a sexual relationship. Lucas may also have attempted to conflate information from two sources into a single story. Evidently, MI5's Kray insider was unable to fathom how the paper could have concluded that Boothby and Kray were lovers unless Lucas's mole had, perhaps, confused Kray and Holt. The source suggested that the newspaper's informant on that score may have been a member of the Nashes, another of London's leading underworld families then in dispute with the Krays. The story went that the Nashes were unhappy about press coverage of their own protection and drug-peddling rackets, so had offered the Kray–Boothby story in return for being left alone. However the mix-up occurred, it proved a crushing blow to any hopes that the newspaper had of fending off Boothby's subsequent demand for recompense. Had Lucas simply stated that the peer and the gangster had been seen socialising together, the story would have still had the potential to badly damage Boothby and the Conservatives. But the room for accusations of libel would have been much reduced, and the allegations themselves easier to prove. The photo of the pair on a sofa, after all, proved an association even as it did not support the claim of a sexual dalliance.

But as it was, Lucas found himself with the building blocks of a story too good not to write. The newspaper's editor, Reg Payne, was keen, too. His relationship with King, however, was tempestuous and there was no guarantee that the proprietor would sign it off. Payne was known for giving his staff raucous dressings down accompanied by the foulest of language but he commanded their broad respect and affection. King, though, did not hold him in much esteem. Moreover, King had been on something of a campaign to 'clean up' Fleet Street, encouraging less reliance on the chequebook journalism of the recent past and reducing emphasis on the details of public figures' private lives.

Nonetheless, King was content that the 'Peer and the Gangster' fitted in with his broad editorial vision for the newspaper, which had recently been renamed from the *Sunday Pictorial* to the *Sunday Mirror*, more closely aligning it with its daily counterpart. The rebranded paper launched with the claim that it was 'the new Sunday paper for The Moderns ... people who not only want to be "with it" but "way out ahead"'.[5]

King was the nephew of two of the biggest names in the newspaper world from a previous era: the brothers Alfred and Harold Harmsworth (later Lord Northcliffe and Lord Rothermere, respectively). As founders of the *Daily Mail* and the *Daily Mirror*, as well as owners of variously *The Times*, the *Sunday Times* and the *Sunday Pictorial*, they remoulded the concept of popular journalism in the Edwardian era. The weight of his forebears' legacy weighed heavily on King, who strove all his life to make a similar impact. Becoming a director of the *Daily Mirror* in 1929, he brought Cudlipp into the business first as a 22-year-old features editor and then, a couple of years later, as editor of the *Sunday Pictorial*. Where King was high-born, Cudlipp was not. Raised in Cardiff, he left school at 14, his shining journalistic instincts unrestricted by a lack of formal education.

During the 1930s, both the *Mirror* and *Sunday Pictorial* exhibited a new and assertively less deferential tone to those in power. Cudlipp temporarily left Fleet Street to serve during the war but returned to King in 1951 as editorial director of both newspapers. Over the next few years, King and Cudlipp oversaw an expansion of their media empire, buying up rivals including the *People* and the *Daily Herald* and a vast array of magazines. By the time King consolidated his various assets into the International Publishing Company, it represented the single largest publishing operation on the planet. Its jewel in the crown, the *Daily Mirror*, was soon the bestselling newspaper in the world, its circulation regularly topping 5 million.

By now, King wanted his flagship titles to pose a real challenge to the status quo in demanding a modern and meritocratic society. It was an attitude that chimed with a growing distrust of the Establishment. The journalist Henry Fairlie had put wind in the sails of the new anti-Establishment movement with a celebrated article in the 23 September 1955 edition of *The Spectator*:

> I have several times suggested that what I call the 'Establishment' in this country is today more powerful than ever before. By the 'Establishment' I do not mean only the centres of official power – though they are certainly part of it – but rather the whole matrix of official and social relations within which power is exercised. The exercise of power in Britain (more specifically, in England) cannot be understood unless it is recognised that it is exercised socially. Anyone who has at any point been close to the exercise of power will know what I mean when I say that the 'Establishment' can be seen at work in the activities of, not only the Prime Minister, the Archbishop of Canterbury and the Earl Marshal, but of such lesser mortals as the chairman of the Arts Council, the Director-General of the BBC, and even the editor of *The Times Literary Supplement*, not to mention divinities like Lady Violet Bonham Carter.[6]

Then, Harold Wilson arrived to become the anti-Establishment's political hero *de jour*. Preparing his pitch for the forthcoming general election, he made a speech at Birmingham's Town Hall on 19 January 1964, in which he laid in to the country's anachronistic system of privilege and entitlement. He said:

> We are living in a jet age, but we are governed by an Edwardian Establishment mentality. Over the British people lies the chill frost of Tory leadership. They freeze initiative and petrify imagination. They cling to privilege and power for the few, shutting the door on the many ... We do not believe that a small minority of the British people, distinguished by their family connections, or educational background, have a unique right to positions of influence and power.[7]

Overlooking his own family background, his Winchester and Oxford education, the choice of Eton for his sons' education and his penchant for weekends shooting on his vast Aberdeenshire hunting estate, King was determined to spearhead the media attack on the Old Guard. The Profumo affair provided the perfect opportunity. Macmillan was there for the taking and the critique of the dissolute lifestyle of Profumo was easy to upscale into a condemnation of the entire ruling class – an elite prepared to endanger the nation for the metaphorical thrill of a frolic in a swimming pool on a country estate with a pretty young woman. Out came King's chequebook to secure Keeler's story in what turned into a 'gloves off' battle. The Establishment failed in what felt like the last whimpering of the Old Boy Network. The Boothby scandal was to have been the final nail in the coffin. But the story played into King's hands in other ways as well. Firstly, it gave him the opportunity to get one up on Cudlipp. The men had worked together with spectacular success for the best part of thirty years but there was a degree of rivalry between them. In particular, King was conscious that there were those who regarded Cudlipp as the born newspaper man, the editorial genius behind the operation, with King little more than a competent executive. With Cudlipp away as the story broke, King could prove his mettle as a *bona fide* Fleet Street legend in his own right.

Additionally, for all that it claimed to be the organ of the 'with it' Moderns, King oversaw a virulently homophobic strand in the *Mirror* papers. It was homophobia in its truest sense – King bought into the idea, *à la* Maxwell Fyfe, that homosexuals were a threat to the nation, especially as subjects of blackmail by hostile states. The *Sunday Mirror's* homophobic outpourings arguably reached their nadir on 28 April 1963, with a piece written by Hollywood reporter Lionel Crane to coincide with the publication of Lord Radcliffe's report into the Vassall affair. Radcliffe gave much anxious thought to the question of Vassall's homosexuality, concluding: 'There was nothing in Vassall's conduct or conversation that indicated, even to a sharp observer, a man addicted to homosexual practices.'[8] Now Crane, under the headline 'How to spot a potential homo', promised a 'short course on how to pick a pervert'. Homosexuals are, he declared, divided into two groups: the 'obvious' and the 'concealed'. While those in the first group 'could be spotted by a One Eyed Jack on a foggy day in Blackwall Tunnel', the latter were elusive but generally fitted into one of eight categories of 'suspects', including those 'with an unnaturally strong affection for their mother', the 'fussy dresser', the 'over-clean man' and the 'man who is adored by older women'.[9] It was desperate stuff but Boothby now gave King another chance to prove his thesis that homosexuality was detrimental to the health of the country.

After the initial 'Peer and the Gangster' splash in the *Sunday Mirror* on 12 July, the *Daily Mirror* took up the story with gusto the following day. 'Coming so soon after the Profumo affair,' ran the editorial, 'any new scandal involving a peer, or other prominent public men, is bound to have wide repercussions.'[10] The Commissioner of the Metropolitan Police, Sir Joseph Simpson, remained poised to report on the issue to Home Secretary Henry Brooke, readers were told. Then on the 14th, the *Mirror* reported that Marcus Lipton, the Labour MP for Brixton, was to raise the matter in the House of Commons, asking Brooke: 'What reports have you received from the Metropolitan Police about the intimidation in the form of protection money extorted from club owners in the West End and what actions are you taking?'[11]

However, the front page also reported Simpson's statement from the previous evening denying knowledge of the newspaper's claims. On the 15th, the *Mirror* responded by urging Brooke: 'If he doesn't know what MPs and the *Daily Mirror* are talking about, let him go down into the heart of the police force and ask the men on the job what they know about the activities of this gang.'[12] The next day, it was reported that Arthur Lewis, the Labour MP for West Ham North, would the following Monday ask Brooke whether he had sanctioned Simpson's statement 'regarding a matter on which Parliamentary questions were pending' and if in future 'Will you require the Commissioner to refrain from making such statements in anticipation of Ministers' answers to Parliamentary questions?'[13]

Evidently, both Westminster and Fleet Street were coming to realise the impact of Simpson's intervention. For the time being, the *Mirror* could not press the issue of the Krays and their links to Boothby any further. On 17 July, coverage focused on Brooke's rather vague reply to Lipton: 'It would not be in the public interest to discuss the progress of particular inquiries.'[14] Meanwhile, a separate editorial took up a hostile position against Simpson:

> Gangsterism and crime in Britain are now winning hands down against the forces of law and order. This is shown by a shock report on the 1963 London crime statistics which was sent to the Home Secretary yesterday by the Metropolitan Police Commissioner, Sir Joseph Simpson. He records a 7% rise in the number of indictable crimes.[15]

The article went on to emphasise an accompanying drop in the clear-up rate, to less than 25 per cent.

The following day, there was a new angle. The recently appointed Director of Public Prosecutions, Norman Skelhorn, was reported to have told all chief constables to seek his advice before launching prosecutions over homosexual offences between consenting adults. Where some saw an admirably progressive gesture, others smelled a rat. Arthur Lewis was among them. 'The police have been – and are – investigating the existence of a blackmail, extortion and protection racket, which I am told is connected with homosexuality,' he said. 'What I want to know is this. Is there any link between the various investigations and the allegations that prominent people are involved, and the Government's change in the administration of homosexuality laws? If there is, it would mean there was a plot – a cover-up – on the part of the government.'[16]

Writing in the *Sunday Mirror* the next day (the day of 'The Picture We Must Not Print'), the Welsh MP Leo Abse was similarly intrigued:

The Director of Public Prosecutions has told police forces to take no proceedings without first sending him a report. Why has the government changed its mind? Are the rumours that widespread protection rackets have been discovered true? Is it correct that it has become known that prominent personalities including a peer and many clergymen have been found to have been ensnared by criminal thugs? Whatever the reasons, the belated step now taken is in the direction of sanity. The disposition of the wretched homosexuals arises from birth or a faulty family upbringing … One day, perhaps, we will have legislation which, while ensuring that juveniles and public decency are protected, will not drive hundreds of thousands of men to live a frightened life in the shadows.[17]

However, by Tuesday the Attorney General, Sir John Hobson, had denied any link between Skelhorn's edict and the *Sunday Mirror*'s revelations. Moreover, Lewis was told that Simpson had been unaware of a pending parliamentary question when he made his public statement. Then, on 23 July, Brooke spoke in the House, telling Lipton that the Chief Commissioner of Police had advised him that the protection racket situation was less serious in London than it had been on several occasions in the past. (The *Mirror* duly pointed out that Scotland Yard did not keep statistics on protection rackets, rendering it 'the Crime that Never Was' and thus making Simpson's statement somewhat redundant.[18]) Brooke also confirmed that there was no police evidence 'to support the allegations published' by the *Sunday Mirror*, to which Reg Payne responded: 'The *Sunday Mirror* stands by its statement that a vicious protection racket is being run – I am surprised to hear the Home Secretary say that the police have no evidence to support this.'[19]

Despite their, for now, spirited defence of the story, the *Mirror* papers were losing momentum. They had played a strong hand but it had been countered by those of Simpson and Brooke, while Boothby, Goodman and Gardiner had still to flourish the ace up their collective sleeve – Boothby's letter to *The Times*. King, Lucas and the rest had been outmanoeuvred, less than a fortnight since breaking the story. The pivotal figure in their strategic defeat was Joseph Simpson, whose interference provided the basis for Brooke's subsequent statements. Between the two of them, they effectively pulled the rug from beneath those working in the Mirror Building.

Simpson had form when it came to interventions on behalf of the government. On 27 March 1963, he had attended a meeting at the Home Office with Brooke, Brooke's Permanent Under Secretary (Charles Cunningham), and the head of MI5 (Roger Hollis).[20] Brooke wanted to explore the possibility of pursuing a criminal case against Stephen Ward, who was rapidly assuming the role of scapegoat in the Profumo affair. Ward knew too much that implicated Profumo and was making noises to various contacts that he might have to tell what he knew. At best, the threat of prosecution might silence him. But even if it did not, he would be a discredited witness. There was also a growing appetite to exact some sort of revenge on a character regarded in certain influential corners as a dangerous moral vacuum.

Keeler had already claimed that Ward had asked her to find out from Profumo when the US would provide West Germany with nuclear warheads. It was an extremely serious accusation – espionage of the highest order – but no one took it seriously. If Ward had indeed made the request, it was surely in jest. Keeler was no trained operative and there was no serious possibility that Profumo would spill the beans on such a delicate issue. Hollis was adamant – Ward did not pose a security risk and would not be pursued for violation of the Official Secrets Act.

Simpson now found himself in a quandary. It was clear that the government would look kindly upon some kind of police action. Nor would he have wanted it to appear that Ward was in any way being protected by the Met. Simpson duly agreed to look into Ward's background, particularly rumours that he ran a network of call girls off whose immoral earnings he lived. The Chief Commissioner's conduct was dubious on several points. Firstly, it looked very much like he was accepting a political order (or, at least, a weighty invitation) to find a way of charging an individual who posed a political threat – undermining the long tradition of the force's independence from political influence. Secondly, it was an utter perversion of the normal pattern of police investigation – the quest to find the culprit of a specific crime. Instead, the police were being charged with seeking evidence of a crime so as to be able to prosecute a specific suspect.

Simpson did not believe there was much prospect of successfully ensnaring Ward but agreed to set up an investigative team under Chief Inspector Samuel Herbert and Detective Sergeant John Burrows. Over the next few months, some 125 witnesses were interviewed, several – like Keeler – on numerous occasions. Others, like Rice-Davies, were encouraged to provide evidence of Ward's supposed misdemeanours in return for having their own minor offences – in Rice-Davies's case, a trumped up allegation of stealing a television – dropped. Meanwhile, reports on the investigation's progress were regularly circulated around Westminster and Whitehall, until the Met finally got their man.

There is further evidence of Simpson's proclivity to do what he deemed to be the bidding of his political masters. Sometime around 1966, a little before the passage through Parliament of the Wolfenden recommendations, he was once more in a meeting at the Home Office, this time with Wilson's Home Secretary, Roy Jenkins, and the Home Office minister, Dick Taverne. Jenkins was concerned that too much police time was being wasted in arresting individuals for cottaging. It was a practice, he said, that he thought ought to be discontinued. Simpson responded: 'Home Secretary, it is quite unconstitutional for you to tell me, as a policeman, how I should operate.' Nonetheless, he continued, he would look into the matter. Then he made a statement that took both Jenkins and Taverne aback. 'As a matter of fact,' Simpson began, 'there are several cottages in Westminster which we don't investigate.' When pressed as to why, he said: 'Because it would be embarrassing.' Embarrassing, why? 'Because they are frequented by celebrities and MPs.'[21]

The Met's blind eye to the misbehaviour of influential people continued afterwards, too. In November 1970, for instance, David Little was a new recruit to the Met, stationed at Gerald Road in Belgravia. One rainy evening his beat took him along Eaton Square, where he glimpsed what he described as a 'dark heap', lying on the road in a gutter. It turned out to be a drunk, so Little called for a van to take in the man. Back at Gerald Street, Little told the assistant station sergeant where he had found the prisoner. The assistant sergeant took a look at the drunk's face, then promptly screamed and ran out – not a practice, Little reflected, that had featured in his training. A minute or so later, the assistant sergeant returned with the station sergeant to inspect the prisoner, who was dressed in evening wear and a long velvet cloak. The station sergeant then told Little to take the drunk back to Eaton Square and replace him in the gutter exactly as he had been found. The prisoner, needless to say, was Boothby. When Little returned to the station, he was told he was only the latest in a line of officers who had done the same over the years. He was also made aware of an unwritten rule: Boothby was not to be picked up if found.[22]

Simpson's unwillingness to upset the political apple cart left King and his lieutenants at the Mirror Building with nowhere to go. By the time that King had authorised the *Sunday Mirror*'s humbling apology and paid off Boothby, his critics were ready to take their own pound of flesh. Randolph Churchill, Winston's son, weighed in with an article on 13 August 1964 in *The Spectator*. He condemned the 'particularly obnoxious article' that had appeared on 12 July, commenting:

> In an article in the *Sunday Times* on April 21, 1963, Mr. King revealed the rules he had laid down for all his papers concerning intrusion into people's private lives ... People who control newspapers ought to be responsible for more than signing apologies: they ought to know what is going into their papers. Otherwise, they must fall under the judgment of Mr. Stanley Baldwin, who said of Lords Rothermere (Mr. Cecil H. King's uncle) and Beaverbrook: 'These men seek power without responsibility – the prerogative of the harlot throughout the ages.'[23]

The following day, Francis Williams – who had variously been the editor of the *Daily Herald*, the wartime controller of press censorship and news at the Ministry of Information, a public relations adviser to Clement Attlee in Downing Street and the governor of the BBC – had his say in the *New Statesman*. Boothby had handled the 'smear' against him admirably, he claimed, in what he cited as 'a classic example of gutter journalism conducted with almost incomprehensible incompetence'.[24]

It was altogether an ignominious and uncomfortable few weeks for King, but a life in Fleet Street had made him nothing if not robust. The *Mirror* papers soon moved on to other stories, other scandals, other targets and by the year's end had played their part in getting the Conservatives out of power and Wilson into No. 10. King spent another four years as the most powerful man at the IPC until his infatuation with what he perceived as Wilson's frailties led to his exit. Cudlipp could shoulder only limited blame for what happened over the Boothby story, having been out of the country at the key moment. Lucas emerged remarkably unscathed, enjoying many more years on the crime desk, his reputation largely intact. Reg Payne somehow ended up as the fall guy at the Mirror Building, removed from a commanding post on Fleet Street's front line and redeployed to the backwater that was *Tit-bits* magazine.

Neither King nor Cudlipp ever publicly mentioned the saga again, their hands tied by Goodman's red tape. And so in less than a month, the *Mirror* papers that had threatened to explode a bomb beneath the Establishment were outflanked and drawn into its conspiracy of silence.

19

Collateral Damage

It was the evening of 9 March 1966 and two friends, George and Albie, were perched on stools at the pub's bar, supping light ales. It was a quiet night at the Blind Beggar in Whitechapel. There were only a few other customers; at one end of the bar was an old man half-reading a newspaper and half-watching the television. The barmaid was washing glasses as the Walker Brothers' 'The Sun Ain't Gonna Shine Anymore' spun on the record player.

Then, at around 8.30, the pub's door opened and in walked two figures. George looked across to them and said, 'Well, just look who's here.' At that instant, one of the arrivals fired a couple of shots into the pub ceiling, while his companion moved towards George. He raised his 9mm Luger revolver and put a bullet in George's forehead, a little above his right eye. As George lay dying on the floor and the bar's other occupants looked on in horror, the two assailants left the pub, got into a Mark 1 Ford Cortina and sped off into the night.

The victim was George Cornell, his killer Ronnie Kray. Kray had brought two members of the Firm with him – the other shooter Ian Barrie and John 'Scotch Jack' Dickson the getaway driver. The slaying represented Ronnie's first known murder. He had, as those in the underworld might have put it, 'made his bones'. Why Cornell was killed remains a subject of debate. He was a member of the rival Richardson gang, and the previous night a Kray associate had lost his life in an altercation with the gang. However, Cornell had not been present at the scene. Another proposed motive is that

Kray held a grudge after Cornell had called him a 'fat poof' when the pair bumped into each other the previous Christmas – it was just the sort of emasculating language that Kray found hard to brush off. A further theory goes that the grudge went back much further, to a fight several years before between two East End gangs during which Cornell gave Kray the hiding of his life.

Whatever the reason, when news reached Kray that night that Cornell was on local turf, he had the scent of blood in his nostrils. For all the violent havoc the Kray gang had caused since the late 1950s, it was the first documented death for which they were responsible. It was a staging post in the upsurge of violence that ensued in the months and years after the suppression of the Boothby scandal. The *Sunday Mirror*'s scoop ought to have marked the beginning of the end for the twins and their criminal enterprise. The press was on to them, the police were too and the net was closing in. But all the progress made in the first half of 1964 to eliminate their threat was undone by the dismantling of the story. The police and Fleet Street almost instantly lost their stomach for the fight. C11's intelligence-gathering operation was fatally undermined, the evidence already accumulated now disregarded and, eventually, lost. The prospect of an imminent prosecution was snuffed out. The press, meanwhile, now treated the twins with the utmost delicacy. There were few proprietors prepared to risk the expensive and embarrassing climb down forced upon the *Mirror* owners for going after them. Lew Chester and Cal McCrystal set the tone when they wrote a piece on the brothers – 'The Charitable Life of the Brothers Kray' – for the *Sunday Times* on 9 August 1964.[1] There was scant mention of the protection rackets, the gambling dens, the long firms and the casual violence. Instead, they were reborn as 'two famous sporting twins' – a description that was knowingly lifted and adapted by journalists any time the Krays featured in a story – and philanthropic ones at that.

The rescuing of Boothby had the knock-on effect of empowering the brothers. Ronnie in particular felt a growing sense of untouchability – just look what they had already got away with. His policy of nurturing friends in high places seemed to be paying off handsomely. His feeling of growing power was bolstered by the emerging mythology building around them. Their circle of celebrity associates was larger than ever. Then there were the iconic images taken by David Bailey – whose photography documented the glamour of London in the Swinging Sixties. His Kray pictures featured in the 1964 'Box of Pin-Ups' collection alongside the likes of The Beatles, Mick Jagger, Jean Shrimpton, Terence Stamp, Rudolf Nureyev and Andy Warhol.

The year 1965 was arguably the high point of the Krays' career. Business boomed (they were by then starting to launder money for the American Mafia) and in the public imagination, they occupied a space shared by the great movers and shakers of the day. They also inflicted another notable defeat on the powers of law and order. In July 1964, statements by the Met chief Joseph Simpson rebutting many of the *Sunday Mirror's* allegations had been pivotal in undermining the Boothby story. However, Simpson was a man wary of accusations of neglecting his duty, and so he charged Chief Superintendent Fred Gerrard with keeping an eye on the twins. He, in turn, put Detective Inspector Leonard 'Nipper' Read on the case, who assembled a handpicked team to assist him.

It was an unenviable task. Read soon learned that the Krays always seemed one step ahead. More often than not, when they were linked to a crime there were no witnesses willing to testify, evidence quickly and efficiently disappeared from crime scenes, and alibis were generally impregnable. (Being twins gave the Krays a particular advantage, too. Where a witness might just identify one brother as the culprit of some wrongdoing, their identification evidence commonly fell apart when presented with the other near-identical brother.) For months, Read's pursuit was frustrated. But then his luck seemed to turn. Against all expectations, a club owner was prepared to give evidence that the twins had been demanding money with menaces from him. But two trials, a nobbled jury and a discredited star witness later, the Krays walked free. The case represented the Met's last serious attempt to take them off the streets until 1967. The jubilant brothers topped off 1965 with a wedding, when Reggie married local beauty Frances Shea. David Bailey was the wedding photographer and Boothby sent the happy couple a telegram of congratulation.

But from the heights of that year, the twins quickly embarked on a downward spiral. Ronnie was increasingly troubled by mental health issues, which manifested in periods of depression and paranoia. He did not help himself by drinking excessively and abusing Stematil, the drug he was prescribed for his schizophrenia. Meanwhile, an example of the Krays' dysfunctional relationship with the police came about in 1966. Word reached Ronnie that an Inspector Townsend was offering the twins immunity from arrest for an unlicensed gambling den they were running in a pub, in return for a small weekly consideration. Ronnie met with the police officer, recorded their conversation and sent the cassette to the Director of Public Prosecutions. Townsend was suspended pending a prosecution, at which Kray was asked to testify. This was a step too far for the twin, though, who refused to assist a prosecution and so was duly subpoenaed. Ronnie then went into hiding until the threat of prosecution for failing to appear passed.

As Ronnie's behaviour became more unpredictable, so did Reggie's. His marriage was quickly on the rocks, undermined by several factors including the deep animosity that existed between his wife and his twin. They could not abide each other. Frances made several attempts to take her own life, finally succeeding in June 1967. By that stage, another gangland victim had died at the instigation of the Krays. Having escaped capture for George Cornell's death when none of the eyewitnesses would identify him, in 1966 Ronnie hit on a bizarre scheme to bust Frank 'the Mad Axeman' Mitchell out of Dartmoor Prison. The two had become friends in the 1950s when they were both imprisoned at Wandsworth. Mitchell subsequently earned his nickname for holding a married couple hostage with a hatchet. The Dartmoor escape plan made little sense from the Krays' point of view. However, Ronnie hoped to help publicise Mitchell's grievance that he had not been given a firm release date despite his relatively good behaviour in prison. Moreover, it represented yet another gesture of defiance towards the authorities and might also strengthen the twins' standing in the underworld, which had taken a knock after the brazen killing of Cornell. Reggie was initially unconvinced but Ronnie won him round.

In December 1966, Mitchell was one of a party of prisoners working out on the moors. On the pretence of going to feed some nearby ponies, he made his way to a quiet local road where, as pre-arranged, a car full of Kray associates was waiting for him. Back in London, however, things soon went awry. Mitchell was physically big and operated on the shortest of fuses. Attempts at persuading the newspapers to print letters aimed at enticing the Home Office to consult on a release date failed – the government was understandably unwilling to be seen to negotiate with an escaped violent convict. Meanwhile, Mitchell was unwilling either to hand himself back to the police or to remain holed up in the flat the Krays had provided for him. As he grew increasingly agitated, they introduced a woman into the flat to keep him 'entertained'. He promptly fell in love with her, further complicating matters. Aware that their involvement in his escape had left them in an awkward position, the twins decided to take out the problem at root. Employing members of the Firm and an associate called Freddie Foreman, they arranged for Mitchell to be killed. He was shot in the back of a van supposedly taking him to a new safe house on Christmas Eve, 1966. According to Foreman, his body was dumped in the English Channel.[2]

After Frances's death a few months later, Reggie came under increasing pressure to join his brother in 'making his bones'. In October of 1967, he did so. This time, the victim was Jack 'the Hat' McVitie. His principal crime was to have failed to fulfil a hit commissioned by Ronnie on the twins' former business adviser, Leslie Payne. Ronnie feared Payne intended to give the police evidence of the Firm's crimes, so paid McVitie £500 up front, with the rest to follow once Payne was dispatched. McVitie was lured to a supposed party at a basement flat in Stoke Newington, where both the brothers were waiting for him. A fight broke out, in which Reggie looked to shoot McVitie in the head, only for his gun to jam. He then set about McVitie with a carving knife in a gruesome and frenzied attack witnessed by assorted members of the Firm and their families. The disposal of the body is indicative of the increasing chaos then enshrouding the brothers. McVitie's body was bundled into the back of a car (he was too big to fit in the boot), which shortly afterwards ran out of petrol. Foreman, who at the time was running a pub in Southwark, was again called into action, removing the corpse, binding it in chicken wire and then supposedly driving to the Sussex coast, where McVitie was cast into the sea.[3]

Cornell, McVitie and Mitchell can confidently be tagged as murder victims of the brothers, all killed in the reign of terror unleashed after the Boothby affair. But few doubt there were others slaughtered at their hands. For a long while it was widely believed that Firm stalwart Teddy Smith was another victim. He went missing in 1967, although more recent evidence suggests he escaped to Australia and built a new life for himself.[4] At the time of his disappearance, he and Ronnie were in a dispute with each other over some 'trouble with a boy'.[5] Then there was the mysterious death of Ernie Isaacs, a career criminal gunned down in his own flat in Shoreditch in May 1966. The word on the street was that the brothers had a hand in that one.[6] In other cases, it is harder to separate fact from mythology. The accusation that they were involved in the death of former boxing world champion and Soho club owner Freddie Mills has, for example, been a particularly enduring rumour though the evidence to back it up is scant.[7] Similarly, it is difficult to know what to make of claims by a former cellmate of Ronnie's that he had admitted to having forced Reggie's wife, Frances, to take an overdose.[8] The truth is that an industry has built around such claims, and in many instances the Krays themselves did not necessarily want to shut down the rumours. To be suspected of certain killings can be positively advantageous to those who ply their trade through fear.

One persistent but unverifiable rumour attached to Ronnie is that he once killed a rent boy during a bout of rough sex.[9] Then, in 2002, a former fellow inmate of Reggie's at Parkhurst and Maidstone called Peter Gillett told a Channel 5 documentary team that Reggie had confessed to shooting a young gay boy, overcome with disgust that he had enjoyed sexual relations with him.[10] In the absence of corroborating evidence, however, the evidence of Gillett – who in 2019 was given an eighteen-year sentence for paedophile offences – must be treated with caution.[11]

There is, though, another source – an associate of the Krays on the outside – who alleged that Ronnie was responsible for the death of a male sex worker. In his 2006 book, *Getting Away with Murder*, Lenny Hamilton alleged that there were in fact seven murder victims in all. He also claimed that a London-based Polish scrap metal dealer used his smelter to dispose of the remains in several cases. For a while, Hamilton – a jewel thief and safebreaker – enjoyed the twins' favour after he intervened in a dispute they had with a police officer attempting to arrest them. Over the years, they had a number of friends in common too. But the relationship went through its ups and downs, the lowest of which saw Ronnie brand Hamilton's face with hot steel for a perceived slight.

Hamilton would give evidence against the Krays at their trial in 1969 and repeatedly went on the record to criticise their antics and the hero worship they incited. According to his book, several times Ronnie paid for the services of a West End rent boy before concluding that he was in love with him. Kray, Hamilton said, bought the lad clothing and jewellery, as well as paying for a flat for him. However, he subsequently heard rumours that the boy was cheating on him. Ronnie took him to his caravan at Steeple Bay in Essex, accompanied by Reggie and a driver. Ronnie knocked back several gin and tonics on the journey and grew progressively more abusive – verbally and physically – towards the lad. Once they arrived at the caravan, Ronnie strangled him as the driver looked on. According to Hamilton, the corpse was then wrapped in bedsheets and driven back to London for disposal.[12]

Hamilton died in 2014 and there is little prospect of verifying his story now. It does nonetheless support the notion that the Krays became, for a while at least, an uncontrollable force; purveyors of extreme violence unanswerable for their actions; savage creatures who used the friendships of celebrities and leveraged the secrets of influential public figures to legitimise their brutality. It was all achieved with relative ease in the aftermath of the Boothby affair, when those who should have been scrutinising them felt it safer to leave them alone. And what was the cost? We can say with assuredness that at least three lives were ended, collateral damage to the twins' quest for wealth and power. In all probability, the figure was much higher and that takes no account of the many more who kept their lives but suffered at their hands in other ways – including as victims of sexual violence.

It was only due to the persistence of Nipper Read and his team, alongside a growing feeling among their associates that the Kray juggernaut was now out of control, that the brothers were arrested in May 1968. (Ronnie was in bed with a youth when he was apprehended.) The previous year, Read had been granted another go at bringing in the twins after a long hiatus. The failure of the 1965 money-with-menaces trial had ended all Scotland Yard interest in the pair in the meantime. Read discovered that there were no police files on them whatsoever in the period between the trial's collapse and his resumption of investigations. Nonetheless, he was able to gather sufficient evidence to ensure that the Krays finally went on trial again in 1969. After thirty-nine days, they were convicted of the murders of Cornell and McVitie, the prosecution relying heavily on the evidence of Firm members. A further trial, this time for the killing of Mitchell, began a few days later but was doomed to failure after the judge condemned the main witness – long-time Kray associate Albert Donoghue – as 'tainted'. In terms of the twins' own long-term prospects, the verdict on that occasion hardly mattered. They had already each been given life sentences for Cornell and McVitie's deaths, to include thirty years without parole – a record sentence for murder at the Old Bailey.

According to Norman Lucas, Kray claimed the police had been hostile to him ever since he was linked to 'a distinguished national servant' in 1964. 'It was a scandalous matter,' Kray said. 'The well-known person got £40,000 and all I got was an apology from a daily newspaper ... Most newspapers have been hostile and the police have been after me ever since the scandal and that is why I am here today.'[13] In truth, though, the Boothby saga was less a drag upon them and more of a boon to the Krays. Had the Establishment not prioritised its self-protection in July 1964, London might have been saved those years of the twins' orchestrated mayhem, preserving an indefinite number of lives in the process.

20

Compromised

For Boothby, the *Sunday Mirror*'s apology and pay-off were at once a vindication and an albatross around his neck. Not least because he had what Ronnie Kray now wanted. And Boothby was only too aware that Ronnie was not a man used to being refused what he desired.

When the 'Peer and the Gangster' story broke, Kray was deeply unhappy to find himself implicated and nervous of wider exposure. When Bernard Black started touting photographs to the *Sunday Mirror*, his ire grew. Black was ordered to go back to the newspaper's offices and tell them they couldn't print the picture because of copyright problems. The following day, a High Court injunction was enacted, hence the famous 'Picture We Must Not Print' headline the following weekend. By the time *Stern* had unmasked Boothby and he, in turn, had his denial of wrongdoing published in *The Times*, Kray decided it was time for action. If his name was to be splashed across the press in such circumstances, he ought to at least get something out of it. So, he struck a deal with the *Express*, which published a photo of Boothby and Kray on a sofa in Boothby's apartment. In return, Kray received £100 – little more than pocket money.

When Boothby then got his £40,000, Kray was determined to share the spoils. It has never been conclusively established how Boothby used his money – he variously claimed to have spent some on property and to have given much of it away to charitable causes – but there is little doubt that several thousand found its way into the Kray coffers.

Leslie Holt was another who was not particularly pleased by the turn of events that summer. MI5 documents reveal that towards the end of August 1964, Holt was 'excessively angry' after Boothby sacked him as his chauffeur by means of a curt letter. Holt apparently told the MI5 source that Boothby had promised him £2,000 from his award but so far he'd received none of it (although the security files state that Holt was in possession of a Jaguar and a Ferrari believed to have been paid for by Boothby). Holt was also said to be 'determined to blow the story in the Press'.[1] By the middle of October, he'd received a £200 payment from Boothby, who, the MI5 source said, had got Ronnie Kray to threaten Holt against saying or doing anything against Boothby.[2]

Boothby could hardly refuse Ronnie or Holt. He knew that either could blow apart his claims of innocence in an instant. Whether or not there was any truly compromising evidence of his wrongdoing (something Boothby could not be sure of), he had hardly been cautious in being seen in their company. Having gone public with a declaration that he had only met Kray a couple of times in 1964 on matters of business, he had put himself at the mercy of countless individuals who might testify that he had known Kray socially since at least 1963. According to Maureen Flanagan – who in her youth was a glamour model known as Flanagan, as well as Violet Kray's hairdresser – Boothby even visited the family home in Vallance Road. Violet would remember him as a 'funny old man with a bow tie'.[3] Members of the Firm, meanwhile, referred to him among themselves as 'the Queen Mother'.[4] He had also taken Kray to lunch at the House of Lords and then to his beloved club, White's, if anyone was interested in checking.[5] There were photos too, of Boothby, Kray and associates at Kray's favourite Society Club, and correspondence, innocent enough in nature, but which nonetheless revealed a pre-existing friendship. For example, a note dated 6 June 1963, addressed to 'Mr Kray' and written on notepaper adorned with Boothby's address, read:

> Thank you for your post-card. I very nearly went to Jersey myself, as I have never been there, and hear from so many people that it is quite delightful.
>
> If you are free tomorrow evening (Friday), between six and seven, do come round for a drink and a chat.
>
> Ever sincerely, Boothby

Boothby may have seen off the immediate threat from the *Mirror* papers, but now he was at the mercy of more malevolent forces. The first challenge he faced was persuading Kray not to sue the newspapers in his own right. Having navigated his way to an outrageous victory at the Mirror Building, the last thing Boothby wanted was for the matter to be immediately raked up again. Yet, on Wednesday, 12 August 1964 – less than a week after Cecil King's apology was published – the *Daily Express* reported intelligence that solicitors had received instructions from Ronnie to launch a libel action against the IPC.[6]

In response, Boothby put down a series of notes on a sheet of House of Lords paper. The document laid out the reasons why he believed Kray should reconsider issuing a writ:

(1) The apology signed by Cecil King is without parallel in the history of Fleet Street. In view of the fact that R.K. and myself were both mentioned in 'The People', and that our photograph appeared together in the 'Daily Express' (joint circulation 10 million), it clearly covers both him and myself.

  No separate apology that he could ever ask for would be anything like as good; and the risk is that they might drag up everything against him in his past.

(2) He has had an extremely good press, particularly in the 'Sunday Times', which referred at length to his charitable work. Why spoil it?

(3) The whole thing is now dead. If he brings an action, it will all be revived again next year. What is the point of this?

(4) As of this moment, both R.K. and myself have emerged from this incident with flying colours, and to the entire satisfaction of the country as a whole. Scotland Yard are happy about it, and no-one wants any more muck-raking. In fact this thing has done far more good to R.K. than myself. There is, at this moment, no stain on his character. Why spoil it all by running the risk of putting one there. The Mirror newspapers are prepared to call it a day; and it is a good one for both of us.[7]

The document raises several points of interest, notably how Boothby knew 'Scotland Yard was happy' and what it was happy about. To hold off further enquiries? It is an extraordinary claim, but further evidences the suspicion that Scotland Yard had not acquitted itself with particular credit in this instance. Whether Boothby's jotted notes were intended to serve as an aide-memoire to himself or perhaps the basis of a note to or conversation with Kray is unknown, but they are indicative of the anxiety he was already suffering in the face of Kray's unpredictability. That the gangster did not proceed with his libel action might perhaps have been the result of Boothby's powers of persuasion or, more likely, because he was provided with a share of the money Boothby had received. It helped, too, that on 19 September the *Daily Mirror* extended the apology previously granted to Boothby alone:

> Although neither the Sunday Mirror nor the Daily Mirror mentioned the name of either party to this alleged relationship, other newspapers did, with the result that on August 6 we acknowledged that what we had reported was wrong, and apologised to the peer concerned. We now wish to apologise to Mr Ronald Kray whom some people identified as the other person concerned, and to state that the allegations contained in our reports were without foundation. We express our regret to Mr Ronald Kray for the embarrassment and distress our reports caused to him.[8]

But by no means was Boothby off the hook.

Another test of nerve came towards the end of 1964. In October, Kray travelled to the US for business but was denied entry on arrival in New York, despite having been granted a visa by the US Embassy in London. Presumably, his reputation had gone before him across the Atlantic Ocean. He was sent back to Britain on the next available flight, whereupon he contacted Boothby to let him know his displeasure at what had transpired. He also complained about police harassment in London. There is no record as to Kray's demeanour as he ran through his complaints with Boothby. However, in early December – by which time the politician was enjoying some medicinal sunshine – there was a letter sent from Barbados's Miramar Beach Hotel to Ronnie from Boothby's long-serving manservant, Gordon Goodfellow. The content illustrates Boothby's desire to be seen as doing everything possible for Kray, who was clearly bringing pressure to bear:

I have just got your letter to L.B. [Lord Boothby] … We are both very distressed that you should feel this way. I have spoken to L.B. and he says that no living man could have done more for you than he has done.

As regards the American visa, he made several representations to the Ambassador, who undertook to look into the matter himself. He has spoken on your behalf to the Chief Commissioner of the Metropolitan Police, and to Chief Inspector Gerrard, who took down the statement he made, in the course of which he said he had found you perfectly straight-forward in any dealing he had had with you and that he firmly believed you were now successfully engaged in business which was absolutely legitimate. L.B. further said that he had reason to believe that the police were 'hounding' you without justification; and Chief Inspector Gerrard included this in the statement which he took down.

He was also instrumental in getting an apology to you from the Editors of the Daily Mirror, with whom he discussed the matter. Finally, L.B. went to much trouble, just before he left, to put Mr Thomas in touch with the right people regarding the ships he wished to buy from the Admiralty, in the belief that you were associated with this project.

He has asked me to say that, for his part, he has no feelings other than those of regard for you; but that, although he can bring such influence as he has to bear, he has of course no control over the actions either of the American Embassy or Scotland Yard. He is, however, a great friend of the Editor of *The Times*, and, if there is any further trouble from this quarter, he will be glad to do what he can when he gets back.[9]

The Establishment had conspired to protect Boothby, and he in turn was exercising his Establishment contacts for all they were worth in Kray's interest. In a single letter, there is evidence that Boothby pressurised an ambassador, police chiefs and a Fleet Street newspaper to appease the gangster, while also offering to leverage a friendship with the editor of the national newspaper of record to the same end. On top of that, he also seems to have sought to assist a suspected Kray contact in the business of procuring warships from the Admiralty – with gun- or drug-running the likely intention.[10] And still Kray demanded more.

Early 1965 witnessed what was surely Boothby's post-Kray scandal low point. The previous year, the son of a baronet called Hew McCowan had bought a Soho club called the Hideaway. McCowan seemingly agreed to a business proposition from the twins that they provide protection in return for a cut of the business, but he quickly decided to back out of the deal. At that stage, he received a visit from the twins' henchman Teddy Smith, who caused damage to the club's interior and generally struck the fear of God into the club owner. McCowan subsequently went to the police and on 6 January 1965, the brothers were arrested. The following day they were remanded into custody on charges of demanding money with menaces. Inspector Gerrard executed their arrests and called for bail to be denied for fear that they would seek to intimidate witnesses. A further bail application to the more senior Divisional Court was also rejected.

On 9 February 1965, Goodfellow wrote to the twins' parents on behalf of Boothby to thank them for the birthday wishes they had sent him. Goodfellow also mentioned the 'unfairness of this treatment of the twins', concluding, 'let's hope all will be well in the end'. Meanwhile, Charlie Kray was keeping up the pressure on Boothby on his brothers' behalf. Two days later, Boothby made an unprecedented intercession in the House of Lords. He tabled a question asking whether it was the government's intention to keep the twins in custody for an indefinite period without trial. Much of the House was appalled, the memories of the previous summer's near scandal still fresh in their minds. Lord Stonham, Under Secretary at the Home Office, explained the matter was not one over which the Home Secretary had any jurisdiction and that the courts' decisions on bail were perfectly legal.

Sensing the climate was against him, Boothby added: 'I would only like to say that I hold no brief at all for the Kray brothers, one of whom I have never met, and the other only twice in my life last July. But I am on the record as having fought continuously ...'

Shouts of 'Order! Order' drowned him out from all sides but Boothby was not to be silenced. 'But I am on the record as having fought continuously ... I am going to ask the Lord Chancellor a question. I am not interested in the activities of the Home Office, which have been characteristic in this case and have done infinite damage to the reputation of this country ...'

More shouts of 'Order! Order!' Boothby carried on. 'My Lords, I am going to ask the Lord Chancellor a direct question. It is this: will he take a sharp and a hard look at our system in Scotland, where the procurators fiscal act under the directions of the Lord Advocate and where this kind of situation could not possibly arise?'[11]

The former Lord Chancellor, Viscount Dilhorne, noted that the matter was still *sub judice*, and the Liberal leader, Lord Rea, protested that 'the question was not in the traditions of the House, and is therefore to be regretted'.[12] Boothby nonetheless continued to defend his position. 'If this kind of question is not allowed to be put on this kind of occasion in one or other House of Parliament, then we might as well pack up and go home.' Even Lord Longford, a noted advocate of penal reform who would in due course attract much criticism for his friendship with Myra Hindley, considered that, 'I think the noble Lord will regret that intervention when he reads it in cold blood.'[13]

It was an abject humiliation for Boothby, who had given the impression of being merely a lackey for the Krays. It must also have been an intensely uncomfortable episode for the Lord Chancellor, who by then was Gerald Gardiner – a man well versed in the complex nature of Boothby's association with the brothers. He heard a bail application from their lawyers the following day – in a landmark case – but rejected their appeal.

The first Hideaway trial ended the following month with a hung jury, a key prosecution witness changing his story late on. It has been strongly rumoured that Boothby's *Sunday Mirror* pay-out significantly contributed to the defence fund. A second trial later in the same month saw the twins acquitted after McCowan received a thorough going-over on the witness stand. It transpired that he had previously made three allegations of blackmail against other defendants and that he had also broken the terms of his probation following a conviction for sodomy in 1953. His credibility shot to pieces, a 'not guilty' verdict was virtually inevitable. On 5 April the newly free twins made their way from court to Vallance Road as returning heroes, a crowd of family, friends, the press and general well-wishers gathering to greet them.

Boothby sent a congratulatory note, in which he talked about the hard time he had received for petitioning the Lords in their interest. To the press, he said: 'I'm delighted. I'll go on fighting to make sure that no one is kept in prison without a quick trial. It is a matter of principle.'[14] Then a few days later, he wrote to Ronnie on House of Lords paper. 'It may interest, and encourage, you to know,' he said, 'that I have had a great many letters congratulating me on the stand I took in the House of Lords on your behalf; and that some of their Lordships are now a bit ashamed of the treatment they gave me.' He also enclosed a poem that 'shows what I believe to be the general feeling', urging that Kray tear it up once he had read it. The note finished: 'I think that they will now leave you alone. And you can never say that I haven't done my best! Don't bother to answer this. Yours ever, Bob B.'[15]

Boothby continued to socialise with the Krays. After wriggling free of the McCowan charges, the twins took control of the Hideaway and renamed it El Morocco. Brian Stratton, an ex-convict, recalled seeing Kray and Boothby in there one night with two boys. Boothby went outside with one of them but could soon be heard calling for Ronnie. The boy, it turned out, didn't want to go home with Boothby but Kray told him that if he did not or if he refused to do whatever Boothby wanted, he would be hurt.[16]

All the while, 'the Queen Mother' might be called into service at any moment. In 1967, according to the Teale brothers, he was responsible for providing a reference for their mother to take up a job as housekeeper to Lord Claud and Lady Violet Hamilton, with whom he was acquainted. A little after Mrs Teale had started working at their home in Russell Court, SW1, not far from St James's Palace, Leslie Holt and Charlie Kray allegedly forced their way past her one evening and burgled the property, taking valuables worth several thousand pounds.[17] It seemed like Boothby's stint in servitude to the Krays might never end. And then, in 1969, it appeared like it had. Yet even as Ronnie Kray stood in the dock facing a double murder charge, Boothby's abasement was not yet quite complete. In a throwaway aside as he gave evidence, Kray commented: 'If I wasn't here I could be having tea with Judy Garland, or having a drink with Lord Boothby.'[18] But the judge, Mr Justice Melford Stevenson, was quick to shut down that particular line of testimony. When the twins were found guilty of the murders and Melford Stevenson passed record sentences on both, he said: 'In my view, society has earned a rest from your activities.'[19] Boothby doubtless felt that he had, too.

Just like Boothby, Driberg found himself burdened with vassal status where it came to the twins. Moreover, their demand for political favours did not cease with their imprisonment. Driberg's correspondence bears witness to the hold they still maintained. When the brothers called, Driberg was quick to respond. In one letter, for example, Ronnie thanked him for journeying such a long distance to visit them, especially since he had a bad foot at the time. There was also a series of missives sent by Ronnie after learning that he needed to submit a list of prospective visitors for prison approval. On 2 August 1969, he wrote to complain 'about the bureaucratic and humiliating procedure my friends will have to undergo in future … I hope you will be able to help me in this matter.' A few weeks later, Driberg received a response from the Home Office to say it was not in the public interest to change the policy. Then in November 1969, Shirley Williams wrote to him in her role as Minister of State for Home Affairs, turning down his request on the twins' behalf that they should be allowed to serve their sentences in the same prison or at least be reunited periodically.

The following year, Driberg received a letter from one Cheryl Huskin, a 19-year-old with an interest in criminology who had struck up a correspondence with Ronnie after he was imprisoned. Much to the disappointment of them both, she was now being prevented from visiting him on the grounds that there was no prior relationship. Violet Kray had also written to Driberg on the same subject. Driberg promised to appeal to the Home Secretary, Reginald Maudling, which he duly did. When Mark Carlisle, the Under-Secretary of State for Home Affairs, replied on Maudling's behalf to refuse Huskin access, Driberg let her know the bad news: 'I am very sorry to send you the enclosed unsatisfactory reply from Westminster …' He then told Carlisle that the decision was both 'absurd and unfair' and could be interpreted as 'arbitrary caprice'.[20] There was another letter to Carlisle a few months later after a visit to Parkhurst where he found Reggie in low spirits. 'Whatever the Krays [*sic*] misdeeds may have been,' he argued, 'and they were indeed appalling ones, they are in prison for a very long time, and should surely not be discriminated against in comparison with other prisoners …'[21]

Clearly, Driberg felt compelled to make representations on the twins' behalf, to be seen to be working in their best interests. The deferential tone he generally adopted points to his determination to keep on their right side, too. But in October 1970, he wrote a letter to the journalist Bernard Levin that encapsulated his predicament – the obligation he felt to do their bidding against his desire to be free of their shadow. Levin had recently published a book called *The Pendulum Years: Britain in the Sixties*, in which he examined the pull of the past versus the pull of the future in the decade just gone. Within its pages was reproduced a photo of Driberg in the company of the Krays, an image originally printed in the *Daily Mail*. Driberg began by praising Levin for the book, then continued:

> ... I am less gratified by the linking of myself with the Krays on p. 384. I cannot altogether blame you for this, since I took no action when the *Mail* – monstrously, as I think – published that photograph without checking with me on the circumstances in which it was taken. I should probably have sued, and may consider having to do so if others, less innocent (in the context) than you, continue to assume that the photograph implied that I was a close friend of the Krays. This is at least as untrue as it was of the photograph in respect of which Bob Boothby got £40,000 from the *Mirror*. (Incidentally, he could confirm that I warned him against the Krays.)

He then gave a detailed account of how he had come to know the brothers. It had been Joan Littlewood, he explained, who introduced him to them: 'One evening I met her in the east end, and she took me to the Krays' club there; we spent perhaps half-an-hour in the club, observing some remarkable fauns among the brothers and their hangers-on.' A few months later, she invited him to meet her at a party the Krays were giving at an East End dancehall before going for a meal in Limehouse. However, Littlewood turned up late so Driberg spent an hour on his own at the party. He claimed to find it an 'an embarrassing and boring experience' but 'because of the one previous meeting at their club, was recognised (as "Joan's mate – the MP"); knew nobody else there; but at one point while waiting was pressed into being photographed in that group. I agreed most reluctantly, but my excuses were not accepted and, even at a party given by villains, it is difficult to insist on such a refusal without seeming, among other things, snobbish.'

It was all rather redolent of Boothby's own narrative concerning the incriminating photo he was too polite to decline at Eaton Square. Also in common with Boothby, Driberg's tale was largely fictitious. As he told Levin:

> The incident may carry the moral that – one in 'public life' – perhaps not even a journalist – should ever associate, even fleetingly, with criminals or potential convicts. The fact remains that I was not an intimate of the Krays. Indeed, I would never have been in that photograph if Joan had been punctual.

While wisely declining to initiate an action against Levin, he did nonetheless request that any reprints of the book should carry a note to the effect that he was: 'All entirely ignorant of the nature of the Krays.' 'Sorry to bother you with this,' he concluded, 'but, in case of any future trouble, I want to get on record exactly how the thing happened – so that it can't be said that I didn't ever object to being bracketed with the Krays.' Whether the ink had dried on this letter before he was dashing another off to the Home Office on the twins' behalf must remain a matter for speculation.[22]

Boothby (and Driberg) may have executed an escape of Houdini-esque proportions in July 1964, but the contortions required to effect it ultimately condemned them to a life sentence of indebtedness to the Krays.

21

Aftermath

In 1971, John Pearson was ready to publish his landmark book on the Krays. He had been asked by the twins a few years earlier to chronicle their lives but what he produced was no hagiography. Instead, he wrote as honest and unflinching an account of their brutal lives as there has ever been. But the genesis of that book would itself become part of the Kray mythology.

After the brothers were imprisoned in 1969, their mother, Violet, gave Pearson a suitcase which she hoped might be useful for his research. Inside were some photographs, an inscribed book and several notes from Boothby to Ronnie Kray. There was nothing much incriminating about the contents of the letters, except for one detail. Some of them dated from 1963. Pearson immediately realised the implications. When Boothby insisted to the world that he had only met Kray in 1964, and then merely to discuss business, he had been lying. Key grounds for his successful challenge to the *Mirror* newspapers were instantly discredited.

Pearson included the evidence in his manuscript. The book was scheduled for a big launch and *The Observer* newspaper paid a hefty sum for serialisation rights. Then Pearson's world fell apart. His literary agent called to tell him that his publisher had been contacted by Arnold Goodman, who warned them that the book was libellous. As a result, they had decided to halt publication. *The Observer*, too, withdrew its offer. Goodman, it just so happened, was chairman of the *Observer* trustees at the time. Then Pearson went on holiday, only to find on his return that he had been burgled. The material that Violet Kray passed to him had mysteriously disappeared. Around the same time, his agent's office was also turned over. Pearson was sure that there were powerful forces at work.[1]

Having devoted years of his career to completing the book, he found himself on the point of ruin. Fortunately, though, a rival publisher swept in at the last moment, agreeing to publish the book as long as all references to the Boothby saga were edited out. Even without that incendiary content, it became a bestseller and, reputedly, the most widely borrowed book from prison libraries for years to come. But to Pearson's enduring anger, his book became part of a whitewash of 'the Peer and the Gangster scandal' that lasted well over twenty years.

Boothby's memoirs made no mention of the episode, nor did those of Tom Driberg, Arnold Goodman, Cecil King or Hugh Cudlipp. It was not present in the biography of Gerald Gardiner written by his wife, or in the official biographies of Alec Douglas-Home, Harold Wilson or Jim Callaghan. It was only after Boothby's death in 1986 – and the consequent end of the risk of libel – that Pearson was able to go public with his evidence of Boothby's deceit. The true nature of the peer's relationship with the gangster emerged in a drip feed of intelligence over many more years, culminating with the release of MI5 files covering the scandal in 2015. There may yet be more revelations to come.

Even after Boothby's death, commentators have tended to treat the saga with a degree of levity when not dismissing it altogether. With larger-than-life figures like the twins, Boothby and Driberg, there was the temptation to see it as some sort of Orton-esque farce in which there were no real victims. Meanwhile, Boothby's official biographer after his death, Robert Rhodes James, portrayed the incident as a great calumny. Boothby was a victim of Fleet Street's post-Profumo 'fevered atmosphere'. Boothby, we are told, at least found it within himself to laugh about it in later years. 'Yet astonishingly and lamentably, some of the mud stuck, and years later one still finds people linking Boothby's name with that of the infamous Krays.'[2] Then, in 2005, there was an article in the *Conservative History Journal*, the official publication of the Conservative History Group. Under the headline, 'Rum, Buggery and the Lash: The truth about my hero, Lord Boothby', Ronald Porter confidently asserted that Boothby was 'never blackmailed by the Krays on account of his sexual flings with lads supplied to him by the Krays'.[3]

Such was the veil drawn over the scandal for decades that most of those involved saw out the rest of their lives virtually without being impacted by it. Arguably, among those public figures mixed up in it, the scandal was to the long-term detriment of only Boothby and Driberg, both forced to maintain a fiction and, for years afterwards, in hock to the Krays. The Krays themselves were, conversely, beneficiaries. But there are also the untold victims of that whitewash – those who directly fell prey to the twins as they enjoyed their period of untouchability, and the many more caught up in the ripples that spread far and wide from the Krays' reign of terror.

Let us begin, though, with the fates of the three Prime Ministers directly implicated in the cover-up: Douglas-Home, Wilson and Callaghan. The rest of Douglas-Home's term was relatively uneventful after that flurry of drama in July 1964. He seemed to have steadied the Conservative ship just as Macmillan had hoped he would when he recommended him to the Queen as his Downing Street successor. That year's general election was expected to be a cake walk for Labour in the weeks leading up to it, but in the end it turned into a remarkably close contest, with Labour claiming only a four-seat majority. Douglas Hurd, who served as Home and Foreign Secretary under Margaret Thatcher and John Major, wrote Douglas-Home's entry for the *Oxford Dictionary of National Biography*. His assessment inadvertently captures the completeness of the Boothby blackout:

> During his premiership Home had gradually asserted himself as an honourable leader, albeit in an unfashionable tradition. The poisons of 1963 slowly drained out of British political life in 1964, making possible a straightforward election with no backdrop of scandal or what was later called sleaze.[4]

In opposition, Douglas-Home soon grew weary of his obligations as party leader and stood down in the middle of 1965. He did, however, remain as shadow Foreign Secretary and became Foreign Secretary proper after Ted Heath's election victory in 1970. But when Heath lost the 1974 election, Douglas-Home called time on his own career, accepting a life peerage and returning to the House of Lords (which he had left in order to become Prime Minister). He died of bronchopneumonia on 9 October 1995, at the age of 92. According to a private memo that Macmillan wrote but never sent to the Queen back in 1963, he was 'clearly a man who represents the old governing class at its best ...'

After coming to power in the October of 1964, Harold Wilson enjoyed a dynamic first eighteen months despite the frailty of his majority. His media management was exceptional and he retained a high level of personal popularity even as he juggled an economy on the point of a currency deval-uation. He called a new election in March 1966 in a bid to strengthen his political hand, winning a majority this time of some ninety-seven seats. But he could stave off the prospect of devaluation no longer, an act that was fol-lowed in short order by a disastrous set of local election results in the spring of 1968. It was around this time that Cecil King spearheaded his campaign against him. Despite, or perhaps because of, these various setbacks, Wilson's tenure gained momentum as another general election approached. The Prime Minister was increasingly seen as a survivor, winning respect from large parts of the electorate for his ability to bounce back. So, it came as a moderate surprise when Heath defeated him in 1970. But Wilson was back again in February 1974, at the head of a minority government cast against the backdrop of the international oil crisis, domestic strikes, power cuts and the three-day week. An attempt to consolidate power with a new election in the October was only partially successful, bringing a majority of just three seats. By now, Wilson was also increasingly paranoid that there were conspiracies afoot against him, with the intelligence services a particular focus of his suspicion.

He stood down as Prime Minister in April 1976, becoming that rarest of things – a premier who determined his own Downing Street exit rather than being pushed out of the door. However, his resignation honours list left a bitter taste. The 'Lavender List', as it came to be known (the original draft was supposedly written on lavender-coloured notepaper) included a number of controversial figures seemingly included more for their financial clout than their closeness to the Labour agenda. Marcia Williams (Arnold Goodman's old nemesis and perhaps Wilson's Achilles' heel too) is widely held to have had a significant influence on deciding who was included.

Williams herself was given a life peerage in 1974 to become Lady Falkender. Wilson retired from the House of Commons at the general election of 1983, subsequently taking the title of Baron Wilson of Rievaulx, and died at St Thomas's Hospital in London on 23 May 1995.

Wilson's replacement as Prime Minister was Jim Callaghan, Driberg's alleged 'Mr Fixit'. On entering No. 10, he became the first man to hold all of the four great offices of state – Home Secretary, Foreign Secretary, Chancellor of the Exchequer and Prime Minister. His was a troubled premiership though, culminating in the freezing 'Winter of Discontent' of 1978/79 when widespread public strikes threatened to bring the country to its knees. At the general election of 1979, the Conservatives under Margaret Thatcher won a landslide. Callaghan stood down as Labour leader in 1980 and as an MP seven years later, when he went to the Lords as Baron Callaghan of Cardiff. He died on 26 March 2005, his ashes scattered around the base of the Peter Pan statue at the entrance to London's Great Ormond Street Hospital for children.

Henry Brooke, the Home Secretary who had the misfortune to find himself contending with the Vassall, Profumo and Boothby scandals, left office after the Conservative electoral defeat in 1964. His lack of personal popularity told, and he lost his Hampstead seat at the 1966 election. He did, however, receive a life peerage and held the title Lord Brooke of Cumnor until his death on 29 March 1984.

As for Harold Macmillan, he stood down as an MP at the October 1964 election and turned down the earldom that was customary for former Prime Ministers. Lady Dorothy died from a heart attack at Birch Grove, the Macmillans' East Sussex estate, two years later. Boothby remained her intimate until the end. By then, he had already burnt some seven hundred letters he had received from her over the years – an act that upset her greatly, as she considered he had no right to destroy '*my* letters'. She, on the other hand, kept his correspondence in the family home. Macmillan discovered them after her death and, without reading them, decided that the stash should not be left to posterity. There were too many to burn in his fireplace, so he lit an incinerator in Birch Grove's gardens one windy day. He was ill-equipped for the job and soon found himself chasing charred fragments as they blew across the lawn. It was a scene he subsequently recounted to

Boothby. 'And so it all ended,' he concluded. Boothby was quiet for a while, then concurred: 'And so it all ended.'[5]

Macmillan's retirement from the political scene did not mark a retreat from work altogether. He was a hands-on chancellor of the University of Oxford and took a great interest in his family's publishing business, of which he was for a time chairman. He published his own diaries and memoirs through the Macmillan company. Then, on the occasion of his 90th birthday in 1984, he at last took his earldom, becoming the Earl of Stockton (his original parliamentary constituency). He was an active member of the Lords until his death at home on 29 December 1986. He is buried next to Dorothy and their daughter, Sarah. She had committed suicide in 1970, her life blighted by alcoholism, the question of her paternity never fully resolved.

Arnold Goodman went from strength to strength for years after his intervention in the Boothby business. He was a chairman of the Arts Council of Great Britain, during which time he also took up Lord Astor's invitation to take the chairmanship of the trustees of *The Observer* (much to John Pearson's chagrin). For three years in the 1970s he was additionally chairman of the Newspaper Publishers' Association, and also became Master of University College, Oxford. All the while, he maintained his successful legal practice, Goodman Derrick, specialising in media and libel law. Politically, Wilson kept him close throughout the 1960s and during the period of opposition in the '70s. He was even dispatched to Rhodesia for secret negotiations with the country's controversial leader, Ian Smith.

Goodman became, in the words of his biographer Brian Brivati, 'the Establishment's lawyer'.[6] As Goodman himself observed: 'Public prominence should not place you at any advantage over the rest of mankind, but it is a craven society where it is allowed to place you at a disadvantage.'[7] It was little surprise, then, when he became involved in the next great British political sex scandal after Boothby: the trial in 1979 of former Liberal leader Jeremy Thorpe for incitement and conspiracy to murder his former lover, Norman Scott.

Goodman and Thorpe went back a long way. In 1957 Goodman had advised him on an issue of libel unrelated to the Scott affair. Thorpe and Scott met sometime in 1961 and their sexual relationship did not last long.

The politician initially tried to help Scott find employment but as time passed, Scott grew resentful of him and blamed him for a number of personal setbacks. He repeatedly suggested he would make public their affair if Thorpe would not help him further, and Thorpe grew increasingly concerned about the threat he posed. He engaged his friend, a fellow MP called Peter Bessell, to try to smooth things over – including a plan to help set him up in work abroad – but with little success. By 1967, Thorpe called on Goodman to send Scott a letter threatening that he might be charged with blackmail. Goodman, however, warned against the strategy, arguing that a successful prosecution was unlikely and that should Thorpe duly decide not to pursue one, it might be regarded as a sign of guilt to the wider world.

Thorpe consulted Goodman several times on the issue over the next decade. There was a new sense of urgency when Scott unsuccessfully attempted to sell incriminating letters to the *Sunday Mirror* in 1974. Then, in March 1976, Scott used an appearance at Barnstaple Magistrates Court in Devon – he was up on charges of social security fraud – to repeat allegations that Thorpe had converted him to homosexuality and then taken his national security card so that he could not earn a living, thus ruining his life.

News of Scott's outburst in the courtroom reached Thorpe while he was at Goodman's office to discuss another matter. Goodman was all for Thorpe issuing a broad denial but the increasingly desperate Liberal leader felt the time had come for more direct action. He wrote a piece for the *Sunday Times* under the headline: 'The Lies of Norman Scott'. The tactic seemed to work, especially when Harold Wilson went on record with his belief that Thorpe was the victim of a smear campaign by South Africa's secret services (an eccentric conspiracy theory that was quickly debunked). Wilson's intervention was also a staging post in his increasingly cool relations with Goodman, who was appalled that the Prime Minister had voiced such opinions.

By now, two investigative journalists – Barrie Penrose and Roger Courtiour – were on the case, and gradually unpicking Thorpe's extravagant web of lies. Then, in May 1976, Scott sued the Metropolitan Police for the return of some letters that he claimed proved his relationship with Thorpe and which he had lodged with them back in 1962. Goodman again swung into action. He wrote to the police to demand the letters be returned to

Thorpe instead, claiming that as their author they were rightfully his. The police refused the request but agreed to send Goodman copies in advance of returning them to Scott. Goodman concluded that a pre-emptive strike was now in Thorpe's best interests. He negotiated a deal with the *Sunday Times* to publish extracts on condition that the general tone of the piece be sympathetic to Thorpe.

The scheme singularly failed, however. One of the letters referred to Scott as 'Bunnies' and confirmed for much of the country that there was something to Scott's claims. Thorpe resigned as the Liberal Party leader but the saga was by no means finished. In August 1978 he was charged in relation to an alleged murder attempt on Scott in 1975 – a bungled attempt to shoot the victim on a dark Dartmoor road that instead resulted in the death of only his dog. Thorpe's old friend, Bessell, was to be the crown's star witness. Having assisted with a campaign to discredit Bessell in advance of his evidence, Goodman then withdrew so that the highly experienced criminal lawyer, David Napley, could represent the politician.

Much to Thorpe's dismay, reporting restrictions were lifted on the proceedings. It also proved to be to Goodman's disadvantage, too. When Bessell gave evidence, he cited a meeting he had had with one of the co-accused, David Holmes, in 1976. Bessell said Holmes told him that Thorpe had met Goodman, who'd agreed that Scott was dangerous and must be prevented from mentioning Thorpe's name when he appeared at Barnstaple court. Bessell continued that he was also told Goodman had suggested to Thorpe that Bessell write a confidential letter to Scott's solicitor alleging that Scott had previously attempted to blackmail him (Bessell) as well as Thorpe. Goodman would then tell the solicitor that if Scott did not mention Thorpe in court, no further action would be taken. However, if Scott did mention him, Bessell would swear an affidavit and Scott would likely face a prison sentence.

Bessell's evidence was widely reported, with the implication that Goodman was the puppet master of another cover-up. Goodman was furious and gave the *Telegraph* an interview. The newspaper took his side, describing him as 'a sane man, of blameless reputation' and concluding that the advice he had provided to Thorpe 'did not remotely relate to those matters discussed in court so far'.[8] That claim was simply not true. He had provided advice for several years that directly impacted on those court proceedings. Thorpe was ultimately acquitted following one of the most wildly unbalanced judicial summings-up ever seen in a British courtroom ('He is a crook, a fraud, a sponger, a whiner and a parasite,' the judge said of Scott. 'But of course, he could still be telling the truth …'⁹). Thorpe was never short of confidence himself. Back in 1976 he had told Peter Hain that he did not intend to resign as Liberal leader as 'I have the three most powerful pillars of the state on my side – Harold Wilson, Arnold Goodman and MI5.'¹⁰

There is evidence, too, that Boothby's connection to the Thorpe scandal does not end with the fact that the two politicians consulted the same lawyer. In 2004, Kray lieutenant Teddy Smith (at the time holed up in Australia) gave a series of taped interviews for a proposed newspaper serialisation that never occurred. In the course of these interviews, he revealed that Ronnie Kray had harboured plans to build an organisation based on the American Mafia's 'Murder Inc.' model, carrying out murders to order. Smith said:

> What you've got to understand is, if this had taken off this would have instituted a reign of terror like London had never seen before … Here he [Ronnie] was talking about men bumping off people who they never even knew for a price. I am telling you, there is people out there you'd be amazed [*sic*]. I mean I can quote an MP who was sizing me up to bump somebody off in north Devon. He come to size me up, I know what he was up to. A very so-called respectable person, who he hoped to proposition me in [*sic*].

Thorpe was the Member of Parliament for North Devon from 1959 until 1979 and his alleged target could only realistically have been Norman Scott. Assuming that Smith is correct in his interpretation of events (and it is impossible to corroborate his claims), the meeting he describes must have occurred at some point before Smith's disappearance in 1967. This would show that Thorpe had been considering an attempt on Scott's life many years earlier than previously believed. Moreover, Boothby (who is known to have had a long association with Thorpe) and/or Driberg must be the most likely contenders to have provided the necessary introduction to Smith and the twins.[11]

In truth though, by the time of the Thorpe affair, Goodman was already falling out of the political limelight. When Wilson got back to Downing Street in 1974, Goodman was no longer at his or the nation's top table. Then, in 1993, crisis threatened when Lord Portman – Goodman's client for more than forty years – began legal action, claiming that the lawyer had siphoned off some £10 million of the Portman family fortune. Goodman died on 12 May 1995 before the issue was resolved, but his firm subsequently settled the claim for £500,000 without admitting guilt.

Gerald Gardiner, meanwhile, generally managed to steer clear of further scandal as he established his reputation as one of the great reforming Lord Chancellors. As well as extensive technical changes to the court system, he oversaw the suspension of the death penalty for murder in 1965 and its final abolition in 1969 – a provision for which the Krays should doubtless have been grateful. Goodman retired from the chancellorship when Labour fell in 1970, and died at his London home on 7 January 1990.

Joseph Simpson spent a good part of the rest of his tenure as the Met's Chief Commissioner arguing that the police complaints procedure ought to remain in-house. Nonetheless, he faced increasing pressure from the Home Office to establish an external tribunal. To the end, he strived to balance the demand for greater public scrutiny of policing against the needs of a police force that often felt overwhelmed and under-equipped. On 20 March 1968 Simpson had the last in a series of heart attacks while at his London home, with the stress of work considered a contributory factor. His death was greeted with an outpouring of grief from those who had served under his command. The *Oxford Dictionary of National Biography*, however, acknowledged his double-edged legacy:

> Simpson's work was, of course, unfinished, and we cannot know how he would have handled the major scandals that afflicted the Met in the 1970s. It is clear, though, that some of the reflexes developed in response to relatively limited criticism in the 1960s – the assumption that public and media attacks were ill informed or even malicious and that wrongdoing could be handled internally – damaged the Met ...

On Fleet Street, Cecil King saw out a seven-year stint as chairman of the Newspaper Publishers Association in 1968, in which role he had given some credibility to the Press Council and for a while looked like he might be stemming the tide of titillation dressed up as journalism. But then came his fall from grace at the IPC after he turned on Wilson. In his subsequent retirement, he wrote occasional articles for *The Times*, as well as publishing an autobiography and his diaries – an action that lost him several friends who felt their confidences had been betrayed. He eventually relocated to Dublin with his wife and died at his home in the city on 17 April 1987.

Hugh Cudlipp never much liked taking over from his old boss (King had even described him on the day of his dismissal as 'a first violin rather than a conductor').[12] Once the IPC had merged with Reed International, he took the opportunity to shed his responsibilities as chairman to focus on the nitty-gritty of what was going on in the company's newsrooms instead. He retired at the end of 1973 and the following year was made a life peer, Baron Cudlipp of Aldingbourne, by Harold Wilson. He briefly and unhappily returned to the Mirror Group in the 1980s to advise Robert Maxwell but soon realised his mistake and resumed his retirement. He wrote a volume of autobiography as well as a book on the newspaper industry, and was also the founding chairman of the Chichester Arts Festival. He died at his home in Chichester on 17 May 1998.

Kray associate and Boothby's lover, Leslie Holt, came to a markedly more tragic and curious end. In 1979 he died from an overdose of anaesthetic during an operation to remove a verruca. A Harley Street doctor, Dr Gordon Kells, was eventually charged with his manslaughter but was acquitted at the Old Bailey in 1981. As well as being his doctor, it is alleged that Kells and Holt had struck up some sort of association whereby Kells would provide Holt with details of society clients who might be suitable targets for burglary. Members of Holt's family became convinced that he was murdered.[13] Years later, the Krays' childhood friend, Laurie O'Leary, wrote that Holt had been nervous of being drawn into the twins' trial after their arrest in 1968 and that he had lodged papers with a solicitor containing information that would 'certainly rock the political world'.[14]

The Krays, meanwhile, never enjoyed freedom together after 1968, although they were both permitted to attend their mother Violet's funeral in 1982. Ronnie was moved to Broadmoor high-security psychiatric hospital in 1979, where he was twice married before a heart attack killed him on 17 March 1995. His funeral was said to be the largest the East End of London had seen since that of Winston Churchill in 1965. Reggie was allowed to attend, as he was for his older brother Charlie's funeral five years later. Reggie married in 1997 and when he was diagnosed with cancer of the bladder in August 2000, he was freed from prison on compassionate grounds. He died in the October. All three Kray brothers wrote books detailing their lives and crimes (some of them anyway), contributing to the growth of the Kray legend. They gave their approval, too, to the first film made about their misadventures, 1990's *The Krays*.

Finally, to Driberg and Boothby, the men around whom the Establishment constructed a conspiracy of silence. Predictably, there was no place for Driberg in Harold Wilson's government in 1964, although he continued to serve on Labour's National Executive Committee until 1972. He lobbied Wilson to appoint him ambassador to the Vatican too, but to no avail. Always battling his ailing finances, he remained a prodigious journalist and in 1974 he retired from the Commons with the plan of completing his memoirs. In 1975 he was granted a life peerage and took his seat in the Lords as Baron Bradwell, of Bradwell juxta Mare in the County of Essex – a flamboyant title for a flamboyant figure. He died on 12 August 1976, suffering a heart attack in the back of a taxi as it drove him to his modest flat in the Barbican. His incomplete memoirs were published in 1977 as *Ruling Passions*, the explicit descriptions of some of his sexual antics (though not those involving Boothby or the Krays) causing a sensation.

Driberg remained a sexual (mis)adventurer almost to the end, even if health problems somewhat slowed him down. In 1968, he wrote to Boothby, commenting on an unspecified 'matter'. '… If you are discussing "that matter" with influential people,' he wrote, 'and disparaging remarks are made, you could say truthfully, that I no longer behave as I used to for years – no "cruising", no casual promiscuity, only (very) occasional old friends. Old age & prostatectomy, if not virtue, forbid more!'[15]

In some lights, he could seem a beacon of sexual liberalism ahead of his time – a man who refused to be cowed from acknowledging those 'ruling passions' that had always guided him. But posthumously, evidence grew of a darker side to his sexual experimentation. In 2015, Simon Danczuk, the then Labour MP for Rochdale – and the author of a book exposing the paedophilia of Rochdale's former Liberal MP, Cyril Smith – was contacted by an ex-policeman called Michael Cookson. Cookson was a CID sergeant in the Met's Central Command. In 1968, he was assigned to a team who surveilled a succession of teenage escapees from what was then Feltham Borstal in West London entering Driberg's home. The police subsequently interviewed several of the boys and in Cookson's words, 'it was clear that Driberg was abusing them'. According to him, a file was prepared and submitted to the then Director of Public Prosecutions, Norman Skelhorn, but the application to charge was rejected on the basis that it was not in the public interest to pursue the investigation.[16] It was a decision that still distressed Cookson almost fifty years after the event, and sadly he died of a heart attack shortly after making contact with Danczuk's office.

A series of freedom of information requests in 2019 to the Metropolitan Police and to the Criminal Prosecution Service (CPS) at first prompted refusals to confirm or deny that such an application had been made and rejected. Then, after an appeals process, both organisations confirmed that they could find no evidence of the application. The CPS noted that it did not exist as an organisation, at least not its current form, in 1968. It was only established in 1986 as a successor to the Office of the Director of Public Prosecutions. The CPS thus suggested that I should contact the Metropolitan Police, who 'should have a record of any charging referrals they had made and their outcomes'.[17] However, the Metropolitan Police conceded that 'Information for the period 1920 to 1976 is likely to have been held in paper records. Given the length of time that has elapsed, records for that period would have been destroyed or transferred to the National Archives, if applicable.'[18] (The National Archives do not hold any relevant records.)

Despite the absence of a paper trail, there is little reason to believe that Cookson simply made up his allegations against Driberg. Skelhorn, too, had form in this area. He was the Director of Public Prosecutions who advised chief constables to pass details to him of any prospective case involving homosexual acts between consenting adults at the time of the Boothby affair. In his memoirs, Skelhorn would write:

The Director, like a judge, must move with the times, and keep abreast of current ideas concerning crime and punishment, economic and social theories and literary and artistic values. There have been important changes in the law during this century, including the abolition of hanging for murder and of flogging; also in the law concerning homosexuality and obscenity ... I was aware that I ... needed to be alive to new thinking and to move with the times.[19]

An admirable aim, it nonetheless seems possible that his reluctance to sanction unnecessary homosexual prosecutions may have persuaded him to rule out charges related to acts that rightly should be seen as predatory rather than consensual. In 1970, for instance, he refused to sanction charges against Cyril Smith after a police investigation concluded that Smith, who by then had served as the Labour Mayor of Rochdale, was hiding behind a 'veneer of respectability' and had targeted young boys at a local hostel.[20] Then, in 1972, Skelhorn declined to prosecute the former Conservative MP, Victor Montagu, despite Montagu admitting to abusing a boy for two years. A note from Skelhorn's office acknowledged the case as borderline but, given Montagu's 'previous good character' and 'no fear of repetition with this boy', advised 'we could caution'.[21] That Skelhorn would also have declined to prosecute Driberg seems highly probable.

Moreover, a statement made in 2019 by a security service witness to the Independent Inquiry into Child Sex Abuse – set up by the British government in the wake of the Jimmy Savile scandal – revealed that in 1981, MI5 received information suggesting that Driberg had engaged in sexual activities with young boys.[22] In his memoirs, Skelhorn explicitly stated, 'I would never have refused to prosecute someone simply because of the position he held.'[23] 'I should like to dispel once and for all,' he said, 'the belief in some quarters that the Director of Public Prosecutions is specially subject to political direction.'[24] Nonetheless, there is a very real possibility that Driberg got away with far more serious crimes in the aftermath of the Boothby affair than merely having a tumble with a willing gangster or two.

And Boothby? He remained a regular in the House of Lords, where he sat as a cross-bencher. In 1967, he married Wanda Sanna, a glamorous, 33-year-old daughter of a Sardinian businessman. As he left his wedding ceremony, he told the waiting crowd of well-wishers: 'Don't you think I'm a lucky boy?' His old radio and television sparring partner, Dingle Foot (the brother of the future Labour leader, Michael), wrote a commemorative verse for the occasion that included the lines:

When libelled he, obtaining just redress,
Took forty thousand smackers from the Press.[25]

Boothby and Wanda had a seemingly very content marriage for more than twenty years. In 1975, he wrote her a heartfelt letter:

This is just to let you know that I love you far more than anyone or anything else in this world: and that I am grateful, from the bottom of my heart, for what you have given me in return – the most unselfish love and devotion that I have ever known.

You did what you set out to do. You saved my life, restored my position in public life, and brought me several more years of existence. You also enhanced the joy of living. I can never thank you enough.

During this period, he published his memoirs, *Recollections of a Rebel*, and maintained a strong media presence until deep into old age. He also campaigned to rectify a regulatory quirk that meant the 1967 act decriminalising consensual homosexual acts did not apply in Scotland. Homosexuality was subsequently decriminalised there too in 1980.

Into his ninth decade, Boothby's health deteriorated markedly. He lost a lot of weight until he was a physical shadow of his younger self. He lived, he said, on whiskey and Complan towards the end.[26] But he remained mischievous and provocative all the way through. When his cousin, Ludovic Kennedy, visited him not long before his passing, Boothby told him he thought euthanasia ought to be optional from the age of 75 but compulsory at 85.[27] An essay he wrote back in 1966 for a collection called *What I Believe* gives us a flavour of Boothby's outlook on life in his later years:

A better title for this essay would be 'What I do not believe'. For the truth is that, in the generally accepted sense of the term, I don't believe in much, beyond the undoubted existence of a life force which carries us, whether we like it or not, upon an irresistible tide. If I thought that the life force itself was eternal, I would try harder to deflect its course, or at least to divert it into more rewarding channels. But I know that it is not.

On 16 July 1986, aged 86, he suffered a heart attack and died at London's Westminster Hospital, close to the parliamentary buildings he had inhabited as an MP and baron for more than sixty years. His ashes were scattered off the coast of his beloved Aberdeen constituency, his secrets still untold.

Epilogue

'The past,' as L.P. Hartley observed in his 1953 classic, *The Go-Between*, 'is a foreign country; they do things differently there.' It is true that in many respects, Britain has changed unimaginably over the decades since the Boothby scandal. The Second World War was then still a recent memory rather than distant history, the pill had only just been legalised, gentlemen commonly wore bowler hats to the office and nervous parents genuinely feared that the Beatles would be the undoing of their children. Yet, in many other respects, we are not so different. The nation is still striving to find its place in a changing world order. There are tensions, too, between liberal progressivism and social conservatism. The battlegrounds may have changed, but many of the same arguments play out. And Britain remains a country hidebound by its class structure. A ten-minute walk through any major city or town will reveal that we are a land of haves and have-nots as much as we ever were. Amid rampant economic and social disparity, the bonds between the classes strain. Largely gone is the once inbred deference that was already waning in the 1960s. Yet in the decade from 2010 to 2020, two from three of Britain's Prime Ministers came from an Eton and Oxbridge background. Everything changes, nothing changes much.

So, what does the Boothby saga have to do with us today? The answer lies with a paradox at the heart of the affair – what constituted its core scandalous element back then is not the same as what disconcerts us now. The essence of the scandal as it was set to be reported in 1964 was that

Boothby and Kray were involved in a homosexual relationship. If the allegations could be proven, both men potentially faced criminal conviction and imprisonment. For Boothby, it would signal the end of his political and media careers, and would likely have ensured his social ostracism, too. His Aberdeen constituents had seen their MP through so many political squalls over the decades, but this would surely have strained their loyalties beyond breaking point. His friends in London, meanwhile, might have extended a sympathetic arm round the shoulders. Poor old Boothby, what terrible bad luck to come unstuck like that after all these years. But there would have been a new cautiousness in aligning too closely with him. While one might have previously put up with, and even rather enjoyed, his frequently erratic behaviour and the constant risk of being dragged into some unforeseen scrape, it would be a different matter to be too tight with the subject of such tawdry tabloid scandal – a scandal, some feared, that would trump even the Profumo affair.

But who would really care now? Homosexual acts between consenting adults have long been legal, and the longstanding demonisation of homosexuality itself has, joyfully, been significantly reduced, if not yet entirely eliminated. Being gay is no longer not merely a crime, it is a protected human right. That Boothby's supposed choice of partner was a ne'r-do-well gangster might still raise eyebrows, it is true. But were the story breaking today in the terms that it was presented in 1964, Boothby would likely be able to shrug it all off. 'Naturally, I had no idea what they were up to. They were introduced to me as legitimate businessmen and there was never a hint to me that they conducted themselves in a criminal manner.' Anyway, Boothby was by no means the first, nor assuredly the last, politician to get rather too pally with characters of dubious reputation.

As it was, Boothby would likely have been left to suffer the consequences of exposure had it not been for the devastation wrought first by Vassall and then by Profumo. Profumo in particular prompted a fundamental undermining of public faith in those charged with executing the government's business. So salacious were its details that the veneer of respectability crucial to upholding the social order was catastrophically damaged. Macmillan's premiership was brought crashing down and politicians had never felt the weight of public scrutiny on their private morality more keenly. The press barons who once upon a time followed an unwritten code of discretion were no longer reliable, nor were the chattering classes so forgiving. This was the context in which the details of Boothby and Driberg's misdemeanours were brushed under the Establishment carpet. Should the full story have been revealed, both main parties would have been subject to genuine existential threat. How the revelation might have impacted their respective performances in the general election due that year was anyone's guess. Coming so fast on the tail of Profumo, the political Establishment would surely be looking at a years-long project to win back public confidence – if it was indeed capable of being won back at all.

But what if the story were breaking today, viewed through the prism of our modern concerns? Boothby's involvement with the Krays would undoubtedly still be a scandal, just for different reasons to those of 1964. In the course of researching this book, it was suggested to me on an online forum that it was inappropriate to delve into the private affairs of an individual who had obviously been committed to keeping his personal life to himself. It is an utterly valid point, and one I wrestled with a lot. But I kept coming back to the same conclusion – the real scandal was not one of sexual orientation but of sexual consent. Boothby's crime – for he was undoubtedly complicit along with Kray – was one of coercion. Using Kray's frightening reputation for violence and the power of Boothby's social status, the pair enjoyed the sexual favours of young men and others who were legally defined as 'young persons' (under the age of 18) who were incapable of freely giving their consent.

For all those who attended Ronnie's Cedra Court parties entirely under their own volition, how many were there against their will? How many hadn't managed to exit the Soho coffee bar or their East End boxing club before Ronnie Kray turned up and let them know he was 'choosing' them? How many quaked as he slipped a £20 note into their pocket, aware that Ronnie never gave you money without strings attached? How many didn't dare risk a 'slap' from the gangster for resisting the advances of a portly, 60-something politician whom they might or might not recognise off the television? How many felt in the slightest that they could say 'no' to the Colonel or his obviously powerful and sophisticated friends?

Having been blindsided by Vassall and Profumo, the political class decided to batten down the hatches when it came to Boothby. They conspired to hide his crimes, and with them those of the Krays too. The twins were left virtually undisturbed to extend their violent hold on London's underworld for years to come. That is why the story remains relevant – not because a politician or a criminal was gay but because it is about the abuse of power in all its senses.

And, as is so often the case, the cover-up was as damaging as the original crime. Rarely in British history has there been such a perfect storm of scandal that its concealment drew in so many pillars of society – the government, the opposition, the intelligence services, the police, the legal profession and the media. The plan worked, too. As a result of their interventions, the Boothby affair failed to take its place in the rollcall of scandals that included Vassall, Profumo and, later, Thorpe. It simply disappeared, only coming to light when it was too late for any of those most closely involved in it to pay a price.

Perhaps even more damagingly, it set a precedent for handling future sex scandals. Where possible, turning a blind eye became the preferred strategy. That was certainly the case with Jeremy Thorpe. In July 1978, Peter Hain – then a Labour activist who would later serve in various senior ministerial positions under Tony Blair and Gordon Brown – wrote a memo that was circulated to, among others, Neil Kinnock and Tony Benn, and which was subsequently retained by MI5. With Thorpe set to be charged with conspiracy to murder, Hain wrote: 'The Labour party and its leadership ought to consider this all very quickly but there must be no pressure for a further cover-up on electorally expedient grounds.' In the same document, he noted: 'There is also clear evidence that leading politicians over the past 15 years, together with civil servants, the police and the security services, have been party to a cover-up surrounding the affair.'[1]

As we are now beginning to understand, a blind eye was also turned in cases of non-consensual and clearly inappropriate sexual interactions, just as had been done for Boothby and Kray. It is why, for instance, the crimes of Jimmy Savile went undiscovered until after his death in 2011. It is why party chief whips have long been in the habit of keeping 'dirt books' detailing the darkest secrets of their party's politicians. The deal is simple: the

MP's problem goes away and, in return, they are expected to tow the party line. As Conservative Chief Whip Tim Fortescue notoriously told a documentary team in 1995:

> Anyone with any sense, who was in trouble, would come to the whips and tell them the truth, and say now, 'I'm in a jam, can you help?'. It might be debt, it might be … a scandal involving small boys, or any kind of scandal in which … a member seemed likely to be mixed up in, they'd come and ask if we could help and if we could, we did.[2]

It is also why the former Liberal leader, David Steel, told the Independent Tribunal into Child Sex Abuse in 2019 that he had assumed since 1979 that the Liberal MP Cyril Smith was guilty of paedophile offences but did not pursue the matter at any point before Smith's death thirty-one years later.[3] Indeed, Steel passed a recommendation that Smith should receive a knighthood in 1988, which he was duly awarded.

Boothby and Driberg had grown used to leveraging their social contacts to smooth things over when their private lives threatened to cause problems – even as both of them railed against the very Establishment that protected them. In both cases there were many attractive aspects to the political stances they adopted over long careers, but they each also displayed an unappealing sense of entitlement – to behave as others were not permitted to behave, and to be protected when they feared being found out. As for the institutions involved in the cover-up, all have shown both a sense of entitlement and a tendency to complacency themselves over the years. From the Met corruption scandals of the 1970s to the Stephen Lawrence debacle in the 1990s, from the parliamentary expenses scandal to the revelations of Fleet Street phone hacking and the intelligence services' mishandling evidence of Iraqi weapons of mass destruction. Each contributed a further step down the path towards popular distrust of the 'powers that be', which culminates in a world where truth becomes a subjective construction and if you want to tell a lie, make sure it's a really big one.

There will always be scandals. If nothing else, the 'Peer and the Gangster' affair serves as a case study in how a cover-up is executed and at what price.

In March 2019, the soon-to-be British Prime Minister Boris Johnson – another scion of the Establishment – appeared on a show on the LBC radio station. He declared that historical child abuse investigations – like the Independent Inquiry into Child Sex Abuse, at which Tom Driberg's name had been brought up several times – represented money 'spaffed up a wall'.[4] It was an extraordinary choice of words given the context. His argument was that such work contributed nothing to protecting the public now. The subtext was that the past has little to teach us. But such a position is wrought with peril. If the mistakes of the past are not learned from, they are doomed to be repeated. That is why Boothby, Kray and 'one of the greatest scandals that never was'[5] deserves proper consideration, albeit belatedly, as an important episode in the history of post-war Britain.

Notes

Prologue

1 *Sunday Mirror*, 12 July 1964, p. 1.
2 Ibid.
3 *The Gangster and the Pervert Peer* (Blakeway Productions, 2009).
4 *Sunday Mirror*, 19 July 1964, p. 1.

Chapter 1

1 The episode of *This is Your Life!* was filmed on 14 October 1963 and transmitted three days later.
2 Barnes, Susan, *Behind the Image: Profiles* (Jonathan Cape, 1974) p. 215. The original piece appeared in the *Sunday Times Magazine* of 1 April 1973. Barnes was the wife of Jim Callaghan's Foreign Secretary, Anthony Crosland.
3 *The Edge of the Sixties* for the BBC.
4 *This is Your Life!*, op. cit.
5 The episode was broadcast on the BBC Light Programme on 23 March 1962.
6 The Beaverbrook Papers (Parliamentary Archives, BBK/C/47c).
7 *This is Your Life!*, op. cit.
8 Campbell, Duncan, *We'll All Be Murdered in Our Beds!: The Shocking True History of Crime Reporting in Britain* (Elliott and Thompson, 2015) p. 129.
9 Boothby, (Lord) Robert, *My Yesterday, Your Tomorrow* (Hutchinson, 1962) p. xi. The volume consisted of personal memoirs, pen portraits of famous figures, and selected speeches and newspaper pieces that Boothby had written over the years.
10 *Good Afternoon* (Thames Television, 9 April 1975).

Chapter 2

1   Barnes, op. cit., p. 217.
2   Hansard (HC, vol. 674, 22 March 1963).
3   *The Times*, 6 June 1963. p. 13.
4   *Statesman Journal*, 24 June 1963, p. 4.
5   *Sunday Mirror*, 26 July 1964, p. 2.
6   The letter, written on House of Lords notepaper, is dated 19 July 1964 and resides in the National Archives (NA), PREM 11/4689.
7   Smith made the claim in a recorded interview of 18 May 2004. A transcript was supplied to the author by Ray Rose in February 2020.
8   The piece appeared under the headline 'Events of the Week'. *Der Stern* noted: 'According to British press tradition, it can be taken as reasonably certain that there is a hardcore of truth in all this.' In the UK, it was *Private Eye* that first named the Krays as the gangsters implicated by the *Sunday Mirror*. Peter Cook was the guest editor while the regular editor, Richard Ingrams, was away. Cook himself then promptly left the country for a holiday, perhaps wisely.
9   Pearson, John, *Notorious: The Immortal Legend of the Kray Twins* (Arrow Books, 2010) p. 121.
10   An editorial note in the diaries refers to a *Spectator* profile of Lord Goodman written by Auberon Waugh and published on 15 April 1978. Waugh wrote that, fifteen years after the trial, Crossman was 'happy to boast to a party of journalists in my hearing that he and Bevan had both been pissed as newts'. See Crossman, Richard and Morgan, Janet (eds), *The Backbench Diaries of Richard Crossman* (Hamish Hamilton, 1981) p. 633.
11   MI5 report dated 10 August 1964 (NA KV 2/4097, #244a).
12   Barnes, op. cit., p. 219.
13   *The Times*, 1 August 1964, p. 7.
14   *Daily Mirror*, 6 August 1964, p. 1. Boothby's boxer dog, Gigi, had gone missing while out for a walk a couple of days earlier and the saga of the hound (who was found by the time of the *Mirror* apology) was discussed in the press, deflecting at least a little of the scandal away from Boothby in the meantime. The 'missing dog' drama was thus, in certain respects, a precursor to the modern 'dead cat' strategy of averting attention from where it is most unwanted.

Chapter 3

1   Dudgeon, Piers, *The Real Peter Pan* (Robson Press, 2015) p. 365.
2   Jerome, Jerome K., *Three Men in a Boat* (Heinemann and Balestier, 1891) p. 232.
3   Boothby, Robert, *I Fight to Live* (Victor Gallancz, 1947) p. 15.
4   James, Robert Rhodes, *Bob Boothby: A Portrait* (Hodder & Stoughton, 1991) p. 19.
5   Boothby, (Lord) Robert, *Boothby: Recollections of a Rebel* (Hutchison and Co., 1978) p. 16.

6   Boothby, *Recollections*, op. cit., p. 24.
7   James, op. cit., p. 40.
8   James, op. cit., p. 41.
9   Boothby made the observation in a piece for *My Oxford*, a collection of recollections from high-profile Oxford graduates edited by Ann Thwaite (Robson Books, 1977).
10   Letter from Boothby to his Aunt Cecil, known in the family as Cass (Robert Boothby Papers, National Library of Scotland, Acc. 12929, General Correspondence, item 1).
11   Boothby made the comments in an interview in 1976. See: Birkin, Andrew, *J.M. Barrie and the Lost Boys: The Real Story Behind Peter Pan* (Yale University Press, 2003) p. 295.

Chapter 4

1   Boothby, *Recollections*, op. cit., p. 110.
2   *The Spectator* (12 February 1965) p. 14.
3   Letter from Boothby to Churchill, 22 January 1932 (Churchill Papers, Churchill Archives Centre, Cambridge).
4   Boothby, *Recollections*, op. cit. p. 16.
5   Bowra, Maurice, *Memories 1898–1939* (Harvard University Press, 1967) p. 123.
6   Quoted in James, op. cit., p. 52.
7   Boothby, *Recollections*, op. cit., p. 33.
8   Churchill, Randolph Spencer and Gilbert, Martin, *Winston S. Churchill, Vol. 5, Part 1* (Houghton Mifflin, 1981) p. 744.
9   Quoted in James, op. cit., p. 88.
10   Tinniswood, Adrian, *The Long Weekend: Life in the English Country House Between the Wars* (Vintage, 2018).
11   Boothby, *Recollections*, op. cit., p. 71.
12   Ibid.

Chapter 5

1   *Daily Mail*, 1 April 1927.
2   Pearson, John, *Notorious*, op. cit., p. 101.
3   Ibid.
4   Thorpe, D.R., *SuperMac: The Life of Harold Macmillan* (Pimlico, 2011) p. 100. Robert Rhodes James told Thorpe that Sarah had come to the attention of Boothby's roving eye, having deemed it too sensitive a subject to include in his own biography of Boothby.
5   Papers of Nancy Astor, University of Reading Special Collections, MS 3748.
6   Quoted in James, op. cit., p. 115.

7   Letter from Boothby to Fisher, 21 October 1977 (Robert Boothby Papers, National Library of Scotland, Acc. 12929, General Correspondence, item 29).

8   Quoted in James, op. cit., p. 116.

9   Hines, Richard Davenport, *The Macmillans* (Random House, 1992) p. 194.

10   Interview with Simon Carey, Boothby's cousin, in *Secret History: Lords of the Underworld* (broadcast on Channel 4, 23 June 1997).

11   Barnes, op. cit., p. 208.

12   The Beaverbrook Papers (Parliamentary Archives, BBK/C/47b).

13   *Daily Mail*, 10 May 1978.

14   Wyatt, Woodrow and Curtis, Sarah (eds), *The Journals of Woodrow Wyatt: Vol. 2* (Macmillan, 1999) p. 546 [entry for 9 July 1991].

15   Bowra, Maurice, *New Bats in Old Belfries* (Hardy, Henry and Holmes, Jennifer (eds); Robert Dugdale in Association with Wadham College, Oxford, 2005) pp. 76–7.

16   Intriguingly, in 1950 Dorothy Macmillan's brother, the Duke of Devonshire, died of a suspected heart attack in the presence of his doctor. The doctor's name was John Bodkin Adams. In due course, Bodkin Adams would be acquitted of charges of murdering another patient but he has long been suspected of being a prolific serial killer. According to Jane Robins, author of *The Curious Habits of Dr Adams: A 1950s Murder Mystery* (John Murray, 2013), between 1946 and 1956, more than 160 of his patients were thought to have died while in a coma, leading to suspicions that he was mis-medicating (a great many of his patients had made him a beneficiary of their wills). In the case of the Duke, no coroner was called (as should have happened) and Bodkin Adams himself signed the death certificate. It has been noted that because the Duke's death was not treated as suspicious, Dorothy escaped the publicity that would surely have come her way in such a sensational case – doubtless a blessing to her given the complexities of her personal life.

Chapter 6

1   *Report from the Select Committee on Conduct of a Member* (HMSO, 1941).

2   Hansard (HC, 28 January 1941, vol. 368, col. 191).

3   Churchill made the comment in an address at Winchester House, Epping, on 23 February 1931.

4   Boothby, *Recollections*, op. cit., p. 128.

5   Ibid., pp. 111–12.

6   Ibid., p. 107.

7   Ibid., p. 109.

8   Quoted in James, op. cit., p. 153.

9   Letter to Stanley Baldwin (31 January 1934).

10   *The Times*, 17 December 1935, p. 15.

11   Boothby, *Recollections*, op. cit., p. 125.

12   Churchill, Randolph Spencer and Gilbert, Martin, *Winston S. Churchill, Vol. 5, Part 1* (Houghton Mifflin, 1981) p. 825.

13   Rasor, Eugene L., *Winston S. Churchill, 1874–1965: A Comprehensive Historiography and Annotated Bibliography* (Greenwood Press, 2000) p. 227.

14   *Sunday Express*, 28 March 1937, p. 9.

15   Letter to Duff Cooper, 11 September 1940.

16   Boothby, *I Fight to Live*, op. cit., p. 164. Chamberlain uttered the famous phrase at Heston Aerodrome on 30 September 1938.

17   Hansard (HC Deb 07 May 1940 vol. 360, col. 1151).

18   Shakespeare, Nicholas, *Six Minutes in May* (Vintage, 2017) p. 285.

19   James, op. cit., p. 242.

20   Boothby, *Recollections*, op. cit., p. 165.

21   James, op. cit., pp. 259–61.

22   Quoted in James, op. cit., p. 279.

23   Interview with Simon Carey, Boothby's cousin, in *Secret History: Lords of the Underworld* (Broadcast on Channel 4, 23 June 1997).

24   *Report from the Select Committee on Conduct of a Member* (HMSO, 1941).

25   Olson, Lynne, *Troublesome Young Men: The Rebels Who Brought Churchill to Power in 1940* (Bloomsbury, 2007) p. 351.

26   *The Times*, 22 January 1941, p. 5.

Chapter 7

1   Boothby, *Recollections*, op. cit., p. 169.

2   Smith, Daniel, *The Spade as Mighty as the Sword: The Story of World War Two's 'Dig for Victory' Campaign* (Aurum Press, 2011) pp. 187–8. I first became familiar with the extraordinary life and times of Lord Boothby via my research into the Dig for Victory campaign. The Bethnal Green Archives provided a wealth of information on efforts towards the campaign in the East End of London.

3   Kray, Reginald, Kray, Ronald and Dinenage, Fred, *Our Story* (Pan Books, 2015) pp. 1–3.

4   Pearson, *Notorious*, op. cit., p. 63.

5   Kray, Kray and Dinenage, op. cit., p. 56.

6   Pearson made the claim in the *Mirror* of 1 September 2015 (www.mirror.co.uk/news/real-life-stories/gangster-twins-ronnie-reggie-kray-6354591).

7   Alleyne, Richard, 'Ronnie Kray in torment over being gay', *Daily Telegraph*, 19 October 2001.

8   Pearson, John, *The Profession of Violence: The Rise and Fall of the Kray Twins* (originally published by Weidenfeld and Nicolson, 1972; republished by William Collins, 2015) p. 69.

Chapter 8

1   Boothby, *My Yesterday, Your Tomorrow*, op. cit., p. 207.

2   Boothby, *Recollections*, op. cit., p. 59.

3   Ibid., p. 63.

4   Boothby, *My Yesterday, Your Tomorrow*, op. cit., pp. 210–11.
5   Thomson, George Malcolm, *Vote of Censure: An Eyewitness Account of the Threat to Churchill's Leadership in 1942* (Stein and Day, 1968) p. 191.
6   Boothby, *Recollections*, op. cit., p. 243.
7   James, op. cit., p. 352.
8   Quoted in James, op. cit., p. 358.
9   *News of the World*, 9 September 1956.
10   Hansard (HC Deb 1 November 1956, vol. 558 col. 1655).
11   Boothby made the comment on *Frankly Speaking*, broadcast on the BBC Home Service, 11 December 1958.
12   Hansard (HC Deb 30 October 1957, vol. 575 col. 254).
13   Cannadine, David, *History in Our Time* (Yale University Press, 1998) p. 277.
14   Quoted in James, op. cit., p. 392.
15   Broadcast on the BBC on 27 May 1959.
16   Pottle, Dr Mark, *Daring to Hope – The Diaries and Letters of Violet Bonham Carter, 1946–1969* (Weidenfeld and Nicolson, 2000) p. 207.
17   The Beaverbrook Papers (Parliamentary Archives, BBK/C/47b).
18   Ibid.
19   *Any Questions?* (BBC Light Programme, 23 March 1962).
20   James, op. cit., p. 412.
21   The Beaverbrook Papers (Parliamentary Archives, BBK/C/47c).
22   Ibid.
23   Quoted in James, op. cit., p. 341.

Chapter 9

1   Hansard (HC Deb 28 April 1954 vol. 526 col. 1749).
2   Boothby, *My Yesterday, Your Tomorrow*, op. cit., p. 43.
3   Griffith-Jones made his observation at the Old Bailey on 2 November 1960.
4   Mitchell, Caroline, *Women and Radio: Airing Differences* (Routledge, 2001) p. 67.
5   Hansard (HC Deb 28 April 1954, vol. 526 col. 1749).
6   Hansard (HC Deb 28 April 1954, vol. 526 col. 1751).
7   Boothby, *Recollections*, op. cit., p. 25.
8   Sent on 7 December 1953 (The Papers of Lord Hailsham, Series: 2, Political correspondence, Box: 25, File: 7, Churchill Archives Centre, University of Cambridge.
9   Jenkins, Simon, 'Make mine a glass of cannabis wine, thank you', *Guardian*, 18 October 2018 (www.theguardian.com/commentisfree/2018/oct/18/britain-war-on-drugs-canada-cannabis).
10   From the so-called 'Little Kinsey' Report, extracts of which were published in the *Sunday Pictorial* between 3 and 31 July 1949.
11   Whitaker, Brian, *Unspeakable Love* (Saqi Books, 2011) p. 237.
12   Wildeblood, Peter, *Against the Law* (Weidenfeld & Nicolson, 1955) pp. 92–3.
13   Boothby, *Recollections*, op. cit., p. 212.

14 Hansard (HL Deb 21 July 1967, vol. 285 col. 523).
15 *The Report of the Departmental Committee on Homosexual Offences and Prostitution* (HMSO, 1957).
16 Hansard (HL Deb 19 May 1954, vol. 187 col. 739).
17 Hansard (HC Deb 26 November 1958, vol. 596 cols 427 and 437).
18 Hansard (HL Deb 4 December 1957, vol. 206 col. 810).
19 *The Times*, 7 March 1958, p. 11.
20 Boothby, *Recollections*, op. cit., p. 212.
21 David, Hugh, *On Queer Street: A Social History of British Homosexuality 1895–1995* (HarperCollins, 1997) p. 179.
22 Williams, Kenneth and Davies, Russell (eds), *The Kenneth Williams Diaries* (HarperCollins, 1994) p. 206.
23 Hailsham, Viscount, 'Homosexuality and Society', in Rees, J.T. and Usill, H. (eds), *They Stand Apart* (Heinemann, 1955).

Chapter 10

1 *Daily Mail*, 28 July 1959, p. 5.
2 Junor, John, *Listening for a Midnight Train* (Pan Books, 1991) pp. 52–3.
3 David Dorward, then a university administrator, made the comment in the 1959 edition of the *St Andrew's Alumnus Chronicle*.
4 Boothby, *My Yesterday, Your Tomorrow*, op. cit., p.13.
5 Email from Linda Mallard to the author, 10 January 2019.
6 Boothby, *My Yesterday, Your Tomorrow*, op. cit., p. 9.
7 The Beaverbrook Papers (Parliamentary Archives, BBK/C/47b).
8 *Daily Express*, 7 May 1963, p. 4.
9 Junor, op. cit., p. 53.
10 MI5 report circulated 24 July 1964 (NA KV 2/4097, #231A).
11 NA MEPO 2/11462.
12 *Essex Chronicle*, 1 February 1950, p. 4.
13 Interview with Ludovic Kennedy, Boothby's cousin, in *Secret History: Lords of the Underworld*.
14 The claim was made in an article published in the *National Socialist* in August 1963, a copy of which was retained by MI5 (NA KV 2/4097, #223A).
15 Boothby, *Recollections*, op. cit., p. 213.
16 MI5 report dated 15 July 1964 (NA KV 2/4097).
17 O'Leary, Laurie, *Ronnie Kray: A Man Among Men* (Headline, 2001) p. 162.
18 MI5 report dated 15 July 1964 (NA KV 2/4097).
19 Boothby sent the note, written on House of Lords paper, to Holt's parents on 18 December 1963 (*Secret History: Lords of the Underworld*).
20 Email from Michael Thornton to the author, 9 September 2018.
21 Thornton, Michael, 'You're in trouble son ... Ronnie Kray fancies you rotten', *Daily Mail*, 14 October 2006. Thornton supplied the author with the unedited original version on 9 September 2018.

Chapter 11

1   Quoted by Adrian Bingham in his article, 'Swinging – only pampas grass is quite as suburban – and as British' in *The Independent*, 4 December 2011.
2   Rice-Davies, Mandy and Flack, Shirley, *Mandy* (Michael Joseph, 1980) p. 78.
3   Denning, op. cit., p. 206.
4   NA MEPO 2/11388.
5   Anthony Daly provided information to the author on Boothby in this period via an email of 18 December 2018. Daly did not knowingly meet Boothby (although retrospectively suspects their paths crossed) but was told about his activities by Tom Driberg. Driberg had been a client of Daly's after Daly was coerced into working as a rent boy in the 1970s. Daly detailed his experiences in *Playland: Secrets of a Forgotten Scandal* (Mirror Books, 2018; republished as *The Abuse of Power* in 2019).
6   Email from Jon Vickers-Jones to the author, 12 November 2019.
7   Quoted in *Secret History: Lords of the Underworld* (broadcast on Channel 4, 23 June 1997).
8   Lucas, Norman, *Britain's Gangland* (W.H. Allen, 1969) p. 240.
9   O'Leary, op. cit., p. 82.
10 *Sunday Mirror*, 3 September 2015 (www.mirror.co.uk/news/uk-news/ronnie-kray-fancied-you-you-6376849), confirmed by Conrad in conversation with the author.
11 Thornton, op. cit.
12 Teale, Bobby, *Bringing Down the Krays* (Ebury Press, 2013) p. 66.
13 *Frankly Speaking*, broadcast on the BBC Home Service, 11 December 1958.
14 Kray, Reg, *A Way of Life* (Sidgwick & Jackson, 2000) p. 162.

Chapter 12

1   Boothby did not realise he was corresponding with an MI5 agent. The agent retained their respective notes from 31 March 1939 for the files (NA KV 2/4095).
2   MI5 memo, 11 June 1936, NA KV 2/4095, #3A.
3   MI5 memo, 14 October 1939, NA KV 2/4095, #11A.
4   MI5 memo, 21 March 1940, NA KV 2/4095, #19A.
5   MI5 memo, 22 June 1940, NA KV 2/4095, #27A.
6   MI5 memo, NA KV 2/4095, #123A.
7   MI5 memo to Home Office, 26 August 1940, NA KV2/2855.
8   NA KV 2/4095, #53A.
9   Hansard (HC Deb 14 August 1940, vol. 264 col. 779).
10 NA KV 2/4095, #63A.
11 www.theguardian.com/books/2006/apr/23/biography.features1 – quoted in a review of *Blackshirt: Sir Oswald Mosley and British Fascism* by Stephen Dorril (Viking, 2006).

12 James, op. cit., p. 103.
13 Ibid.
14 Letter from Boothby to Christopher Mayhew, Under-Secretary of State at the Foreign Office, 10 May 1949, NA KV 2/4096, #909A.
15 Note on Boothby, 24 August 1951, NA KV 2/4096.

Chapter 13

1   www.telegraph.co.uk/news/uknews/1423933/Macmillan-apology-to-the-Queen-over-terrible-Profumo.html
2   https://media.nationalarchives.gov.uk/index.php/scandalous-case-john-vassall
3   *Daily Express*, 8 November 1962, p. 1.
4   *Sunday Pictorial*, 28 October 1962, p. 1.
5   Davenport-Hines, Richard, *The Macmillans* (Heinemann, 1992) p. 304.
6   Horne, Alistair, *Harold Macmillan, Vol. II: 1957–86* (Penguin, 1989) p. 461.
7   Hansard (HOC 14 November 1962, vol. 667 cols 393 and 401).
8   media.nationalarchives.gov.uk/index.php/scandalous-case-john-vassall/
9   www.dailymail.co.uk/news/article-2251958/Why-historian-blackening-Mail-reporter-went-jail-betray-source.html
10 Cudlipp, Hugh, *At Your Peril* (Weidenfeld & Nicolson, 1962) p. 25.
11 Deedes, W.F., *Dear Bill: A Memoir* (Macmillan, 1997) p. 162.
12 Diary entry for 7 July 1963.
13 Hansard (HC Deb 17 June 1963, vol. 679 col. 99).
14 In *The Secret Worlds of Stephen Ward* (Headline, 2013), for example, Anthony Summers and Stephen Dorril cite a former MI6 agent, Lee Tracey, claiming Ward was given a lethal dose of barbiturates by an MI5 operative. Meanwhile, journalist Tom Mangold – who saw Ward on the night he overdosed – has described the claims as 'junk journalism at its very worst, complete piffle, a disgrace to our trade' (see www.independent.co.uk/voices/comment/stephen-ward-wasnt-murdered-i-was-there-8990737.html)
15 Denning, Lord Alfred Thompson, *Lord Denning's Report* (HMSO, 1963) p. 2.
16 Davenport-Hines, R. (3 October 2013). Ward, Stephen Thomas, *Oxford Dictionary of National Biography*.
17 Kennedy, Ludovic, *The Trial of Stephen Ward* (Victor Gollancz, 1964) preface.
18 Crossman, Richard and Porter, Janet (eds), *The Backbench Diaries of Richard Crossman* (Hamish Hamilton, 1981) p. 997.
19 Jordan, Colin, 'Behind the Democratic Curtain' in the *National Socialist*, vol. 1 no. 5, August 1963 (NA KV 2/4097, #223A).
20 Ibid.
21 The romantic intrigues drawing in Boothby, Macmillan and Kennedy are dealt with in impressive detail in Farris, Scott, *Inga: Kennedy's Great Love, Hitler's Perfect Beauty, and J. Edgar Hoover's Prime Suspect* (Lyon's Press, 2016).
22 Ibid., p. ix.
23 Dawson, Mackenzie, 'This accused spy had a fling with JFK and stole Hitler's heart', *New York Post*, 23 October 2016.

24 Scott, op. cit., p. 334.

25 Horne, Alistair, *Harold Macmillan, Vol. II: 1957–86* (Penguin, 1989) p. 495.

Chapter 14

1   *New Society*, 4 October 1962, vol. 1, iss. 1, p. 20.
2   www.theguardian.com/news/2006/jun/30/guardianobituaries.obituaries
3   21 July 1964, NA PREM 11/4689.
4   Note from Martin Redmayne to the Home Secretary and copied to Timothy Bligh, 30 July 1964, NA PREM 11/4689.
5   Secret memo, 28 July 1964, NA PREM 11/4689.
6   Note on meeting in Home Secretary's office, 21 July 1964, NA PREM 11/4689.
7   Ibid.
8   *The Times*, 14 July 1964, p. 10.
9   Confidential memo written by Roger Hollis, 4 November 1963, NA KV 2/4097, #223Z. Hollis, incidentally, was a golfing chum of Colin Coote, the newspaper editor in whose company Boothby was when the scandal broke.
10 Note written by Roger Hollis, 22 July 1964, NA KV 2/4097, #227A.
11 Bligh's 'Note for the Record' was marked 'Secret'. NA PREM 11/4689.
12 Note on meeting in Home Secretary's office, 21 July 1964, NA PREM 11/4689.
13 Email from John Jackson to the author, 24 September 2018.
14 Note for the Record, 21 July 1964, NA PREM 11/4689.
15 *Daily Mirror*, 23 July 1964, p. 24.
16 Note written by Roger Hollis, 22 July 1964, NA KV 2/4097, #227A.
17 Note for the Record, 21 July 1964, NA PREM 11/4689.
18 Note on meeting in Home Secretary's office, 28 July 1964, NA PREM 11/4689.
19 Note on meeting in Home Secretary's office, 21 July 1964, NA PREM 11/4689.
20 Ibid.
21 *Daily Mirror*, 23 July 1964, p. 24.
22 Ibid.
23 Note for the Record, 22 July 1964, NA PREM 11/4689.
24 Note on meeting in Home Secretary's office, 28 July 1964, NA PREM 11/4689.
25 *Daily Mirror*, 6 August 1964, p. 1.

Chapter 15

1   Pearson, *Notorious*, op. cit., p. 122.
2   Goodman, Arnold, *Tell Them I'm on My Way* (Chapmans Publishers, 1993) p. 209.
3   Ibid., pp. 206–9.

4   Ibid., p. 197.
5   Ibid., p. 195.
6   Ibid., p. 198.
7   Ibid., p. 206.
8   Ibid., p. 212.
9   Archive of Harold Wilson (Oxford, Bodleian Libraries, MS. Wilson c 764).
10   Ibid.
11   Butler, D.E. and King, Anthony, *The British General Election of 1964* (Macmillan, 1965) p. 120.
12   Haines, Joe, *Glimmers of Twilight: Harold Wilson in Decline: Murder, Intrigue and Passion at the Court of Harold Wilson* (Politico's Publishing, 2003) p. 54.
13   Goodman, op. cit., p. 188.
14   Letter from Gardiner to Boothby, 19 August 1964 (Robert Boothby Papers, National Library of Scotland, Acc. 12929, General Correspondence, item 29).
15   Archive of Harold Wilson (Oxford, Bodleian Libraries, MS. Wilson c 764).
16   Private letter from Boothby to 'Dear P.M.', 12 November 1964, NA PREM 13/81.
17   Archive of Harold Wilson (Oxford, Bodleian Libraries, MS. Wilson c 1484).

Chapter 16

1   McKenzie, Compton, *Thin Ice* (originally published by Chatto & Windus in 1956; reprinted by Penguin in 1977) p. 167.
2   Driberg, Tom, *Ruling Passions* (Quartet Books, 1978) pp. 144–6.
3   Pearson, *Notorious*, op. cit., p. 104. However, others – notably, true crime researcher Ray Rose – is sceptical as to whether there was a sexual relationship between Smith and either of Driberg or Kray. Certainly, there is nothing in the way of documentary evidence to confirm so, although that is hardly surprising.
4   Driberg, op. cit., p. 8.
5   Wheen, Francis, *Tom Driberg: His Life and Indiscretions* (Chatto & Windus, 1990) p. 40.
6   Driberg, op. cit., p. 16.
7   Ibid., p. 92.
8   Ibid., p. 84.
9   Ibid., p. 123.
10   Boothby, *Recollections*, op. cit., p. 213.
11   Driberg, op. cit., p. 132.
12   Wheen, op. cit., p. 98.

Chapter 17

1   FBI memorandum dated 5 September 1946.
2   Driberg, op. cit., p. 41.
3   Ibid., p. 48.

4   The Oxford student weekly, *Cherwell*, reported Driberg's comments on
     15 June 1963.
5   Driberg, op. cit., p. 143.
6   Ibid.
7   Ibid., p. 13. The Labour politician Woodrow Wyatt, meanwhile, told a story that
     Driberg had once been travelling back to London from a long meeting with
     Jim Callaghan when both men felt the need to urinate at the roadside. Driberg
     allegedly grabbed Callaghan's penis and said, 'You've got a very pretty one there.'
     Callaghan promptly retreated back to their vehicle.
8   Ibid., p. 350.
9   Timothy Bligh's Note for the Record, 21 July 1964, NA PREM 11/4689.
10   Note on conversation between Rees-Davies and fellow Conservative MP,
     Anthony Bourne-Arton, 20 July 1964, NA PREM 11/4689.
11   MI5 intelligence report, 15 July1964, NA KV 2/4097.
12   Email from Haines to the author, 26 July 2018.
13   www.romeospy.co.uk/Pages/sunny_jim.htm
14   Diary entry for 30 January 1979 in Donoghue, Bernard, *Downing Street Diary:
     With James Callaghan in No. 10, Vol. 2* (Jonathan Cape, 2008) p. 435.
15   Note for the Record, 22 July 1964, NA PREM 11/4689.
16   Hansard (HC Deb 29 October 1946, vol. 428 col. 499).
17   *Report of the Royal Commission on the Press, 1947–1949* (HMSO, 1949).
18   Wheen, op. cit., p. 266.
19   Ibid., p. 281.
20   Lownie, Andrew, *Stalin's Englishman: The Lives of Guy Burgess* (Hodder &
     Stoughton, 2016) p. 279.
21   Pincher made the case against Hollis most stridently in *Treachery: Betrayals,
     Blunders, and Cover-ups: Six Decades of Espionage Against America and Great Britain*
     (Mainstream, 2012).
22   Wheen, op. cit., p. 191.
23   In his memoirs, Kingsley Amis also noted the 'complete and baffling immunity
     [Driberg] enjoyed from the law and the Press to the end of his days' (*Memoirs*,
     Hutchinson, 1991) p. 311. He also described how a night out with Driberg in
     the mid-1970s had ended up back at Driberg's Barbican flat, with the politician
     chasing the young Martin Amis around the bedroom as he attempted to ring for
     a cab home.
24   Abse, Leo, 'The Judas Syndrome', *The Spectator*, 20 March 1982, p. 11.

Chapter 18

1   Cudlipp, Hugh, *Walking on the Water* (The Bodley Head, 1976) pp. 326–7.
2   *Daily Mirror*, 10 May 1968, p. 1.
3   According to Butler, D.E. and King, Anthony, *The British General Election of 1964*
     (Macmillan, 1965) p.151: 'It was the *Daily Mirror* rather than Mr. Wilson which
     sustained the Labour campaign to a polling day climax.'

4   Interview with Norman Lucas in *Secret History: Lords of the Underworld* (broadcast on Channel 4, 23 June 1997).
5   *Sunday Pictorial*, 31 March 1963, p. 1.
6   *The Spectator*, 23 September 1955, p. 5.
7   Wilson, Harold, *The New Britain: Labour's Plan* (Penguin, 1964) pp. 9–10.
8   media.nationalarchives.gov.uk/index.php/scandalous-case-john-vassall
9   *Sunday Mirror*, 28 April 1963, p. 7.
10 *Daily Mirror*, 13 July 1964, p. 1.
11 *Daily Mirror*, 14 July 1964, p. 1.
12 *Daily Mirror*, 15 July 1964, p. 24.
13 *Daily Mirror*, 16 July 1964, p. 2.
14 *Daily Mirror*, 17 July 1964, p. 2.
15 *Daily Mirror*, 17 July 1964, p. 5.
16 *Daily Mirror*, 18 July 1964, p. 20.
17 *Sunday Mirror*, 19 July 1964, p. 11.
18 *Daily Mirror*, 23 July 1964, p. 24.
19 Ibid.
20 There is a good account of the meeting in: Knightley, Phillip and Kennedy, Caroline, *An Affair of State: The Profumo Case and the Framing of Stephen Ward* (Guild Publishing, 1987) p. 163.
21 Independent Inquiry into Child Sex Abuse, Allegations of Child Sexual Abuse linked to Westminster, Public Hearing 5 March 2019 (transcript available at www.iicsa.org.uk/key-documents/9655/view/public-hearing-transcript-5-march-2019.pdf) pp. 192–7.
22 Email from Little to the author, 4 December 2018.
23 Churchill, Randolph, *The Spectator*, 13 August 1964 (see *The Spectator*, F.C. Westley, 1964, vol. 213, p. 203).
24 Williams, Francis, *New Statesman*, 14 August 1964.

Chapter 19

1   Chester, Lew and McCrystal, Cal, *Sunday Times*, 9 August 1964, p. 4.
2   Fido, Martin, *The Krays: Unfinished Business* (Carlton Books, 2000) p. 250.
3   Foreman, Freddie, *The Godfather of British Crime: The Autobiography of the Krays' Enforcer* (John Blake, 2008) p. 187.
4   In 2019, the writer Clare Campbell raised the possibility that Smith might have been a mole for MI5 within the Kray operation (www.dailymail.co.uk/news/article-6738091/Kray-Brothers-henchman-Teddy-Smith-MI5-spy-fleeing-Australia.html). Meanwhile, Ray Rose has dedicatedly built a compelling case that Smith did not die but instead disappeared to Australia, returning to Britain only shortly before his death in 2004. Rose is also sceptical of the claim that Smith was MI5's mole. For instance, Rose points out that the mole in MI5's Boothby files gives Leslie Holt as his source for intelligence that Boothby and Kray had been photographed together in 'a normal, social pose'. Yet Teddy Smith was present at the meeting at which the photographs of Boothby and Kray (the

ones later given to the *Sunday Mirror*) were taken. In other words, Smith did not need Holt to tell him about the photographs, as he was witness to them. The fact that the source credits Holt for the intelligence suggests that the source was not personally present and was not, therefore, Teddy Smith.

5   Pearson, *Notorious*, op. cit., p. 223.
6   Morton, James, *Krays: The Final Word* (Mirror Books, 2019) pp. 333–4.
7   In 2018, a BBC4 documentary *Murder In Soho: Who Killed Freddie Mills?* (produced by Phoenix Television) suggested Mills did not commit suicide, as was officially recorded, but was likely murdered on the orders of American Mob boss Meyer Lansky. The programme alluded to rumours of the Krays' involvement but suggested it was unlikely, even given their association with Lansky intermediaries. The Krays themselves denied any involvement and were indeed known to be admirers of Mills.
8   So claimed Bradley Allardyce, who inhabited a cell on the same landing as Reggie Kray at Maidstone Jail for three years. Allardyce subsequently claimed the pair were lovers and that Reggie confided in him that Ronnie had forced Frances to take an overdose. (See: http://news.bbc.co.uk/1/hi/england/1756592.stm)
9   Morton, op. cit., p. x. See also: Connor, Michael, *The Soho Don* (Mainstream, 2002).
10 Gillett made his claim in *The Krays: Their Empire Behind Bars* (Real Life Media Productions for Channel 5 Television, 2002).
11 www.cps.gov.uk/south-east/news/rapist-gangland-links-jailed-18-years
12 Hamilton, Lenny and Cabell, Craig, *Getting Away with Murder* (John Blake, 2006) pp. 109–11.
13 Lucas, op. cit., p. 274.

Chapter 20

1   MI5 report, 11 September 1964, NA KV 2/4097.
2   MI5 report, 16 October 1964, NA KV 2/4097.
3   Flanagan, Maureen, *One of the Family: 40 Years with the Krays* (Arrow Books, 2015) p. 102. Flanagan was a friend of the family and Violet Kray's hairdresser. She was also a celebrated glamour model who went by the single name of Flanagan.
4   Pearson, *Notorious*, op. cit., p. 110.
5   Ibid., p. 106.
6   *Daily Express*, 12 August 1964, p. 1.
7   Full text provided by private source.
8   *Daily Mirror*, 19 August 1964, p. 3.
9   The precise date is obscured but 'Dec. 64' is visible. MEPO 2/10763.
10 This was the assessment of Simon Carey, whose father Boothby had approached, as detailed in an interview for the documentary, *Secret History: Lords of the Underworld* (broadcast on Channel 4, 23 June 1997).

11 Hansard (HL Deb 11 February 1965, vol. 263 cols 271-2) and *Daily Mirror*, 12 February 1965 p. 2.

12 Hansard (HL Deb 11 February 1965, vol. 263 cols 272).

13 Ibid.

14 *Daily Express*, 6 April 1965, p. 9.

15 Full text provided by private source.

16 Interview with Brian Stratton in *Secret History: Lords of the Underworld* (broadcast on Channel 4, 23 June 1997).

17 Teale, op. cit., pp. 233–4.

18 Pearson, *Notorious*, op. cit., p. 335.

19 *Daily Mirror*, 6 March 1969, p. 6.

20 The Papers of Tom Driberg, Christ Church Archives, Oxford (SOC.Driberg K 2).

21 Ibid.

22 The Papers of Tom Driberg, Christ Church Archives, Oxford (SOC.Driberg L 17).

Chapter 21

1 Pearson, Notorious, *op. cit.*, pp. 345–6.

2 Quoted in James, op. cit., pp. 419–20.

3 Porter, Ronald, 'Rum, Buggery and the Lash', *Conservative History Journal*, Winter 2004/2005, p. 13.

4 Hurd, D. (9 January 2014). Home, Alexander Frederick [Alec] Douglas, *Oxford Dictionary of National Biography*.

5 Quoted in James, op. cit., p. 129.

6 Brivati, Dr Brian, 'A Good Man Who Couldn't Help Himself', *The Guardian*, 24 January 1999 (www.theguardian.com/politics/1999/jan/24/uk.politicalnews).

7 Brivati, Dr Brian, *Lord Goodman* (Richard Cohen, 1999) p. 250.

8 *Daily Telegraph*, 22 November 1978.

9 Shrimsley, Robert, 'Jeremy Thorpe: a political scandal from a desperate time', *Financial Times*, 27 April 2018 (www.ft.com/content/13b45fa2-4818-11e8-8ae9-4b5ddcca99b3).

10 Penrose, Barrie and Courtiour, Roger, *The Pencourt File* (Secker & Warburg, 1978) p. 22.

11 A transcript of the recording from 19 June 2004 was provided to the author by Ray Rose in February 2020.

12 Howard, A. (8 January 2009). Cudlipp, Hubert Kinsman [Hugh]. *Oxford Dictionary of National Biography*.

13 Holt's sister, Pat Melbourne, and his niece, Tricia Heppel, claimed as much in interviews for *Secret History: Lords of the Underworld* (broadcast on Channel 4, 23 June 1997).

14 O'Leary, op. cit., p. 153.

15 Quoted in James, op. cit., pp. 431–2.

16 Cookson's claims are contained in Simon Danczuk's statement to the Independent Inquiry into Child Sex Abuse, provided on 27 November 2018 (www.iicsa.org.uk/key-documents/10433/view/INQ003692.pdf).

17 CPS correspondence with the author.

18 Metropolitan Police correspondence with the author.

19 Skelhorn, Norman, *Public Prosecutor: The Memoirs of Sir Norman Skelhorn* (Harrap, 1981) p. 74.

20 Swinford, Steven, 'Cyril Smith: the predatory paedophile protected by establishment', *Daily Telegraph*, 18 April 2014 (www.telegraph.co.uk/news/politics/liberaldemocrats/10775341/Cyril-Smith-the-predatory-paedophile-protected-by-establishment.html).

21 Laville, Sandra and Travis, Alan, 'Tory MP Victor Montagu escaped child sex abuse trial in 1970s', *The Guardian*, 15 May 2015 (www.theguardian.com/politics/2015/may/15/tory-mp-victor-montagu-escaped-child-sex-abuse-trial-in-1970s)

22 Independent Inquiry into Child Sex Abuse, Allegations of Child Sexual Abuse linked to Westminster, Witness Statement of Security Service Witness, 6 February 2019 (www.iicsa.org.uk/key-documents/9774/view/INQ004032.pdf, p. 13).

23 Skelhorn, op. cit., p. 70.

24 Skelhorn, op. cit., p. 72.

25 Quoted in James, op. cit., p. 428. Dingle Foot served as Solicitor-General in Harold Wilson's government in 1964–67. He had regularly appeared with Boothby on television and radio panel shows. Michael Foot was another of Boothby's good friends and sent his congratulations after Boothby extracted his apology from Cecil King.

26 Interview with Ludovic Kennedy, Boothby's cousin, in *Secret History: Lords of the Underworld* (broadcast on Channel 4, 23 June 1997).

27 Ibid.

Epilogue

1 Hain memo sent to Tony Benn, Dick Clements, Neil Kinnock, Tom Jackson and Audrey Wise, dated 4 July 1978 (NA PREM 16/2237).

2 Fortescue was a whip in the government of Edward Heath between 1970 and 1973. He was interviewed for the documentary, *Westminster's Secret Service*, broadcast on BBC2 on 21 May 1995.

3 Independent Inquiry into Child Sex Abuse, Allegations of Child Sexual Abuse linked to Westminster, Public Hearing 13 March 2019 (www.iicsa.org.uk/key-documents/9810/view/public-hearing-transcript-13-march-2019.pdf) pp. 66–165.

4 Interview with Nick Ferrari on LBC on 13 March 2013.

5 The words of Dr Richard Dunley, records specialist at the National Archives, as quoted in a BBC News article of 23 October 2015 (www.bbc.co.uk/news/uk-34612729).

Selected Bibliography

Amis, Kingsley, *Memoirs* (Hutchinson, 1991)

Andrew, Christopher, *The Defence of the Realm: The Authorized History of MI5* (Penguin, 2010)

Arnott, Jake, *The Long Firm Trilogy* (Sceptre, 2005)

Barnes, Susan, *Behind the Image: Profiles* (Jonathan Cape, 1974)

Bingham, Adrian, *Family Newspapers?: Sex, Private Life, and the British Popular Press 1918–1978* (Oxford University Press, 2009)

Birkin, Andrew, *J.M. Barrie and the Lost Boys: The Real Story Behind Peter Pan* (Yale University Press, 2003)

Bloch, Michael, *Jeremy Thorpe* (Abacus, 2016)

Boothby, (Lord) Robert, *Boothby: Recollections of a Rebel* (Hutchison and Co., 1978)

Boothby, (Lord) Robert, *My Yesterday, Your Tomorrow* (Hutchinson, 1962)

Boothby, Robert, *I Fight to Live* (Victor Gallancz, 1947)

Bowra, Maurice, *Memories 1898–1939* (Harvard University Press, 1967)

Bowra, Maurice, *New Bats in Old Belfries* (Hardy, Henry and Holmes, Jennifer (eds); Robert Dugdale in Association with Wadham College, Oxford, 2005)

Brivati, Dr Brian, *Lord Goodman* (Richard Cohen, 1999)

Butler, D.E. and King, Anthony, *The British General Election of 1964* (Macmillan, 1965)

Callaghan, James, *Time and Chance* (HarperCollins, 1987)

Campbell, Duncan, *We'll All Be Murdered in Our Beds!: The Shocking True History of Crime Reporting in Britain* (Elliott and Thompson, 2015)

Cannadine, David, *History in Our Time* (Yale University Press, 1998)

Chibnall, Steve, *Law-and-Order News: An Analysis of Crime Reporting in the British Press* (Routledge, 2001)

Churchill, Randolph Spencer and Gilbert, Martin, *Winston S. Churchill, Vol. 5, Part 1* (Houghton Mifflin, 1981)

Clark, Colin, *Younger Brother, Younger Son: A Memoir* (HarperCollins, 1997)

Collins, Damien, *Charmed Life: The Phenomenal World of Philip Sassoon* (William Collins, 2017)

Coote, Colin, *Editorial* (Eyre & Spottiswoode, 1965)

Coote, Colin, *The Other Club* (Sidgwick & Jackson, 1971)

Crossman, Richard and Morgan, Janet (eds), *The Backbench Diaries of Richard Crossman* (Hamish Hamilton, 1981)

Cudlipp, Hugh, *At Your Peril* (Weidenfeld & Nicolson, 1962)

Cudlipp, Hugh, *Walking on the Water* (The Bodley Head, 1976)

Cullen, Pamela, *A Stranger in Blood: The Story of Dr Bodkin Adams* (Elliott & Thompson, 2004)

Daly, Anthony, *Playland: Secrets of a Forgotten Scandal* (Mirror Books, 2018)

Danczuk, Simon and Baker, Matthew, *Smile for the Camera: The Double Life of Cyril Smith* (Biteback, 2014)

Davenport-Hines, Richard, *The Macmillans* (Heinemann, 1992)

David, Hugh, *On Queer Street: A Social History of British Homosexuality 1895–1995* (HarperCollins, 1997)

Deedes, W.F., *Dear Bill: A Memoir* (Macmillan, 1997)

Denning, Lord Alfred Thompson, *Lord Denning's Report* (HMSO, 1963)

Donoghue, Bernard, *Downing Street Diary: With James Callaghan in No. 10, vol. 2* (Jonathan Cape, 2008)

Douglas-Home, Alec, *The Way The Wind Blows: An Autobiography* (HarperCollins, 1976)

Driberg, Tom, *Ruling Passions* (Quartet Books, 1978)

Dudgeon, Piers, *The Real Peter Pan* (Robson Press, 2015)

Edwards, Ruth Dudley, *Newspapermen: Hugh Cudlipp, Cecil Harmsworth King and the Glory Days of Fleet Street* (Secker, 2003)

Egremont, Lord, *Wyndham and Children First* (Macmillan, 1968)

Farris, Scott, *Inga: Kennedy's Great Love, Hitler's Perfect Beauty, and J. Edgar Hoover's Prime Suspect* (Lyon's Press, 2016)

Fawcett, Micky, *Krazy Days* (Pen Press, 2014)

Fido, Martin, *The Krays: Unfinished Business* (Carlton Books, 2000)

Flanagan, Maureen, *One of the Family: 40 Years with the Krays* (Arrow Books, 2015)

Foreman, Freddie, *The Godfather of British Crime: The Autobiography of the Krays' Enforcer* (John Blake, 2008)

Freeman, Simon and Penrose, Barrie, *Rinkagate: The Rise and Fall of Jeremy Thorpe* (Bloomsbury, 1997)

Goldie, Grace Wyndham, *Facing the Nation: Television and Politics, 1936–76* (The Bodley Head, 1977)

Goodman, (Lord) Arnold, *Not For the Record: Selected Speeches and Writings* (Deutsch, 1972)

Goodman, (Lord) Arnold, *Tell Them I'm on My Way* (Chapmans Publishers, 1993)

Greenslade, Roy, *Press Gang: How Newspapers Make Profits from Propaganda* (Macmillan, 2003)

Haines, Joe, *Glimmers of Twilight: Harold Wilson in Decline: Murder, Intrigue and Passion at the Court of Harold Wilson* (Politico's Publishing, 2003)

Hamilton, Lenny and Cabell, Craig, *Getting Away with Murder* (John Blake, 2006)

Harris, Walter, *Yesterday Calling* (Patagonia Press, 2017)

Higgins, Patrick, *Heterosexual Dictatorship: Male Homosexuality in Postwar Britain* (Fourth Estate, 1996)

Hines, Richard Davenport, *The Macmillans* (Radom House, 1992)

Horne, Alistair, *Harold Macmillan, Vol. II: 1957–86* (Penguin, 1989)

Horrie, Chris, *Tabloid Nation: The Birth of the Daily Mirror to the Death of the Tabloid* (Andre Deutsch, 2003)

Hyde, H. Montgomery, *The Love that Dared Not Speak Its Name: A Candid History of Homosexuality in Britain* (Little, Brown, 1970)

Jackson, Paul, *Colin Jordan and Britain's Neo-Nazi Movement: Hitler's Echo* (Bloomsbury Academic, 2016)

James, Robert Rhodes, *Bob Boothby: A Portrait* (Hodder & Stoughton, 1991)

Jameson, Derek, *Touched by Angels* (Ebury Press, 1988)

Junor, John, *Listening for a Midnight Train* (Pan Books, 1991)

Keeler, Christine, *Secrets and Lies* (John Blake, 2012)

Kellner, Peter and Hitchens, Christopher, *Callaghan: The Road to Number 10* (Cassell, 1976)

Kennedy, Ludovic, *On my Way to the Club* (William Collins, 1989)

Kennedy, Ludovic, *The Trial of Stephen Ward* (Victor Gollancz Ltd, 1964)

King, Cecil, *Strictly Personal* (Weidenfeld & Nicolson, 1969)

King, Cecil, *The Cecil King Diary 1965–1970* (Jonathan Cape, 1972)

Knightley, Phillip and Kennedy, Caroline, *An Affair of State: The Profumo Case and the Framing of Stephen Ward* (Guild Publishing, 1987)

Kray, Charlie and Fry, Colin, *Doing the Business* (John Blake, 1993)

Kray, Kate, *The Twins: Men of Violence* (Blake Publishing, 2002)

Kray, Reginald, *A Way of Life* (Sidgwick & Jackson, 2000)

Kray, Reginald, Kray, Ronald and Dinenage, Fred, *Our Story* (Pan Books, 2015)

Lambrianou, Chris and McGibbon, Robin, *The Kray Madness* (Pan, 2016)

Levin, Bernard, *The Pendulum Years* (Jonathan Cape, 1970)

Lownie, Andrew, *Stalin's Englishman: The Lives of Guy Burgess* (Hodder & Stoughton, 2015)

Lucas, Norman, *Britain's Gangland* (W.H. Allen, 1969)

Margach, James, *The Abuse of Power: The War Between Downing Street and the Media from Lloyd George to James Callaghan* (W.H. Allen, 1978)

McKenzie, Compton, *Thin Ice* (Chatto & Windus, 1956)

Molloy, Mike, *The Happy Hack: A Memoir of Fleet Street in Its Heyday* (John Blake, 2016)

Morgan, Kenneth O., *Callaghan: A Life* (Oxford University Press, 1997)

Morton, James, *Krays: The Final Word* (Mirror Books, 2019)

O'Leary, Laurie, *Ronnie Kray: A Man Among Men* (Headline, 2001)

Olson, Lynne, *Troublesome Young Men: The Rebels Who Brought Churchill to Power in 1940* (Bloomsbury, 2007)

Parkin, Sophie, *The Colony Room Club 1948–2008: A History of Bohemian Soho* (Palmtree Publishers, 2012)

Pearson, John, *The Cult of Violence* (Orion, 2002)

Pearson, John, *Notorious: The Immortal Legend of the Kray Twins* (Arrow, 2011)

Pearson, John, *The Profession of Violence: The Rise and Fall of the Kray Twins* (Weidenfeld & Nicolson, 1972)

Pearson, John, *Stags and Serpents: A History of the Cavendish Family and the Dukes of Devonshire* (Country Books, 2002)

Penrose, Barrie and Courtiour, Roger, *The Pencourt File* (Secker & Warburg, 1978)

Pimlott, Ben, *Harold Wilson* (HarperCollins, 1992)

Pincher, Chapman, *Too Secret Too Long* (Sidgwick & Jackson, 1984)

Pincher, Chapman, *Treachery: Betrayals, Blunders, and Cover-ups: Six Decades of Espionage Against America and Great Britain* (Mainstream, 2012).

Pottle, Dr Mark, *Daring to Hope – The Diaries and Letters of Violet Bonham Carter, 1946–1969* (Weidenfeld & Nicolson, 2000)

Preston, John, *A Very English Scandal* (Penguin, 2016)

Rasor, Eugene L., *Winston S. Churchill, 1874–1965: A Comprehensive Historiography and Annotated Bibliography* (Greenwood Press, 2000)

Read, Leonard and Morton, James, *Nipper* (Sphere, 1992)

Reid, Jeremy, *The Dilly: A Secret History of Piccadilly Rent Boys* (Peter Owen Publishers, 2014)

Report from the Select Committee on Conduct of a Member (HMSO, 1941)

Rice-Davies, Mandy and Flack, Shirley, *Mandy* (Michael Joseph, 1980)

Robins, Jane, *The Curious Habits of Dr Adams: A 1950s Murder Mystery* (John Murray, 2013)

Root, Neil, *The Murder Gang: Fleet Street's Elite Group of Crime Reporters in the Golden Age of Tabloid Crime* (The History Press, 2018)

Sandbrook, Dominic, *Never Had It So Good: A History of Britain from Suez to the Beatles* (Little, Brown, 2005)

Sandbrook, Dominic, *White Heat: A History of Britain in the Swinging Sixties 1964–1970* (Little, Brown, 2006)

Sandford, Christopher, *Harold and Jack: The Remarkable Friendship of Prime Minister Macmillan and President Kennedy* (Prometheus Books, 2014)

Selbourne, David, *Not an Englishman: Conversations with Lord Goodman* (Sinclair-Stevenson, 1993)

Shakespeare, Nicholas, *Six Minutes in May* (Vintage, 2017)

Skelhorn, Norman, *Public Prosecutor: The Memoirs of Sir Norman Skelhorn* (Harrap, 1981)

Smith, Daniel, *The Spade as Mighty as the Sword: The Story of World War Two's 'Dig for Victory' Campaign* (Aurum Press, 2011)

Stuart, James, *Within the Fringe* (The Bodley Head, 1967)

Summers, Anthony and Dorril, Stephen, *The Secret Worlds of Stephen Ward* (Headline, 2013)

Teale, Bobby, *Bringing Down the Krays* (Ebury Press, 2013)

The Report of the Departmental Committee on Homosexual Offences and Prostitution (HMSO, 1957)

Thompson, Douglas, *The Hustlers: Gambling, Greed and the Perfect Con* (Pan, 2008)

Thompson, Douglas, *Stephen Ward: Scapegoat* (John Blake, 2013)

Thomson, George Malcolm, *Vote of Censure: An Eyewitness Account of the Threat to Churchill's Leadership in 1942* (Stein and Day, 1968)

Thorpe, D.R., *Alec Douglas-Home* (Sinclair-Stevenson, 1996)

Thorpe, D.R., *SuperMac: The Life of Harold Macmillan* (Pimlico, 2011)

Thorpe, Jeremy, *In My Own Time: Reminiscences of a Liberal Leader* (Politico's Publishing, 1999)

Thwaite, Ann (ed.), *My Oxford* (Robson Books, 1977)

Tinniswood, Adrian, *The Long Weekend: Life in the English Country House Between the Wars* (Vintage, 2018)

Vassall, John, *Vassall: The Autobiography of a Spy* (Sidgwick & Jackson, 1975)

West, Rebecca, *The Vassall Affair* (Sunday Telegraph, 1963)

Wheen, Francis, *Tom Driberg: His Life and Indiscretions* (Chatto & Windus, 1990)

Wildeblood, Peter, *Against the Law* (Weidenfeld & Nicolson, 1955)

Williams, Kenneth and Davies, Russell (eds), *The Kenneth Williams Diaries* (HarperCollins, 1994)

Wilson, A.N., *Our Times* (Arrow, 2009)

Wilson, Harold, *The Labour Government, 1964–70: A Personal Record* (Penguin, 1971)

Wilson, Harold, *The New Britain: Labour's Plan* (Penguin, 1964)

Wyatt, Woodrow and Curtis, Sarah (eds), *The Journals of Woodrow Wyatt: Vol. 2* (Macmillan, 1999)

Ziegler, Philip, *Wilson: The Authorised Life* (Weidenfeld & Nicolson, 1993)

Index

More from The History Press

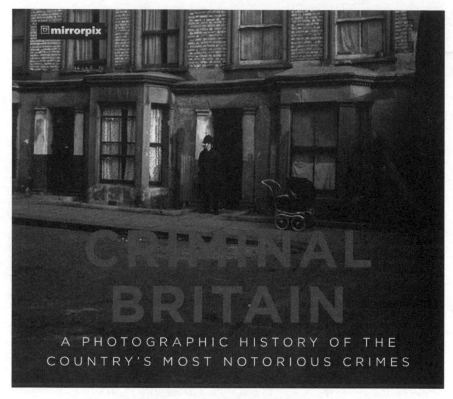

978 0 7509 9074 5